The Pleasures of Reading

The Pleasures of Reading

A Booklover's Alphabet

Catherine Sheldrick Ross

 LIBRARIES UNLIMITED

AN IMPRINT OF ABC-CLIO, LLC
Santa Barbara, California • Denver, Colorado • Oxford, England

Library of Congress Cataloging-in-Publication Data

Ross, Catherine Sheldrick.
   The pleasures of reading : a booklover's alphabet / Catherine Ross.
      pages cm
   Includes bibliographical references and index.
   ISBN 978–1–59158–695–1 (paperback) — ISBN 978–1–61069–433–9 (ebook) 1. Books and reading. 2. Reading interests. 3. Reading—Social aspects. 4. Popular literature. 5. Public services (Libraries) 6. Libraries and community. I. Title.
   Z1003.R74   2014
   028′.9—dc23   2014008161

ISBN: 978–1–59158–695–1
EISBN: 978–1–61069–433–9

18 17 16 15 14   2 3 4 5

This book is also available on the World Wide Web as an eBook.
Visit www.abc-clio.com for details.

Libraries Unlimited
An Imprint of ABC-CLIO, LLC

ABC-CLIO, LLC
130 Cremona Drive, P.O. Box 1911
Santa Barbara, California 93116-1911

This book is printed on acid-free paper ∞

Manufactured in the United States of America

Contents

Acknowledgments

Thanks are owing to a great many people, not least of which are the 302 avid readers whose talk about their reading experiences is a core element of this book. I am equally indebted to the 276 interviewers in successive offerings of my graduate course on genres of fiction and reading, who recruited the avid readers, interviewed them, and transcribed the interviews (see QUESTIONS ABOUT READING). I would especially like to thank Kim Kofmel, who made available for my use her 32 interviews with avid readers from her science fiction, fantasy, and horror study. The research program of interviewing readers was supported in part by a grant from the Social Sciences and Humanities Research Council of Canada (SSHRC). Thanks also to these reading experts who have made suggestions, read sections of this book, provided helpful suggestions and examples, or agreed to be interviewed: Mary K. Chelton, Delilah Dean Cummings, Keren Dali, Simon Davies, Rosemary Lewis, Lynne McKechnie, Cindy Orr, Nancy Pearl, Jen Pecoskie, Paulette Rothbauer, Jake Ross, Sarah Ross, Joyce Saricks, Nancy Schiefer, Lucia Cedeira Serantes, Nancy Tausky, Ase Kristine Tweit, Elizabeth Waterston, and Neal Wyatt. And finally, as always, thanks are due to my editor Barbara Ittner, who got me started on this ABC project over coffee at an American Library Association Conference and has waited so patiently for its completion.

Introduction: 30 Ways of Looking at the Reading Experience

At the very heart of this book is the reader who reads for pleasure. Imagine a circle with the reader at the center. Around the circumference of the circle, visualize as nodes all those interrelated agents, processes, and activities geared to bringing about a happy encounter of reader and book. What are some of these nodes? There are the authors, who write manuscripts within the conventions of their chosen genre, whether epic poem, literary fiction, a vampire story, or a self-help book. There are the publishers and editors, who choose, shape, package, and publicize the books they publish. Intermediaries write the reviews and award the prizes that attract readers' attention to particular titles. Librarians and booksellers are agents of distribution as they order, display, and recommend particular books to readers. Changing technologies affect every phase of book production, distribution, and consumption from the composition of the manuscript to the reading of the book, now happening increasingly on-screen. And, crucially, there are the hidden structures, from the neurons in the brain to the literacy practices of schools and families, that are preconditions for the reader to be able to make sense of the black marks on page or screen. In this book, I offer 30 ways of looking at the experience of reading. The reader is the hero of this story, with the various entries exploring the relation between the reader and one or more of these other nodes. In the end, everything is connected.

The first entry, ABC AND COUNTING BOOKS, tips my hand about my attraction to alphabetic organization—its arbitrariness, inclusiveness, circularity, and intimate connection with the processes of reading itself. While I was trying to write this introduction, I answered a phone call from my daughter, who invited my 23-month-old grandson Cormac to sing the ABC song. He started out strongly, faltered and trailed away in the middle, and rallied at the close—"ABCDEFG mumble, mumble, mumble/Now I know my ABCs/Won't you sing along with me." Beginning readers all start their journey into literacy with the ABCs. Eventually, reading, whenever it is pleasurable, seems automatic and effortless. It's only when the invisible and taken-for-granted brain processes involved in reading break down that they come to our attention, as happens in the case study of the man who forgot how to read (see ALEXIA). You can start reading this book with the A entries, but you don't have to. You can start anywhere and end anywhere, pursuing your interests and skipping from one entry to another by following the cross-references formatted in small caps.

Like the authors of alphabet books for children, I have been forced into selectivity. Other contenders for B, which didn't get into the book, were Being Read To, Bestsellers, Bibliotherapy, and Boys' Reading. Other contenders for P include Perfect Book, Places to Read, Prison Reading, and Prohibited Reading. In the end, I opted for topics that allowed me to consider the experience of pleasure reading from as many different perspectives as possible, while always keeping the reader somewhere in the picture. Even the eight entries on popular genres— DETECTIVE, MYSTERY, AND CRIME FICTION; GOTHIC; HORROR; NONFICTION; RAGS TO RICHES; SELF-HELP; VAMPIRES, ZOMBIES, AND THE UNDEAD; and WESTERNS—are not *just* about texts. They consider the reading experience in relation to certain kinds of stories, characteristic literary conventions and tropes, and particular landmark authors. They are about the ways in which a well-executed example of the genre satisfies its contract with the reader and sometimes goes beyond it.

If you are curious about the avid readers whose reading accounts I freely quote, you might want to start with QUESTIONS ABOUT READING. My research interest in the reading experience was jump-started when I interviewed my first reader, Elizabeth (PhD candidate in English, age 35), years ago as an exercise when I was teaching a graduate course on research methods. This interview, which lasted over an hour, started with childhood reading and progressed through a series of open-ended "what-happened-next" questions to cover such topics as the importance of reading aloud to children, the parental taboo against comic books, continuities between childhood reading and adult reading, binge reading, choosing a book to read, recommending books to others, identification with a central character, rereading, indiscriminate reading, "safe" reading, and favorite books and genres. Are these responses shared by other readers, I wondered. Do other readers approach books written by women differently from the way they approach books by men (in Elizabeth's case, by reading biographies of female, but not male, writers)? Do other readers check to see if a book is "safe" by reading the ending before committing to a book? Do other readers describe themselves as "indiscriminate" and "voracious" readers (see IMPORTANT BOOKS VERSUS INDISCRIMINATE READING)?

To explore these questions and others, my research project of interviewing avid readers grew like Topsy to the current total of 302 open-ended interviews, which I have drawn on, where relevant, to illustrate aspects of the pleasures of reading. What becomes clear from these interviews is the diversity of the reading experience: one reader's favorite is another reader's BAD READING. But at the same time, common patterns emerge. Readers construct and remember their own versions of the books they read. They read themselves into books by identifying with characters, and they read the books back into their own lives (see CHANGING LIVES). In addition to my own interviews, I have rounded out the evidence about readers and their reading experience by drawing freely from other available sources: online postings by readers on discussion groups; self-reports by people who have written books or blog entries about their reading;

other people's empiric research with readers, especially recent work reported in doctoral theses; and published research on readers and reading.

This book is intended as a celebration of readers and the pleasures of reading. I invite readers to join the party.

ABC and Counting Books

Alberto Manguel (2006, 269–70) retells a Talmudic legend of creation in which God in effect said, not "Let there be light," but "Let there be words":

> [W]hen God sat down to create the world, the twenty-two letters of the alphabet descended from his terrible and august crown and begged him to effect his creation through them. God consented. He allowed the alphabet to give birth to the heavens and the earth in darkness, and then to bring forth the first ray of light from the earth's core, so that it might pierce the Holy Land and illuminate the entire universe.

Since then, alphabets have conjured up multiple worlds and universes and have given rise to dreams of creating books that can contain all knowledge. As an ordering principle, the alphabetic arrangement offers the serendipity of arbitrariness. Things can be juxtaposed—bean beside bear, ABC books beside Alexia—without the need to make logical connections (although everything in the end turns out to be connected).

Equally attractive to the imagination is the possibility of all-inclusiveness—of containing everything—promised by the alphabetic arrangement. The letter A can give us aardvark, abacus, absinthe, acorn, adder, alabaster, anchovy, ankle, Antarctic, anteater, apron—all kinds of animals, vegetables, minerals, and much more besides. And it's always possible retroactively to slip in a forgotten topic among the completed entries. Avid readers sometimes report that as children they tried to swallow the entire world by reading encyclopedias. Robert (English professor, age 57) recalled, "When I was a child, the *World Book* was absolutely crucial in the development of my reading. I lived in that encyclopedia. I'd look up things and reread many things in it, but I'd also simply read out of delight. I'd read in sequence sometimes. I'd look up something under P and then keep reading one thing after another. An encyclopedia is another form of the epic, of course; it's how you think of all knowledge in relation to a total containing form."

Before child readers get to an encyclopedia with its impossible promise of inclusiveness, they are introduced to the sparser form of ABC and counting books. In ABC books, authors have to make a choice—A is for Aardvark *or* A is for Apple. That selectivity is their charm. These are the foundational books that have introduced generations of children to the secret codes of letters and numbers that contain the universe.

Something about Alphabet Books

In *The Story of A*, Patricia Crain (2000, 4) has written compellingly about "the alphabet's intimate relationship with childhood and children." Beginners are often first introduced to letters as material objects: magnetized letters on the refrigerator or alphabet building blocks. During the Renaissance, Erasmus recommended baking letter-shaped cookies (Crain 2000, 19). As the most popular way of teaching the proper order of the letters, the alphabet song represents A to Z as a repeatable cycle: "Now I know my ABCs/Next time won't you sing with me?" Then come books. Alphabet and counting books are among the first books read to beginning readers, often before they are two years old. In fact, alphabet books have a long and distinguished history in teaching children to read, from the tablet-style hornbooks common in Shakespeare's time to the primers and spellers of the seventeenth and eighteenth centuries to the situation today where hundreds of illustrated alphabet and counting books vie for the book-buying adult's attention. For a sample of early alphabet books, check out the digitized collection, "Looking Glass for the Mind: Alphabets," at the University of Washington Library.

Most accounts of alphabet books start with the picture alphabet in *The New England Primer*, which uses rhyming couplets and woodcut pictures to illustrate each letter (see digitized images at Lilly Library 2009). *The New England Primer*, printed by Benjamin Harris of Boston around 1687, was the first reading primer used in the 13 colonies. It was reprinted many times thereafter, with textual emendations to suit changing conditions (Monaghan 2005, 99). By 1830, it had sold an estimated 6 to 8 million copies and had taught many generations of children how to read. Now the best-remembered element in the primer is its picture alphabet. Modern readers are usually struck by the way the rhyming couplets intended to teach the alphabet also manage to convey an entire world and worldview. Many children's books do this—remember *The Little Engine That Could* with its message of individual achievement and positive thinking: "I think I can. I think I can." But it's easier to see when the embodied worldview is no longer shared. In the case of the picture alphabet in *The New England Primer*, the couplets speak strongly of Puritan themes of original sin and redemption, the savagery of the natural world, the shortness of human life, and education as a matter of obedience and submission. Here's a sample of what children had the opportunity to learn:

A   In Adam's fall,
         We sinned all.

B   Thy Life to mend,
         God's Book attend.

. . .

F   The idle Fool,
         Is whipt at school.

. . .

T   Time cuts down all,
         Both great and small.

. . .

X   Xerxes the great did die,
         And so must you and I.

More fun is the British alphabet book *Tom Thumb's Play-Book* (1786), which teaches upper- and lowercase letters by personifying the letters and turning them into active characters in the story of "Aa Apple Pye." The apple tree of Adam's fall has become secularized and domesticated as apple pie. This text has lived on in other versions including Kate Greenaway's *A Apple Pie* (1886): "B BIT IT, C CUT IT, D DEALT IT, E EAT IT," and so on.

For later authors of alphabet books, the challenge has been to accompany each letter with words—nouns and verbs, often alliterating—that can be illustrated with verve and originality. The key in learning to read is repetition, and so the pages must be made sufficiently interesting and surprising to entice parents and children to multiple rereadings. One of my own favorites is Maurice Sendak's *Alligators All Around* (1962), which features alligators doing a lot of un-alligator-like activities: "B bursting balloons, C catching colds, D doing dishes, E entertaining elephants, F forever fooling, G getting giggles," up to "Z zippity zound/Alligators all around."

As a companion genre to the alphabet book, the counting book introduces children to counting and numbers. With its 10 numbers rather than 26 letters, the counting book is a more austere challenge, but inventive children's books authors and illustrators have risen to the challenge. See the childrensbooksguide.com Web site for an annotated list, showing cover art, of 43 all-time best alphabet books and 63 all-time best counting books.

What about the Child Reader?

Children encounter alphabet and counting books through the mediation of parents, relatives, and family friends, who buy these books, give them as gifts, or borrow them from the children's library. So we might ask: What about the child readers? What do they learn from these books that are intended to teach as well as amuse? As part of the answer, here is one story of a child reader's engagement with a counting book reported by Lynne McKechnie (2000). She conducted an ethnographic study of what 30 preschool girls do during a visit with their mothers to the local children's library and what they do with the library materials when they take them home. The girls, who were all within three months of their fourth birthday, were each outfitted with a sweatshirt that contained audio-recording equipment so that the library visits could be recorded and transcripts made. In the example that follows, Elissa and her mother are browsing the picture book collection to find books to borrow. Elissa spots Eric Carle's *The Very Hungry Caterpillar* (1969), obviously an old friend.

This counting book was a good choice. It is sixth in the childrensbooksguide.com list of "100 Children's Books of All-Time." By its 40th anniversary in 2009, *The Very Hungry Caterpillar* had sold over 29 million copies. With brilliant illustrations and a book design that features different-sized pages, each with a hole in it, Eric Carle's book tells the story of a caterpillar who eats his way through the days of the week, eating more and getting bigger with each day. On Monday he eats one apple, on Tuesday two pears, on Wednesday three plums, and by Saturday he munches through chocolate cake, a pickle, Swiss cheese, and a lot more.

There is much to be learned from this book: counting, the days of the week, different kinds of foods, and the life cycle of the caterpillar. What Elissa chooses to focus on is transformation (McKechnie 2000, 65–66):

Elissa: [Pulling *The Very Hungry Caterpillar* off the shelf] You know what?
Mother: What?
Elissa: This is it. This is the caterpillar one.
Mother: What happens to him?
Elissa: Gets big.
Mother: And then what?
Elissa: Then . . . he gets more bigger.
Mother: Uh, huh?
Elissa: And then he gets fat.
Mother: Right! And then when he finishes eating and getting big and fat, what happens at the very end?
Elissa: Butterfly! [Elissa and her mother both laugh joyfully]

References

Children's Books Guide. *"The Very Hungry Caterpillar* by Eric Carle."* http:// childrensbooksguide.com/reviews/the-very-hungry-caterpillar-by-eric-carle.

Crain, Patricia. 2000. *The Story of A: The Alphabetization of America from* The New England Primer *to* The Scarlet Letter. Stanford, CA: Stanford University Press.

Greenaway, Kate. 1886. *A Apple Pie: An Old Fashioned Alphabet Book.* Facsimile available in *A Celebration of Women Writers,* edited by Mary Mark Ockerbloom. http://digital.library.upenn.edu/women/greenaway/pie/A-Apple-Pie.html.

Lilly Library, Indiana University. 2009. "The New England Primer." http:// www.indiana.edu/~liblilly/NewEnglandPrimerWeb/alpha.html.

Manguel, Alberto. 2006. *The Library at Night.* Toronto: Alfred A. Knopf Canada.

McKechnie, Lynne (E. F.) 2000. "Ethnographic Observation of Preschool Children." *Library and Information Science Research* 22, no. 1 (February): 61–76.

Monaghan, E. Jennifer. 2005. *Learning to Read and Write in Colonial America.* Amherst: University of Massachusetts Press, American Antiquarian Society.

University Libraries, University of Washington. "Looking Glass for the Mind: 350 Years of Books for Children: Alphabets." http://content.lib.washington.edu/child-rensweb/alphabets.html.

Alexia

One morning Howard Engel, Canadian author of many Benny Cooperman DETECTIVE novels and an omnivorous reader, woke up to find that his world had completely changed. He got dressed, went outside to get his newspaper, and discovered that he couldn't read. As Engel (2007, 27–28) recalled the incident later:

> The July 31, 2001 *Globe and Mail* looked the way it always did in its make-up, pictures, assorted headlines and smaller captions. The only difference was that I could no longer read what they said. The letters, I could tell, were the familiar twenty-six letters I had grown up with. Only now, when I brought them into focus, they looked like Cyrillic one moment and Korean the next. . . . At first I thought it might be a trick. Was I the victim of a practical joke?

Engel noticed that the room looked normal, and he could read his clock—it was just print that was behaving badly. And the problem was not just with his newspaper but also with the books in his library, which similarly seemed to be written in some "Oriental" script. A stroke, he thought. Panicking, he woke up his son, and together they took a cab to the hospital. A stroke was indeed diagnosed, and Engel was told that the damage was to the visual area in the left part of the brain. It emerged that he had other problems as well, apart from not being able to read print—problems with recognizing colors, faces, and everyday objects; problems with finding his way around; and problems with remembering. Familiar objects such as apples, oranges, and tomatoes suddenly looked strange and had to be sorted out by touch or sniff. But, surprisingly, he could still write. He had, he was told, "alexia sine agraphia." This acquired alexia is to be distinguished from dyslexia, which is a puzzling condition that some people are born with. While in rehab, Engel mounted heroic efforts to find workarounds, using his other senses to supplement his damaged visual sense and fill in the holes in his memory. Eventually, through therapy, he got so that he could puzzle out words, sounding the words slowly and one letter at a time, like a kid first learning the ABCs.

The one thing he refused to do was give up on his identity as a writer. A breakthrough came when his therapists suggested that he keep a "memory book" to keep track of appointments and record his thoughts. In a memoir titled *The Man Who Forgot How to Read* (2007), Engel says, "The memory book gave a lift to my sense of being in the driver's seat of my life. [It] became my constant companion: part diary, part appointment book, part commonplace book." One big advantage of the memory book was that it got him to write everyday. Initially with no thought of writing another book, he found that images, plots, characters, and situations were coming to him. He began a novel, drawing closely on his own experience. Engel (2007, 107) says that in writing this book he "was trying to do for stroke victims what Dr. Temple Grandin did for autism." He wanted to tell a "ramping, stamping, thumping good story," but a secondary purpose was to "show what the world looked like through my eyes, the world as filtered through a battered brain" (107). His book was another Benny Cooperman novel called *Memory Book*, in which Cooperman has alexia sine agraphia and experiences problems with his memory, difficulty finding his way through hospital floors and corridors, and distortions in how things look. Circles look bent out of shape "like bicycle wheels that have been in an accident."

Left for dead in a dumpster in the company of a dead woman, the private detective Benny Cooperman ends up in hospital dealing with neurological damage caused by a bludgeoning to the head (detectives in books have to be felled by something more heroic than a stroke). In featuring a detective who solves the crime from a hospital or nursing home bed, Engel can look to some celebrated models such as Josephine Tey's *The Daughter of Time* (1951), Peter Dickinson's *One Foot in the Grave* (1979), and Colin Dexter's *The Wench Is Dead* (1999). Engel (2007, 106–7) explains, "I remembered Josephine Tey's wonderful mystery novel *The Daughter of Time*. Tey's detective is recovering in hospital from a serious accident in the line of duty and bored out of his mind while recuperating. He becomes fascinated by a picture of the infamous English king and child murderer, Richard III. The policeman sets out, metaphorically speaking, to find out the truth about history's most notorious uncle."

Physically confined and barely ambulatory, detectives Grant, Pibble, and Morse in their respective novels at least have the use of their mental powers, but Benny Cooperman has to crack the case with his memory shattered and his power of reading gone. He describes a new attempt in hospital to read *The Globe and Mail*:

> I kept hoping that the next thing I tried to read would be easier. It never was. I tried to sound out the words and the meanings of the headlines.
> "Con ... Coined ... Council ... Ignores ... Idiot ... Inject ... Ann ... Andrew ... Angry ..." I took a breath and tried again. Eventually I made out "COUNCIL EJECTS ANGRY COUNSEL-LOR." I had no difficulty with the sense of the words once I had decoded them. Language wasn't my problem; it was breaking the alphabet code that dogged my progress. (Engel 2005, 61)

Benny Cooperman describes to a visitor the unruly behavior of letters: "the letters keep changing shape on me, *r*'s becoming *p*'s without warning and *j*'s turning into *h*'s." He notes the way his injured brain is "democratic" in its confusion, not just mixing up *p*'s and *q*'s or *b*'s and *d*'s but "treat[ing] all letters equally" (Engel 2005, 71).

Word Blindness

Engel's two books, *The Man Who Forgot* and *The Memory Book*, together provide an insider's account of what it feels like to forget how to read. For an explanation of what is actually going on inside the brain of persons with alexia, we need to turn, as Engel himself did, to Oliver Sacks, noted author of case studies of neurological oddities published in a series of books, including *The Man Who Mistook His Wife for a Hat* (1985), *An Anthropologist on Mars* (1995), and *The Mind's Eye* (2010). While convalescing, Engel wrote to Sacks, the two men corresponded, and eventually they met. The upshot was that Sacks wrote an Afterword to *The Memory Book*, which was reprinted in Engel's *The Man Who Forgot How to Read* (2007). This is how Sacks begins his Afterword:

> In January of 2002, I found myself thinking about the problem of alexia, an inability to read resulting from damage to a particular area in the occipital cortex, the visual part of the brain. I had been seeing a patient, an eminent pianist, who had become unable to read music, and then to read words. She saw them as clearly as ever, but now they had become "unintelligible ... meaningless ... just marks on paper." All this my patient explained to me in a letter, for she was perfectly able to write, though unable to read what she had written.
> Shortly after this ... I received a letter from the Canadian novelist Howard Engel and soon afterward I met him. (Engel 2005, 238)

Later Sacks included Engel's case in *The Mind' Eye*, which tells the stories of people who navigate the world lacking one or another sense or ability that most people take for granted. The chapter, "A Man of Letters," is centered on Howard Engel's alexia but includes parallel cases of acquired alexia, including Sacks's own experience of looking at New York street signs and being surprised to find them written in some undecipherable script, "Phoenician, perhaps" (2010, 67). In Sacks's case, the alexia was part of a migraine aura and was short-lived. But it gave him a personal as well as professional interest in the problem.

Sacks's Afterword to Engel's book together with "A Man of Letters" make a good introduction to what neurologists know about alexia. Sacks says, "Alexia, or 'word-blindness,' as it was originally called, has been recognized by neurologists since the late nineteenth century, and has always been a source of fascination, for one thinks of reading and writing as going together, and it seems bizarre, counterintuitive, that someone should be able to write but be quite unable to read what they have just written. . . . It has often been observed that [alexia sine agraphia] is a purely visual problem; people with alexia have no difficulty, for instance, recognizing letters or words if they are traced on the hand" (Engel 2005, 240). Engel's problem was not with language in general but, according to Sacks, "a pure word blindness, the result of certain areas of the visual cortex being cut off, by the stroke, from the language areas on the same side of the brain" (240). Sacks (2010, 56) calls alexia a special case of visual agnosia, a condition in which people can have "perfectly normal visual acuity, color perception, visual fields, and so on—yet be totally unable to recognize or identify what they are seeing."

Engel's experience throws into high relief a process that is so automatic and effortless for fluent readers that it normally escapes attention. It appears that a number of regions of the brain interact simultaneously to perform most complex functions such as reading. When an injury happens to one region, the "seemingly automatic processes can fall apart and have to be reconstructed in other ways" (Sacks 2005, 243). As Sacks (2010, 56) puts it:

> We think of reading as a seamless and indivisible act, and as we read we attend to the meaning and perhaps the beauty of written language, unconscious of the many processes that make this possible. One has to encounter a condition such as Howard Engel's to realize that reading is, in fact, dependent on a whole hierarchy or cascade of processes, which can break down at any point.

References

Engel, Howard. 2005. *The Memory Book*. Toronto: Penguin Canada.

Engel, Howard. 2007. *The Man Who Forgot How to Read: A Memoir*. New York: Thomas Dunne Books.

Sacks, Oliver. 2005. "Afterword." In Howard Engel. *The Memory Book*. Toronto: Penguin Canada.

Sacks, Oliver. 2010. "A Man of Letters." In *The Mind's Eye*, 53–81. New York and Toronto: Alfred A. Knopf.

Bad Reading

Not long ago, a friend named Lynne said, "You should do some work on the topic of BAD reading experiences." "What do you mean—bad reading?" I wondered. This question launched a 10-minute description of her recent, horrible, no good, very bad reading event. The experience in itself was bad enough, she said, but she also wondered about the long-term effects on readers. Can the bad reading experience spread, like a wine stain on a white tablecloth, and affect a person's enjoyment of reading in general? Might bad reading, she speculated, turn people off reading, making them less likely to pick up a book in future? Or do readers try to erase the memory of the bad experience by choosing for their next reading a surefire book that they know will satisfy.

So this is what happened with Lynne's very bad reading. She told me that normally she likes to read books that have "meaning." (I knew this was so because she had been recently reading books and watching films that deal with the Holocaust.) But occasionally she is in the mood to read a lighter sort of book. With some anticipated time available for pleasure reading, she went to a big-box bookstore deliberately to pick out a book—the only requirement was that it had to be engaging. In the bookstore, she browsed for a new author, using the various clues available: she looked at the "Highly Recommended" shelves, noted which books were on the *New York Times* best-seller lists, and looked at JACKETS and cover blurbs and dipped into likely books to sample them.

Eventually, she found a book that looked promising. It starts out at a birthday party where a six-year-old, fatherless boy, Charlie, gets badly burned in an unsupervised campfire accident and his single mother is called in to take him to the hospital. Lynne likes medical mysteries, and the hook that had attracted her was the hurt child and the single mother. In the beginning, the book unfolds in a satisfying way: Charlie is rushed to the emergency room and the plastic surgeon is compassionate. But then the little boy drops out of the story, and attention turns to the growing romantic relationship between the single mother and the doctor. Complications arise because the plastic surgeon is married with two children and a wife who is part of a group of wives who are gossip mavens. With nothing more revealed about Charlie, the book turns into "gossip that I don't want to hear." It was "not the kind of reading experience I wanted. It was a lot of running around in circles. I could predict the ending. This was making me madder and madder and madder and madder."

So what was really going on that made this choice such a bad reading experience for this particular reader? It was a "betrayal," said Lynne. "I had been duped." What made things even worse was that she had paid $15 for the book and didn't have anything else in the house that would do what she wanted a book to do. So she didn't just stop reading when it took a wrong turn, despite "hating it so much that I felt like throwing the book across the room." In fact she persisted right up to page 200, page after horrible page of gossip about the lives of suburban women. The book that was supposed to be a medical thriller featuring a child turned out to be totally different genre: not exactly a romance but "everyday life with a romantic edge." "It was the *wrong* genre and the *wrong* sort of book for what I wanted."

By now, Lynne was getting riled up all over again in telling me the story: "I was misled"; "I was ripped off, led astray"; "It was like wanting comfort food and finding none in the house"; "I wanted a good story, but I've never hated a book so much"; and so on. Yikes! So she went to the library the very next day and "picked up a John Grisham because I knew it would give me a good plot line. I wanted pleasure and relaxation and ease." In hindsight, she thinks it would have been better if, in the first place, she had "gone to the shelves and picked out an old friend." Her need to erase the bad experience with a Grisham novel is analogous to riders who get back on a horse (in this case a different horse) after being thrown.

Keen to purge her house of the offending book, Lynne interrupted her account to go to her bedroom to retrieve it. She said the book could be the first trophy in a bad book research collection that I could start. In this case, the bad book was Emily Giffin's *Heart of the Matter*, not to be confused with Graham Greene's *The Heart of the Matter*. The paperback cover of the Giffin book is a light mauve with little ornamentation—the words "*New York Times* Bestselling Author" plus the author's name in deep purple, plus the book's title in gold, with the O in the title formed from a key-ring holding two keys. "Why would you think this could be a medical thriller?" I demanded. "What about this light purple cover? What about this description on the back cover, 'A powerful, provocative novel about marriage and motherhood, love and forgiveness'?" Somehow these genre clues were missed. This bad reading experience was a case of mistaken identity and a mismatch of genre and reader.

When I sent this account to Lynne later to ask if I got it right, she said: "Well, you must have got it right because I got madder and madder and madder as I read the story of my bad reading. The only thing I would add is that from now on I am taking my chances at the public library. This is a safe place for risky reading behavior—you can simply return the book and choose another." Several aspects of this case are interesting: the risks of picking a book outside of one's comfort zone, false expectations arising from a misidentification of genre, the way that external constraints to keep reading the unsatisfying book make the whole experience much worse, the intensity of the negative emotion induced by the bad experience, the need to erase the bad reading experience by jumping right back into reading with a surefire reading choice, and the reduction of risk when the book is borrowed from the public library (you don't feel as obligated to keep reading).

Heart of the Matter became the inaugural book in my research collection of bad books and the beginning of my investigation of the bad reading experience. To qualify, the reader has to enter into the reading transaction with an initial expectation of pleasure. We're not talking here about a reluctant reader who is required to read something he or she expects to be bad and then finds to be so. So if you had to read *The Scarlet Letter* in high school English class and hated it, that experience can be added to a database of things that discourage pleasure reading, but it doesn't count as bad reading in the specialized sense being considered here.

Nellie's bad book qualifies because of her high expectations of pleasure. She had waited 13 years for Anne Michaels's *The Winter Vault*. She had loved Michaels's previous book *Fugitive Pieces* and had found its writing style "clear, moving, and just beautiful"—it would "leave me breathless at times." Nellie had so looked forward to reading *The Winter Vault* that, when it finally appeared, she deliberately deferred her reading for a year until she had the best possible situation for luxurious reading enjoyment. She waited until she was on a summer holiday at the family cottage when she could "linger and luxuriate" in the prose. But, alas, the book still sits unfinished on the shelf. With high expectations, she had "started it with gusto" but couldn't get into the narrative, found that she didn't care about the characters or what happened to them, and felt "hammered over the head with the writing style—it seemed the author was just trying too hard." Not only is the book "only half-read and . . . a disappointment," but Nellie's sense of herself as a reader was shaken. She says, "I think I felt disappointed in myself too for a while, until I realized (I have to learn this again and again), that I'm allowed to dislike books even by authors that I used to really, really like, revere even."

The Broken Contract with the Reader

The second bad book I collected was Agatha Christie's *Postern of Fate*, given to me in paperback by Nancy, who usually enjoys Christie's crime fiction but wondered if this last book in the Christie oeuvre was some misguided attempt at parody or perhaps a crossover into some other genre featuring the repartee of a married couple. Or perhaps it was evidence that Christie had lost her famous powers of intricate plotting and was suffering from dementia. "Nothing happens," Nancy complained. "Tuppence says, 'I like to look into things' and then Tommy says, 'Yes, Tuppence, you do like to look into things.' " Nancy felt that the contract with the reader had been broken: there is an implicit promise that an Agatha Christie book makes—that there will be a well-constructed plot with clues, that the clues make sense, and that the clever solution results from detective work and not by accident (see DETECTIVE, MYSTERY, AND CRIME FICTION). And this promise was broken all along the line. Amazon customer reviews generally agreed with Nancy about *Postern of Fate*, most giving it a one or two on a five-point scale. But one Amazon reader, Molly, gave the book six out of a possible five. She read the Tommy and Tuppence conversations as "the essential last chapter of her autobiography"—"probably near-verbatim transcripts of conversations between Agatha and her husband Max [Mallowan] in her later years."

So the "nothing happens" complaint really means that nothing happens that the reader expects or wants to happen in the genre that she thinks she is reading. In effect, we read according to expectations we have *before* we start reading— expectations based, among other things, on genre (see BEFORE READING). In Lynne's case, she misidentified the genre due to her own lack of familiarity with books focusing on women's everyday lives in suburbia. In Nancy's case, she had read all the genre cues correctly, but the author hadn't delivered on the promised genre of detection fiction. Genre is a contract that the author makes with readers, promising a particular kind of experience. When the contract is broken, readers feel betrayed.

In *Before Reading*, Peter Rabinowitz (1987, 43) argues that competent readers are helped to make sense of texts because they have internalized certain rules of reading: "The rules ... serve as a kind of assumed contract between author and reader—they specify the grounds on which the intended reading should take place." Confronted with the myriad of details in any long text, readers use rules of reading to decide what they should pay close attention to and what they can safely skim or jump over. The rules of reading are genre-specific—when reading a classic detective story, we know that we should pay close attention to the murder method, clues, suspects and their alibis and motivations, inconsistencies in testimony, and so on. In the first chapter of *Postern of Fate* titled, "Mainly Concerning Books," *nothing* happens—that is, nothing happens that *should* happen in a detective novel. Tuppence sorts books to put on the shelves in her new home and talks to Tommy about her childhood reading. In the second chapter, Tuppence recalls books that were her childhood favorites ("Oh, here's *The Amulet* and here's *The Psamayad*. Here's *The New Treasure Seekers*"). How differently we would attend to these details in a memoir on the formative influences of childhood reading.

Abandoning a Book

When you start a book, do you feel impelled to read it to the bitter end, however little you are enjoying it? Some readers say that they aren't quitters.

They owe it to the author and to themselves, they say, to finish the book. They remain hopeful. Maybe the book will get better. Maybe the slog will be redeemed finally by a fabulous ending that catches up everything in a satisfying pattern. For example, June (homemaker, age 50) believes that she *must* finish every book, even ones she does not enjoy. She has been reading *Moby-Dick* off and on for a year and is grateful to be "getting near the end."

But some books are risky. The bad book can sometimes blindside readers with something that reaches right into their lives and disturbs or scares them or evokes painful memories. Jerome's bad book was Frank McCourt's *Angela's Ashes*, a memoir of growing up dirt-poor in the slums of Limerick, Ireland. Details of a hardscrabble childhood cut too close to the bone, with the result that Jerome couldn't read past page 45 and still has painful backflashes when he thinks of that book. Reading about a childhood similar to his own experience of growing up with no money and an absent father was "too disturbing personally." The problem often is that the bad book contains unsettling elements that the reader is not expecting and is not prepared for. When Sally was pregnant with her first child, a neighbor strongly recommended a book called *Mothers Who Think—Tales of Real-life Parenthood*. Sally bought the book and read the first essay, which was "all about this woman who must have been suffering from very severe postpartum depression—that, coupled with having one of the most colicky babies imaginable." Sally began to worry that "having a baby— something that I had been looking forward to—was actually going to make me feel miserable. I was a sixth-month pregnant, ticking bomb." Her worries were unfounded, but the bad reading experience "added a lot of unnecessary anxiety" to her pregnancy. In these cases, the reader was vulnerable, undefended against the dark possibility presented in the book.

The willingness to abandon a book is a protective measure that can reduce the risk of a really bad reading experience—the reader closes the book before too many negative emotions are engendered. Some readers, like Jen, are doubly vigilant, careful about picking books and willing to abandon bad choices. She says, "Sure I've started books and not enjoyed them—David Lodge's *Small World* is one example." But that book has been abandoned. Jen thinks of reading as a luxury, and she calculates the cost in time against the expected pleasure. She is very careful about her choices: "I think I have worked so hard to determine what I consider 'good' that I bypass reads that I don't believe will conform. To protect myself from bad reading experiences, I listen very carefully to 'literary authorities,' including friends and critics I enjoy." The person who recommended *Small World*, she says, was "a new-to-me advisor as opposed to a vetted advisor," whose advice will be taken a lot more cautiously in future.

Necessary Conditions

So what are the conditions that are required for a genuine bad reading experience? First, expectations need to be high—you expect something wonderful and you are betrayed. Second, there's no easy escape hatch. For one reason or another, you can't just abandon the book after 15 pages and never think about it again. You keep reading because you are the sort of person who never abandons a book. You keep reading, thinking it has to get better. You keep reading because you have already invested a lot of emotional energy in this book. You keep reading because you are on a train and have nothing else to read. You keep reading because you know the author and feel obligated.

It is striking that in each case, the bad book is someone else's favorite. At the end of a meditation on the theme of "I hate this damn book so much," Lev Grossman (2012) says: "Maybe it's just me": "Maybe other people will find joy and sadness and richness and beauty in this book, even though I didn't. . . . Probably it's not the book, it's just me." But actually it's the fatal conjunction of the "bad book" with the individual reader, who enters the reading encounter with a particular and idiosyncratic set of expectations, vulnerabilities, and personal history. Lynne's comment after she had read this meditation on bad reading that she had encouraged me to write: "I had almost forgotten how much I hated that book! But I loved *Angela's Ashes*—I have no idea what that fellow was talking about. This is a fine cautionary tale for readers advisers everywhere."

References

Grossman, Lev. 2012. "I Hate This Book So Much: A Meditation." *Time Entertainment*, July 25. http://entertainment.time.com/2012/07/25/i-hate-this-book-so-much-a-meditation/.

Rabinowitz, Peter. 1987. *Before Reading: Narrative Conventions and the Politics of Interpretation*. Ithaca, NY, and London: Cornell University Press.

Before Reading

Think of the last book that you read for pleasure. What had to happen *before* that book was in your hands or on your e-reader, ready for you to read the first sentence? Your answer is likely to involve a complex tangle of things as you try to answer the "Why I picked it up" question. Influencing your choice will be some factors that you can talk about and others of which you may not be aware. I have borrowed the title "Before Reading" from Peter J. Rabinowitz (1987), whose excellent book of the same title examines the way that our prior knowledge of literary conventions and how stories work help us make sense of narratives. We can think of reading in terms of three time periods, as Jean (teacher–librarian, age 44) describes them:

> That's the whole aura of reading. Some of it is *retrospective* because you deliberate on what you have read. It's *current* because you're experiencing. And also it's *anticipatory* because you know what you want to read.

As an illustration of how prior knowledge is crucial to the anticipatory, or before-reading, phase, consider this response as James (computer programmer, age 24) examines a book that he has not seen before. An interviewee in Kim Kofmel's 2002 study of science fiction and fantasy readers, James has said that he enjoys fantasy but sees no point to HORROR. Kofmel has asked James to take a look at Nancy Baker's *The Night Inside* and talk about what kind of book he would expect it to be:

James: [Takes the book in hand] It looks like a horror book based on the JACKET [which is black with red lettering]. "Vampire thriller." Maybe it's not horror. Okay, a vampire might not be horror. VAMPIRES are popular, I hate vampires. [Reading book jacket] "This is consummation as bloodbath." "Unique tale of gripping suspense." "Unrelenting tension between the monstrous." "Just as Clive Barker showed in his *Books of Blood* series, the real monsters are not necessarily the biological freaks." Yeah, I'd say that this is a horror book. I don't really particularly want to read it.

Pre-reading encompasses those crucial elements that, taken together, allow you to scan shelves of books in a library or bookstore and pick one that is likely to provide pleasure and reject others. It involves a combination of things: the knowledge that you already have in your head about particular authors, types of books, and genres; what you remember about a particular book from reviews, recommendations of friends, and publicity; what attracts you initially to pick up the book such as the TITLE or jacket; your assessment of the cover blurb (e.g., "consummation as bloodbath"); your reading of a sample paragraph or two; and of course the match between what is offered by the book and what you are in the mood for at the time of choosing. The successful encounter of a reader with a book he enjoys is the end point toward which an enormous number of institutional and individual activities converge: family structures that foster reading; the education system that teaches literacy; publishing houses that select certain authors' work to publish and promote; publicity, prizes, and reviewing structures that focus attention on certain books; bookstores, bookclubs, and libraries that make the physical or electronic book accessible to readers; and, finally, the individual reader's interests, reading skills, and previous experience with genres, literary conventions, authors, and books.

Making Choices

Novice readers often have trouble choosing enjoyable books because they have not yet accumulated the bulk of reading experience that would allow them to interpret available clues. Experienced readers, on the other hand, say that they have developed a system that almost always works for them and seems intuitive because it depends on their broad familiarity with books and authors. As

Rebecca (social worker, age 34) says, "I'm pretty good at telling what will work out. Maybe because of all these years of persisting through books." Paul (librarian, age 42) says, "I get a feel for a book. I am sometimes wrong but rarely."

So what systems do these experienced readers use? It's not a single element but a whole cascade that involves the reader's prior knowledge of the author and the genre as well as information on the book. Marsha (student, age 26) says that she uses an array of cues: previous experience with the author ("It's very safe to know that you've got an author that you like, and there are more books sitting there waiting. . . . I like the fact that LeCarre is still writing"); the reputation of the book ("I always thought I should read important books"); the reputation of the publisher ("I decided that Penguins . . . were important books"); recommendations of friends and family ("I very rarely pick up a book that I've never heard of"); and clues provided by the packaging of the book itself ("I always read the blurbs on the back. I'm easily put off or become very cynical of something that's too glowing"). Paul also puts a book through a series of tests and filters:

> I read the first few pages, look at the back cover, look at the front cover, read what I can about the author, and get an impression of the book. . . . The cover is important. The title. What I know about the author. What other people have said about it. Who it was that said that—is it *The Times Educational Supplement* or it is *The Kodiak Daily Fishwrapper?* I read all the information that is designed to make you interested in the book. Then I'll open it just at random and read one paragraph on each page and then open it again. Maybe three or four times I'll do that and just dip in. So the book is auditioning for me. It's like an audition: the book reads a very small part but it's only got that one chance to succeed.

Selection Strategies

Readers overwhelmingly report that they choose books according to their mood and what else is going on in their lives—short books, easy reads, and old favorites are reread when they are busy or under stress; more demanding and unfamiliar material when their lives are calmer. As one reader explained, "It depends on my mood. . . . Some days you don't want a book that reaches too deep into you and other days you do." Readers use tried-and-true strategies to maximize their ability to find books they are in the mood to read. Here are the most common:

• *Author*

The single most important strategy for choosing is to look for a book by a known and trusted author. Reading books published in a series—especially common with children's books, fantasy novels, and detective fiction—is an intensified version of the strategy of following an author. Readers' major complaint is that favorite authors are dead, are no longer writing, or else are publishing new books at a glacial pace. Rene (physician, age 32) said, "When I'm looking for a new mystery writer, if I see ten books by an author, I'll go 'Ah ha! I'm going to read her, because there are a lot of them.' " Other avid readers said, "It's like finding a gold mine and following a vein when you find a good author like Salman Rushdie"; "I think first of authors and then when I have exhausted those possibilities, I'll think of types. If a library has books divided into genres then that makes it easier for me." A few readers, like Sarah (library assistant, age 40), are remarkably single-minded about following authors:

> I remember at one stage I decided I was going to read the whole library entirely—all the fiction. I never read nonfiction. I would start at the A's and I would work down to the Z's. After a few months I realized I was never going to finish the A's so I started to be more selective. It took me five years to reach the D's. I never got past the D's because then I read Dickens and Dostoevsky and I got held up on them [laughter] another five years.

• *Genre*

After author, genre is the second most important factor in helping narrow down choices. When readers don't have author names handily in their heads, which is often the case, they browse. Shelving books by genre helps readers by narrowing down options to a manageable number. Morag (publishing company employee, age 35) says that when she is looking for fantasy titles, "I'll go into a bookstore with a feeling. It's sort of like 'What do I want to read? What world do I want to be taken to?' " Genre is often used in conjunction with author as a two-step filter: start with genre and then, within genre, look for a favorite author. Lynnette (retired, age 65) reports, "If I am looking for something light to read like a mystery novel, I will look at the authors—I have certain authors I like—and I look to see if there's something I haven't read before." Fiona (information specialist, age 31) says that in a general bookstore, she goes right to the science fiction section: "Either I am looking to see 'has so-and-so written a new book' or I start with A and scan through the section." Contrariwise, readers use genre to eliminate from consideration whole categories of books that they don't enjoy. Maurice (professional engineer, age 57) says, "There are some words that turn me off—you know like 'psychological thriller' or 'horror.' If I see that, it goes straight back on the shelf."

• *Clues Provided by the Book Itself*

Once the reader starts to browse within a range of books, then the clues provided on the book itself become important. As Charles (program coordinator, age 23) explained, "When you're as genre-specific as I guess I am, and read as voraciously as I do, you're looking for some quick identifiers on what's a good book. It'll take me ten minutes to go in [to the science fiction section], get five books, and leave because I'm just so familiar with the genre in general." Readers mentioned most often the importance of the JACKETS AND BOOK COVERS, the blurb on the back, and reading a sample page. TITLES are important—readers said they were drawn both to an unusual, catchy title (in the case of an unfamiliar book) and to a familiar title that they had heard about before. A feature that strongly attracts one reader equally strongly puts off another, but in each case the information has been helpful in matching the book to the reader who will enjoy it. One reader said, "Another way that I choose books is if they have won prizes," whereas another said he is *less* likely to pick prizewinners because the basis for awarding prizes is usually "a type of literary excellence that doesn't particularly make for enjoyable reading."

• *Sample Page*

A final test for many is to read a sample paragraph or page. Maurice says, "I can tell within one paragraph whether I like the person's style or not." This strategy is a version of Ford Madox Ford's famous page 99 test: "Open the book to page ninety-nine and read, and the quality of the whole will be revealed to you." The point about page 99 is that it is arbitrary and under the control of the typesetter and book designer, not the writer. Authors polish and work over the opening and closing pages of a work, knowing that they will receive special attention and be given extra weight. A random page is a good indicator of the general writing style as well as the level of literary competence demanded by the book. With some genres, checking out the diction is a useful filter for what Morag complains about as "a lot of made-up words, concepts, and character names." She says, "I don't want to spend my entire book reading something like, 'Tarnsman of Gor picked up his yakting and walked to the pingting.' I like my science fiction written in English with the occasional foreign place name."

• *Recommendations and Reviews*

Recommendations are important, but only from trusted sources whose tastes are known to be compatible, such as certain reviewers, family members and "friends that know my taste," some rare but treasured bookstore staff and librarians, and some social media acquaintances. Readers sometimes complain that their particular favorite genre is not adequately reviewed: "not a lot of mainstream magazines review science fiction unless they either have a movie deal pending or they're written by a well-known author." It's easier for readers of literary fiction to find helpful reviews. Jean described having sampled little bites of a book through reviews until she felt desperate to eat the whole cake:

> When I read the fifth review of Umberto Eco's *The Name of the Rose* I was so burned up with desire to have that book I was just about crazy.

I actually went out and bought it in hard cover—which I very rarely do. And then I gave it to as many people as I could to justify the price! But I had to have that book because I felt so frustrated. I had tasted enough of the bits and pieces [through reading the reviews] and I needed to have the whole cake, not just a piece of it!

Serendipity

Strategies of looking for new books by known authors or browsing within preferred genres tend to produce selections that are more of the same. But what if the reader wants to break out into something new? Readers also reported that they sometimes acted on sheer impulse to introduce novelty into their reading and discover new authors. One reader said she always checks the just-returned section of the public library first because "I place faith in people having chosen the popular novels and returning them." Another described how she would occasionally "just walk along an aisle in a library, run my finger along the spines of the books and just go, 'Stop now' and pull it out." Unless she can tell it's going to be something completely unappealing "like a war story," she'll read it, just as an experiment. Other tactics used to enhance serendipity included randomly picking a different letter each time and examining fiction with authors' names beginning with a random letter, say A or S. Readers adopt various strategies to establish the right balance between safety and the certainty of success on the one hand and novelty and surprise on the other.

Because readers are reluctant in bookstores to shell out hard cash on a "cold buy," libraries and thrift stores support readers in taking risks with new and unfamiliar authors, genres, or subject areas. Daphne (student, age 29) describes herself as a voracious reader who tries for "huge variety" in the fiction she reads. She and a friend invented the "Dollar Book Deal" as a way to introduce variety and surprise into their reading choices:

I have one friend who also reads a lot and we have sort of a Dollar Book Deal going on. When we go to rummage sales or a thrift store, the rule is: If you find a book that is a dollar or less and you've never heard of it before, then you buy the book, based on pretty much the cover. She'll read it and I'll read it, and we will discuss the book afterwards. That is probably my favorite way to get books because they are always kind of a surprise. I have found some of my favorite books of all time that way and I've also found some of the worst books on the planet that way [laughter]. But, either way, it's a lot of fun.

References

Kofmel, Kim Grace. 2002. "Adult Readers of Science Fiction and Fantasy: A Qualitative Study of Reading Preference and Genre Perception." Doctoral dissertation. London, Ontario: The University of Western Ontario.

Rabinowitz, Peter J. 1987. *Before Reading: Narrative Conventions and the Politics of Interpretation*. Columbus: Ohio State University Press. https://ohiostatepress.org/index.htm?/books/complete%20pdfs/rabinowitz%20before/rabinowitz%20before.htm.

Books about Books and Reading

There are two kinds of bibliographies: those that dream of being exhaustive and listing everything and those that are selective and use strict criteria to list a particular kind of "best." Because the bibliography of reading is enormous and growing all the time, I am going for the selective list and restricting things even more with the extra challenge of the alphabetic arrangement—only one book for each letter. To see the origin of this idea, see Z TO A, A TO Z READING.

Some letters are clearly harder than others, because there are either too few (the letters I and X) or too many. For the letter S, for example, I have an embarrassment of riches, including among others Dai Sijie's *Balzac and the Little Chinese Seamstress* (2002), Francis Spufford's *The Child That Books Built* (2002), Joyce Saricks's *The Readers' Advisory Guide to Genre Fiction* (2009), Nina Sankovitch's *Tolstoy and the Purple Chair* (2011), Patricia Meyer Spacks's *On Rereading* (2011), and Will Schwalbe's *The End of Your Life Book Club* (2012)—each different and each a treasure worth tracking down.

The alphabetic rule is ruthlessly restrictive, but I have been catholic and expansive in the topics covered. Some of these books are about the passion for collecting books or ordering and displaying them on bookshelves. Some are about the industries and institutions that promote books and reading: authorship, publishing, bookselling and bookstores, and libraries. Many are about the experience of reading itself as it is shaded by a particular interest (e.g., childhood reading, women's reading, rereading) or a particular activity (e.g., talking about books, recommending books, remembering books that are lost or neglected, exploring the influence of a particular author, collecting sightings of people reading). Some are about the reading brain or about the emerging technologies that enable reading in new ways. And some are included because they are delightfully offbeat. Most are NONFICTION, but I have included three works of fiction that are variously about storytelling or reading. When making tough choices, I mostly gave the nod to more recently published books and to books that haven't been discussed extensively elsewhere. Hence reluctantly I have left out Italo Calvino's wonderful novel about reading, *If on a Winter's Night a Traveller*, and Alberto Manguel's endlessly engaging *The History of Reading*. And of course a key selection criterion for the chosen books is that they have to offer pleasure to booklovers.

A   Ash, Russell, and Brian Lake. 2007. *Bizarre Books: A Compendium of Classic Oddities*. New York: HarperCollins. Ash and Lake have collected hundreds of examples of book TITLES that are unintentionally amusing. Some are odd author/title combinations (e.g., *Your Teeth* by John Chipping; *A Treatise on Madness* by William Battie). Some involve double entendres (*Making It in Leather*; *Suggestive Thoughts for Busy Workers*). Many titles are oddly specialized (*Cooking with God*; *Harnessing the Earthworm*; *Do-it-yourself Coffins*; *Truncheons: Their Romance and Reality*; *Encyclopedia of Shampoo Ingredients*).

B   Bayard, Pierre. 2007. *How to Talk about Books You Haven't Read*. Translated by Jeffrey Mehlman. Vancouver: Raincoast Books. In 12 chapters with such titles as "Books You Don't Know," "Books You Have Skimmed," "Books You Have Forgotten," and "Inventing Books," this witty book celebrates the creativity of the reader, the skimmer, and, yes, the nonreader.

C   Collins, Paul. 2003. *Sixpence House: Lost in a Town of Books*. New York: Bloomsbury. When bibliophile Collins and family moved from San Francisco to Hay-on-Wye, a small village in Wales with 40 secondhand bookstores, his experiences became material for this book, which is part travel writing, part memoir, and part meditation on books and reading. His bookish topics include biblio-obsession, book binding, literary frauds (e.g., *I Was Hitler's Maid*), book JACKETS, titles, forgotten books, remaindered books, and negotiations with editors as Collins completed his first book, *Banvard's Folly*.

D   Dehaene, Stanislas. 2009. *Reading in the Brain: The Science and Evolution of a Human Invention*. New York: Viking. Drawing on brain imaging studies, cognitive psychology experiments, and case histories of stroke victims, Dehaene discusses such topics as primate evolution, brain circuitry, and neuroplasticity in his exploration of what he calls the "reading paradox": reading is only 5,000 years old and yet we do it with a brain that is the product of millions of years of evolution in a world without writing.

E   Epstein, Jason. 2001. *Book Business: Publishing Past Present and Future*. New York and London: W.W. Norton. This insider account of the publishing business is an expanded version of Norton Lectures delivered in 1999 at the New York Public Library. An editorial director at Random House for 40 years, Epstein recalls landmark publishers, authors, and books and anticipates great changes in store for the publishing business on the brink of an enormous technological transformation. Book publishing, he says, is "by nature a cottage industry, decentralized, improvisational, personal," and after a period of domination by conglomerates it may "become once more a cottage industry of diverse, creative autonomous units."

F Fforde, Jasper. 2011. *One of Our Thursdays Is Missing*. New York: Viking. This is the sixth novel in a series featuring the ace literary detective, Thursday Next, who vanishes a week after she has been called in to avert a genre war. The series includes other bookish titles such as *Lost in a Good Book*, *The Well of Lost Plots*, *First among Sequels*, and *The Woman Who Died a Lot*. Recommended for readers who enjoy a playful, fantasy bookworld full of literary allusions, puns, and overturned literary conventions.

G Gorra, Michael. 2012. *Portrait of a Novel: Henry James and the Making of an American Masterpiece*. Gorra brings extensive scholarship and critical flair to telling the story of how James came to write *The Portrait of a Lady* (1881). One of the many fairly recent books that explore the Henry James theme (for others, check out these biographical novels featuring Henry James: Emma Tennant's *Felony*, 2002; David Lodge's *Author, Author*, 2004; and best of all, Colm Toibin's Booker-shortlisted *The Master*, 2004).

H Hornby, Nick. 2012. *More Baths Less Talking*. San Francisco: Believer Books. The fourth collection of *Believer* magazine monthly columns on "Stuff I Have Been Reading" continues in the same invigorating and funny spirit as the previous collections, *The Polysyllabic Spree* (2004), *Housekeeping vs. the Dirt* (2006), and *Shakespeare Wrote for Money* (2008). Each month Hornby records the books he has bought; the books he has downloaded for free; the books he has read, skimmed, or rejected; and how these books have intersected with his life. A decade of *Believer* columns has been collected in *Ten Years in the Tub: A Decade Soaking in Great Books* (2013).

I Iyer, Pico. 2012. *The Man within My Head*. New York: Alfred A. Knopf. Novelist and travel writer Iyer takes us on a journey into his past, into places he has lived and visited—Bolivia, Mexico, Saigon, Ethiopia, Cuba, Sri Lanka, Colombia, Bhutan, California—and into his lifelong fascination with Graham Greene, whose stories of lonely and displaced outsiders seem to have anticipated Iyer's own "deepest life story." With his memory stored with scenes from *The Quiet American*, *The Comedians*, *Stamboul Train*, *The End of the Affair*, *Our Man in Havana*, and so on, Iyer finds that Greeneland provides a kind of map to make sense of his own dislocated world and his relationship with his dead father.

J Jack, Brenda. 2012. *The Woman Reader*. New Haven, CT, and London: Yale University Press. Jack begins her scholarly account of the woman reader with 28,000-year-old cave paintings and works forward through episodes of struggle that have included restrictions on a woman's education, censorship of what she can read, the upsurge in female novel reading in the eighteenth century, and thereafter the emergence of women as transgressive readers and writers.

K Kingsolver, Barbara. 2004. Foreword. In *Book Sense Best Books: 125 Favorite Books Recommended by Independent Booksellers*. New York: Newmarket Press. One of a growing subgenre of books that winnow out the "best of" for people who want informed suggestions about what to read, this slender volume excels in its selectiveness: 10 works of adult fiction from *Atonement* to *Secret Life of Bees*; 5 adult nonfiction suggestions from *Devil in the White City* to *Seabiscuit*; 10 children's books from *The Bad Beginning: A Series of Unfortunate Events* to *The Sisterhood of the Travelling Pants*; 50 top reading group recommendations from *All the Pretty Horses* to *Three Junes*; and 50 top classics to share with your children and grandchildren from *Bark, George* to *Whale Talk*.

L La Force, Thessaly, ed., and Jane Mount, illust. 2012. *My Ideal Bookshelf*. New York: Little, Brown and Company. Asked to pick a small shelf of books that mattered most in their lives, more than 100 chefs, graphic designers, illustrators, writers, professors, and musicians chose books that inspired them, and they each talked about their chosen books in an interview with Thessaly La Force. Each spread, alphabetically arranged by readers' last name, consists of a reader's bookshelf illustrated by Jane Mount as a spine-out display of titles plus a one-page distillation of the reader's interview with Thessaly La Force. Sally Singer, editor, whose shelf includes Grace Paley's *Collected Stories*, said, "I think I saw myself as a Grace Paley character." Oliver Jeffers, illustrator, who argued that books should be judged by their covers, picked his titles by spine color—red, yellow, orange, blue. Pico Iyer included Graham Greene's *The Quiet American*, which he calls his "uncertain Bible" that he turns to every few months. Coralie Bickford-Smith, book designer for Penguin, described why the pattern she created for Dracula is "composed of garlic flowers."

M Marcus, Leonard S., ed. 2012. *Show Me a Story: Why Picture Books Matter. Conversations with 21 of the World's Most Celebrated Illustrators*. Somerville, MA: Candlewick Press. These illustrators of children's picture books, including Mitsumasa Anno,

Quentin Blake, John Burningham, Eric Carle, Tana Hoban, Helen Oxenbury, James Marshall, Robert McCloskey, Maurice Sendak, William Steig, and Rosemary Wells, provide an insider's view of the craft of picture-book making. Anno says, "In my books, I don't want to teach. What I have done might better be described as 'teaching without teaching'—providing the conditions that allow children to learn for themselves."

N   Nafisi, Azar. 2003. *Reading Lolita in Tehran.* New York: Random House. Perhaps the most celebrated of the books about reading groups, Azar Nafisi's memoir foregrounds a group of her seven most engaged female students who meet every Thursday morning for two years in Nafisi's living room to read and talk about forbidden Western classics. They read *Lolita* (in Xeroxed copies because censors had banned un-Islamic texts), *Mme Bovary, The Great Gatsby, Daisy Miller, Pride and Prejudice,* and others. In that living room, these young women are free to imagine and dream, in contrast to what is happening outside. Nafisi's memoir describes the darkening reality of post-1979 Iran: decreasing access to Western books, censorship, prohibited reading, turf wars over university curricula, her resignation from her university job, the eight-year war with Iraq, attacks on students by the Revolutionary Guard, and the murder of dissidents.

O   Ondaatje, Michael, Michael Redhill, Esta Spalding, and Linda Spalding, eds. 2000. *Lost Classics.* Toronto: Alfred A. Knopf Canada. Seventy-four writers from Margaret Atwood to Ronald Wright provided interesting, quirky essays on books that influenced them but are now lost, hard to find, or underappreciated. The editors' introduction begins, "A book that we love haunts us forever; it will haunt us, even when we can no longer find it on the shelf or beside the bed where we must have left it."

P   Piper, Andrew. 2012. *Book Was There: Reading in Electronic Times.* Chicago and London: The University of Chicago Press. Forget about all those books about the death of reading/death of the book/death of deep thinking, and read this balanced discussion of the gains and losses of print reading versus E-READING. Chapters on the differing sensory experiences of interacting with e-books and print books—holding them, facing the page, turning the page, writing notes, sharing books with others—add up to a phenomenology of the differing kinds of reading made possible by different technologies of the book.

Q   Queenan, Joe. 2012. *One for the Books.* New York: Viking. A grumpy, voracious, opinionated, and idiosyncratic reader, Queenan is fervent about what he likes and dislikes. Detective fiction is "piffle." He would rather have his "eyelids gnawed on by famished gerbils than join a book club." He won't read books with ugly covers or e-books. He has taken up various reading challenges: spending a year reading only short books, spending a year reading books picked with his eyes closed, and so on.

R   Rushdie, Salman. 1990. *Haroun and the Sea of Stories*. London: Granta Books. A children's story with crossover appeal for adults, this multilayered fable is about storytelling itself. Haroun's father Rachid used to open his mouth and "out would pop some brand-new saga, complete with sorcery, love-interest, princesses, wicked uncles, fat aunts, mustachioed gangsters in yellow check pants, fantastic locations, cowards, heroes, fights, and half a dozen catchy, hummable tunes." When Rachid loses his gift, Haroun and his father journey to the realm of the Sea of Stories, where something is very wrong. The "Arch-Enemy of All Stories" has masterminded a thick, dark poison that is gumming and tangling up the Streams of Story and turning them into sludge. For example, "Certain popular romances have become just long lists of shopping expeditions." An exuberant, fantastical, and story-affirming *tour de force*.

S   Spufford, Francis. 2002. *The Child That Books Built*. London: Faber and Faber. A reading memoir in which Spufford rereads the books that he read so voraciously as a child as a way of coping with the family tragedy of his younger's sister's kidney failure: "I am reading to banish pity and brittle bones. I am reading to evade guilt, and avoid consequences."

T   Talmadge, Eva, and Justin Taylor. 2010. *The Word Made Flesh: Literary Tattoos from Bookworms Worldwide*. HarperCollins. In this curated collection of literary tattoos, booklovers wear their favorite quotations or book illustrations on their skin. The authors have assembled more than 150 color photographs of literary tattoos together with, in some cases, statements about the personal significance of the chosen work. Check out the Web site at http://tattoolit.com/.

U   Urquhart, Jane. 2009. *L.M. Montgomery*. Toronto: Penguin Canada. In this deft and moving biography of Lucy Maud, a strong thread ties the elements together: Montgomery's life, motherless and raised on an island raised by stern grandparents; the sources of the biography, which were 50 years of keeping scrapbooks and journals in which LMM recorded and transformed events of her life; and the novels in which Anne, Emily, Jane, and all the others inspired readers everywhere to think of themselves as kindred spirits. Alice Munro was one such reader, who has said that *Emily of New Moon*, which is about the development of a girl child into a writer, was "the watershed book" of her life. Award-winning novelist Jane Urquhart ends her biography of Montgomery by imagining another small-town Canadian girl, aged 11—her own mother—who had discovered by her summer reading of the *Emily* trilogy that riveting stories didn't need to be set "in faraway England" but could be told about characters living in Canada in "plain brick and clapboard houses." She announced, "I'm going to write a novel."

V   Van Riel, Rachel, and Olive Fowler. 1996. *Opening the Book: Finding a Good Read.* Bradford, West Yorkshire, England: Bradford Libraries in association with Morley Books. Library consultant Rachel Van Riel has worked for decades with U.K. public libraries to help transform them into reader-centered places. This book is aimed at helping individual readers discover themselves as readers and have the confidence to expand their reading choices. What is your reading type? Are you a thrill seeker, or do you want something comforting? Van Riel and Fowler give tips on how to take risks in book choices and how to know when to quit.

W   Wilson, Julie. 2012. *Seen Reading.* Calgary, Alberta, Canada: Freehand Books. Wilson is, she says, a "literary voyeur." From her collection of 700 plus sightings of people reading on Toronto subways, streetcars, and buses, she offers 83 readers. For each there is a brief description of the reader (e.g., "Caucasian male, wearing black knitted cap with Canadian crest, Sony headphones, brown cords, green plaid dress shirt, and black West Beach jacket"), information about the book (*Slaughterhouse-Five*, Kurt Vonnegut, Dial Press Trade Paperback, 1999, 48), and a microfiction in which Wilson imagines who the reader might be.

X   Xenophon. *Anabasis.* In 400 BC, Xenophon was a leader of the Ten Thousand soldiers of the Greek army as they beat a perilous, nine-month retreat some 1,500 miles through upper Iraq, Syria, and eastern Turkey northward to the Black Sea, beset by snow and ice, famine, and enemy ambushes. When at last from the top of a mountain they spotted the Black Sea, the army shouted out jubilantly, "*thalatta, thalatta*," "the sea, the sea," a refrain of relief that has echoed intertextually down through subsequent literature, especially Victorian adventure stories of surviving peril in the East. In Chapter 1 of James Joyce's *Ulysses*, Buck Mulligan says, "Ah,

Dedalus, the Greeks. I must teach you. You must read them in the original. *Thalatta! Thalatta!* She is our great sweet mother."

Y   Yardley, Jonathan. 2011. *Second Reading: Notable and Neglected Books Revisited*. New York: Europa Editions. Marketed as an ideal guide for reading groups, this book is a collection of 60 reviews that Yardley wrote originally for the *Washington Post*. Yardley provides an entertaining tour through books that he found even better the second time around (most of them) and some that that disappointed—notably *The Catcher in the Rye*, which proved to be an unpalatable combination of Salinger's "execrable prose" and Holden Caulfield's "jejune narcissism" (137).

Z   Zusak, Markus. 2005. *The Book Thief*. New York: Alfred Knopf. Narrated by Death, who had his work cut out for him in Nazi Germany during the war, this story is about "Some words, An Accordionist, Some Fanatical Germans, A Jewish fist fighter, And quite a lot of thievery." Or you could say the story is about a parentless girl who steals a book, is adopted by a family on the outskirts of Munich during the dark days of Nazi book-burnings and death camps, learns how to read, steals more books, becomes a writer, and discovers the power of words.

Changing Lives

We all have categories for books. There is the well-known Three-Books-I-Would-Take-to-a-Desert-Island category. There's the Three-Books-I'm-Glad-I-Read-Before-I-Die category. For list makers, there's the Best-Book/Worst-Book/First-Book-I-Have-Ever-Read. For worriers, there's the Book-I-*Should*-Read (but probably won't because it's too long or too boring). And then of course there is the Book-That-Changed-My-Life. For we *do* believe that books change lives. And it's not just because through reading we acquire skills that are useful in coping with living in a modern society where almost every activity assumes literacy, although that's true too. At a Thanksgiving dinner party, I mentioned that I was working on this Books-Change-Lives section but acknowledged that some people think the whole concept silly. Kristine, who was visiting from Oslo, said, "Well, a book changed my life—it's what prompted me to become a Catholic." She said that the life-changing book was written by the Norwegian Nobel-awarded author Sigrid Undset (1882–1949).

Undset is best known for her historical, medieval novels such as the trilogy *Kristin Lavransdatter*, but she also wrote contemporary novels, among which is the life-changing book, *Gymnadenia, or The Wild Orchid* (1931). Kristine read *The Wild Orchid* when she was 21, while going through a period of confusion about religion and the "hundreds of interpreters of Christianity, who all proclaimed their version as the only acceptable one." When Kristine's aunt lent her *The Wild Orchid*, she was expecting a medieval epic told with Undset's signature storytelling sweep and her extensive knowledge of history. Instead she got something completely different: a contemporary story set in Oslo between the world wars. The novel traces the religious journey of the main character, Mr. Paul Selmer, and his conversion to Roman Catholicism, which paralleled Undset's own conversion. Here's how Kristine described her memory of this transformative book:

> When I recall the novel, what comes to my mind is the color grey and dark green, rainy weather, and the sense of silence and loneliness. The book was not enjoyable, passionate, cruel, and colorful like Undset's stories set in medieval Norway. Still, I was not disappointed, because there was something else going on when I read: a growing sense that the silent life of this Mr. Selmer was a matter of importance to me. Although the two of us had absolutely nothing in common in any other respect, I came to identify with his vague search for a possible meaning of life, and his experience of getting closer to the church. The reading of this novel ended my state of confusion on religion, and I decided eventually to convert to the Roman Catholic church myself, which I did a couple of years later.
>
> I do not think I want to read the book again. In fact I did not really like it, as literature or as art. Still I did read it, as I understood that the book had something important to offer me. I think I stayed with it because I was always a reader. Through my childhood and youth, I had read stacks of books, both fiction and nonfiction, series books and serious writings. Maybe this variety taught me something about different modes of reading and helped me persist with a book that did not give me the expected experience. I suppose that if the book had reached me at another age or in another state, I may have given up on it after the first few chapters. In this case, it turned out to be a match.

Kristine's reading story is a case of what I have called elsewhere "finding without seeking" (Ross 1999). She didn't seek out this book as a way to help clarify ideas about religious faith. But when *The Wild Orchid* was not what she had expected, she stuck with it long enough to see that the book spoke directly to her concerns. Her own preoccupations at the time of reading mediated how she related to the central character, Mr. Selmer, and his spiritual journey. In such cases, readers play a crucial role in enlarging the meaning of the text by reading it within the context of their own lives.

Such stories of the happy conjunction of reader and book are common—so common in fact that when bookseller Roxanne J. Coady and editor Joy Johannessen asked various prominent people to support literacy by supplying a short essay on their life-changing book, the contributors knew what was expected and obligingly came through. Their essays are collected in a book titled *The Book That Changed My Life* (2006). The collection provides a cloud of witnesses in support of the idea that books can be transformative. The great thing about the topic of the life-changing book is how it elicits stories. People can't just say, "Such-and-such book changed me." They have to say variously: I was in this particular situation or facing this decision or crisis. Here's how I came upon the transformative book. This is what happened in my life as a result of my reading. Here's the element in the book—its language, a particular character, a life situation, a decision, a recognition—that moved me, changed me, helped me, made me the person I am, or gave me the gift I needed at just the right time.

Claire Cook, author of *Must Love Dogs*, locates her transformative reading at a time of huge personal crisis: "When my mother died suddenly just before my eleventh birthday, I decided that spending time with Nancy was preferable to inhabiting my own life" (Coady and Johannessen 2006, 53). She read her "mother's worn blue copy of *The Mystery of Lilac Inn*," followed by all the rest of her mother's Nancy Drew collection and knew even then that "you could always imagine something better than reality." Carlos Eire, author of an award-winning memoir of the Cuban Revolution, *Waiting for Snow in Havana*, tells the story of his arrival in the United States as an orphaned 11-year-old with only one thing in his pocket that he was allowed to bring into the country: Thomas à Kempis's *The Imitation of Christ*. He says, "As I bounced around from foster home to foster home in the United States, I grew attached to the book, not because I liked to read it—hell, no—but simply because it was one of the very few mementos that linked my physically with my family" (Coady and Johannessen 2006, 73). He embraced it first as a physical object, a talisman, but later he started to read it at random, one or two sentences at a time, until slowly the book began to speak to him. What it told him was that pain can be redeeming and that God can be found in small details. Eire says, "Books have made me who I am" (72).

When the testimonial providers are writers, the gift offered by the life-changing book is often a discovery of the power of language or the confidence to find one's own voice or an invitation to become a writer. Asked to talk about influences following the release of his novel *Dissident Gardens*, Jonathan Lethem (2013) said, "[W]hat I deeply believe to be the case . . . is that the life of a writer extends directly out of their reading lives." This was true of many of the writers interviewed by Diane Osen (2002) in *The Book That Changed My Life*. Diane Johnson (Osen 2002, 45) said she wrote her first novel of 30 pages when she was 9 or 10: "It seems to have been very heavily influenced by the Bobbsey Twins books, because it has triplets—Dan, Don, and Dell" whose parents "have conveniently been lost." Biographer David Levering Lewis (Osen 2002, 74) said that the watershed book for him was W. E. B. Du Bois's *The Souls of Black Folk* because of the way it articulates the problem of race as "a tool of analysis to understand not only one's personal dilemma and one's group dilemma, but also a global dilemma." Cynthia Ozick (Osen 2002, 123) recalled that when she was 17 her brother brought home a library book that contained Henry James's story "The Beast in the Jungle": "Reading it, I felt it to be the story of my own life—which was strange, since it's about an elderly gentleman who suddenly discovers that he has wasted his years."

The framing is important. A bare list of life-changing books is bound to be unsatisfying. We want to know the connection between the book and the reader's life. Kate Atkinson began her essay this way: "I read my way through a solitary childhood. Books were the bedrock of my emotional and intellectual life, books that proscribed no limit to the imagination, books that were full of resourceful girls, princesses and goatherds and Victorian maidens, not to mention the sand fairies, the talking animals, the scheming stepfamilies and the handsome men who had been transformed into beasts" (Coady and Johannessen 2006, 4). But then she left childhood entrancement behind, and "books" became "literature" to be studied and appreciated but not loved—until she read Robert Coover's *Pricksongs & Descant*, a collection of stories, myths, allegories, fairy tales, "a box of ludic tricks and delights," a world of thresholds and doors opening into worlds where "anything can happen" (5). Her own reading story is a tale of a treasure, found in childhood, lost, and then found again but transmuted into a new form as she finds the source of her own creativity: "then one day I woke up and wrote my first story. . . . It opened a door."

Of course all these special books have been read by thousands of other readers who didn't experience the life-changing effect. It won't work to give *The Wild Orchid* to some other 21-year-old who is troubled by religious doubt. It's not the book alone but the conjunction of the book and the particular reader at just the right time in the reader's life when she is primed for what the book has to offer. Prefacing his own story of the life-changing book, physician Bernie S. Siegel said, "I must begin by saying I do not believe any book can change your life; only you can. Two people read the same book, one is inspired while the other is bored. The issue is not the book but the person—what lies within each of us. The author's wisdom combined with the reader's inspiration and desire to change can lead to a new life for the reader" (Coady and Johannessen 2006, 154). And so, although there are many Web sites with names like 20 (or 50) Books That Will Change Your Life, they probably won't. You have to find your own book. David (student, age 26) warns that the life-changing book is a serious business: "There are some books you read that are not going to change your life. Other books are going to change your life, so you should be careful before you open the cover."

And for some readers, it may not be a single book that changes a life. What changes a life is reading itself. It is knowing oneself as a person who reads. It is discovering one's identity as a person who shamelessly chooses to read over any other activity. When asked what factors would prompt her to pick up a book rather than doing something else, Sarah (library assistant, age 40) answered, "Reading is so much a part of the fabric of my life that I would approach that question from the other end and say, 'What are the things that would interfere with my reading?' " Anna Quindlen's book *How Reading Changed My Life* (2006) is about that kind of voracious reading. Quindlen (2006, 4) says she grew up in a pleasant place outside Philadelphia but lived somewhere else: "I lived within the covers of books and those books were more real to me than any other things in my life." When she read, "it never seemed to me like a book, but like a place I had lived in, had visited and would visit again, just as all the people in them, every blessed one—Anne of Green Gables, Heidi, Jay Gatsby, Elizabeth

Bennet, Scarlett O'Hara, Dill and Scout, Miss Marple, and Hercule Poirot—were more real than the real people I knew." She offers a phenomenology of reading, starting with the club chair she read in as a child—"a big one, with curled arms and a square ottoman." In her case, the tension between movement and stillness, travel and staying at home was reconciled in the act of reading: "The stories about my childhood, the ones that stuck, that got told and retold at dinner tables . . . are stories of running away" (1–3). She was, she says, a restless spirit, always with the "sense that I ought to be somewhere else. So I wandered the world through books."

References

Coady, Roxanne J., and Joy Johannessen, eds. 2006. *The Book That Changed My Life: 71 Remarkable Writers Celebrate the Books That Matter Most to Them.* New York: Gotham Books/Penguin Group.

Lethem, Jonathan. 2013. "The Influence Interview: 'You've Got to Be into Old, Weird Books.' " *The Globe and Mail,* November 9. http://www.theglobeandmail.com/arts/books-and-media/which-writers-influenced-jonathan-lethem-youve-got-to-be-into-old-weird-books/article15347630/.

Osen, Diane, ed. 2002. *The Book That Changed My Life: Interviews with National Book Award Winners and Finalists.* New York: The Modern Library.

Quindlen, Anna. 2006. *How Reading Changed My Life.* Bloomington: Indiana University Press.

Ross, Catherine Sheldrick. 1999. "Finding without Seeking: The Information Encounter in the Context of Reading for Pleasure." *Information Processing and Management* 35: 783–99.

Detective, Mystery, and Crime Fiction

Of all the popular genres, detective fiction is the one about which readers have felt the least guilt in reading. When academics and serious writers seek out leisure reading, they often choose detective stories, mysteries, or crime novels as they are variously called. They also write them, and they write about them. Although Dorothy L. Sayers considered her translation of Dante's *Divine Comedy* to be her most important work, she is remembered and loved mostly for her detective fiction featuring Lord Peter Wimsey and Harriet Vane. With readers generally, the mystery genre is in the top two or three most popular genres of fiction (Createc 2005). Mystery fans often say that they first got turned on to the genre in childhood, reading *Nancy Drew*, the *Hardy Boys*, *Encyclopedia Brown*, or even Agatha Christie, and they never stopped (Clark 2008, 166–67). Once hooked on mystery stories in childhood, they just keep on reading them, moving on to grown-up versions of the genre they had enjoyed in childhood. Devoted mystery readers are aware of the various subgenres—cozies, hard-boiled, serial killers, historical, police procedurals, and paranormal mysteries. Some may read selectively across the whole continuum, and they may also read the related, but distinct, genres of the thriller, the spy novel, and romantic suspense. From wide exposure to crime novels as well as to crime movies and television series, readers have a well-elaborated mental model of the various conventions used in their favorite subgenres.

The Bargain between Reader and Writer

In general, mystery readers know what to expect when they pick up a detective story. As Elizabeth (PhD candidate in English, age 35) said, "You know exactly what you're getting. The bargain between the reader and the writer is very clear." A murder has been committed, and the reader is involved, along with the detective, in sifting through clues to uncover a hidden, anterior story that happened before the detective arrives on the scene. As Frank Kermode (1983, 56) puts it, "The detective story is much more concerned than narratives normally are with the elucidation of a series of events which closed either before or only shortly after its own starting point." The writer needs to provide all the evidence concerning the truth of those earlier events but do so in a way that keeps the reader guessing right to the end. Much of the mystery reader's engagement is hermeneutic, involved with the interpretation of signs and clues. Bulgarian narratologist Tzvetan Todorov (1977) has pointed out that the classic detective story is really two stories. There is the hidden story of the crime, which the detective is trying to piece together from the available evidence, working from effect to cause. Then there is the story of the investigation itself, which works toward the unmasking of the murderer. As the novelist David Lodge (2006, 260) observes, "The second story is often reported by a friend of the detective (e.g., Watson) who acknowledges that he is writing it, while the story of the crime never admits its literariness."

Writing a successful detective story requires skilful interlinking in the telling of these two stories. The exciting action—the murder—has already happened. So how to keep up the pacing and interest when telling the second story of the investigation? One way is to sequence the unfolding of the clues so that the first set of clues uncovered seems to point to one suspect, but the discovery of a new clue changes everything and requires a new interpretation, a new patterning of the clues, a new prime suspect, and a new version of the motive and the means of the crime. At the hands of a skilful plotter, the reader has considered and rejected two or three different interpretations, each with a different culprit and a different arrangement of the clues, before the detective finally reveals the hidden story of how the crime was actually committed. In detective fiction that draws on elements of the thriller, the author may ratchet up the suspense by putting the detective at physical risk, by introducing a second murder, by using the "child in jeopardy" device, or by upping the ante by means of a ticking-clock deadline, after which time another person will be killed. Agatha Christie's Hercule Poirot and Miss Marple are never personally threatened as they go about talking to people and gathering clues. But in more recent works, investigators are on the firing line and may end up, like Sara Paretsky's V. I. Warshawski, bound and thrown into Lake Michigan, stowed in the trunk of a car, beaten black and blue, and shot at. In Patricia Cornwell's mystery series, threats against Chief Medical Examiner Kay Scarpetta include both physical attacks and assaults on her personal and professional integrity.

To limit the field of suspects to a manageable number, the murder has traditionally taken place in an enclosed setting such as a country house, a passenger ship or train, or an institution such as a hospital, university department, island resort, or monastery. For example, in Louise Penny's *The Beautiful Mystery* (2012), the dead body of a monk is discovered in an enclosed garden in a fortress-like monastery on an island in a remote lake in the wilderness of northern Quebec, which is home to two dozen cloistered, contemplative monks and entirely barred to the outside world—until the arrival of Chief Inspector Armand Gamache and his investigative team. The main cast of characters of a detective novel is as formulaic as the characters in the *commedia dell'arte*: the dead body, the detective(s), and the suspects.

The detective's pursuit of the hidden truth involves witnesses, clues, motives, and means. It may also require specialized knowledge about such things as railway schedules or the effects of poisons or the splatter patterns of blood. Describing the classic detective story, P. D. James (2009, 9) says, "What we can expect is a central mysterious crime, usually murder; a closed circle of suspects, each with motive, means and opportunity for the crime; a detective, either amateur or professional, who comes in like an avenging deity to solve it; and, by the end of the book, a solution which the reader should be able to arrive at by logical deduction from clues inserted in the novel with deceptive cunning but essential fairness." Success is achieved if the reader closes the book saying, "There it was under my nose the whole time; I should have realized."

Rules of the Game

In the 1920s and 1930s, when the genre was being consolidated, mystery authors amused themselves by writing "rules." These rules specified the role of the detective, the need to introduce the criminal as a character early on, the requirement to play fair with the reader when presenting clues, and the need to solve the mystery by logical means. Specifically excluded were irrational elements such as supernatural agents, love interest, and solving the crime by accident, by intuition, or by Ouija board. Love interest was outlawed as a distraction in a genre supposedly focused on ratiocination, analytic skill, and the logical examination of clues. The creator of the fictional detective Philo Vance, S. S. Van Dine (1928), generated 20 rules, including "There must be but one detective," "There must be but one culprit, no matter how many murders are committed," "A crime in a detective story must never turn out to be an accident or suicide," and "The motives for all crimes ... should be personal. International plottings and war politics" belong in spy stories. In 1929, Ronald Knox, a mystery author and theologian, came up with his "Ten Commandments" of detective fiction. In addition to the rule that "The detective must not himself commit the crime," Knox banned "supernatural agencies," more than "one secret room or passage," "hitherto undiscovered poisons," and "twin brothers, and doubles generally." These interdictions were largely critiques of the detective fiction of the day, many of which sacrificed plausibility for ingenious solutions.

In "The Simple Art of Murder," Raymond Chandler (1946) famously argued that the classic detective story, with its many rules, had turned into an artificial intellectual game played out in drawing rooms and country houses. In welcome contrast, he thought, the American writer Dashiell Hammett "gave murder back to the kind of people that commit it for reasons, not just to provide a corpse; and with the means at hand, not with hand-wrought dueling pistols, curare, and tropical fish" (234). Hence Chandler's insistence that, in addition to playing fair with the reader over clues, the story "must be about real people in a real world" and "be realistic as to character, setting, and atmosphere." In his posthumously published *Notebooks*, Chandler (1976, 35–40) provided 12 notes on the mystery story (supplemented by 12 additional notes), which emphasized plausibility and realism: no elaborately constructed scenario such as is found in Agatha Christie's *Murder on the Orient Express* and no "fantastic poisons" or "snakes climbing bellropes" such as are found in Conan Doyle's "The Speckled Band." In addition, "It must have a sound story value apart from the mystery element; i.e., the investigation itself must be an adventure worth reading" and "It must punish the criminal in one way or another" because the detective's failure to solve the crime "is an unresolved chord and leaves irritation behind it."

It wasn't long before every single rule was broken. Agatha Christie has made the narrator of one of her novels the murderer. The courtship of Peter Wimsey and Harriet Vane is a treasured element in five Dorothy Sayers novels— this from a writer (Sayers 1929, 39) who primly said "the less love in a detective-story the better." Love interest may dilute the austere rationality of the problem–solution plot, but it pleases readers like Rene (physician, age 32), who says, "I much prefer the mystery stories that have a little bit of a sideline romance in them." Whole subgenres such as the police procedural with its teams of police investigators have risen up in defiance of the strange rule requiring "but one detective." The conception of the detective story as essentially a puzzle or intellectual game was challenged by subgenres that feature serial killers as well as pathologists who cut up bodies with Stryker saws. The growing trend to paranormal mysteries has challenged the embargo on supernatural elements and solutions. In 1973, Josef Skvorecky published *Sins for Father Knox*, a collection of stories in which each of Knox's 10 rules is broken. Umberto Eco's runaway best-seller *The Name of the Rose* (1983) breaks the most sacred rule of all: that the essence of the genre is analysis and rationality. Eco's novel is an antidetective story in which clues lead nowhere, reason is inadequate, and order is illusory. At the novel's end, the detective Brother William of Baskerville reflects on what happened: "There was no plot . . . and I discovered [the solution] by mistake."

Something about the Detective/Mystery Genre

No other genre, with the possible exception of science fiction/fantasy, has generated such a wealth of secondary critical materials and tools about it. Successful mystery writers themselves, such as Dorothy L. Sayers (1929), Raymond Chandler (1946), Carolyn G. Heilbrun (1990), and P. D. James (2009), have written about the genre, but that's just the tip of the iceberg. Literary critics have analyzed detective fiction through many lenses, including historical, biographical, Marxist, Freudian, feminist, and postmodernist. Richard J. Bleiler's *Reference and Research Guide to Mystery and Detective Fiction* (2004) is an impressive work of bibliographic control of the genre, well indexed to allow multiple access points. It lists and describes encyclopedias, bibliographies, readers' guides, and lists of authors and series broken into numerous categories (e.g., college mysteries, gay and lesbian mysteries, gothic mysteries, locked-room mysteries, medical thrillers, and music mysteries). Also included are biographical dictionaries of crime writers; guides to the genre for readers' advisors; collections of interviews with mystery writers; biographical and critical studies of individual authors such as Edgar Allan Poe, Arthur Conan Doyle, and Agatha Christie; character indexes; and lists of awards bestowed by various national crime writers associations. Guides to the mystery genre have been written for readers' advisors such as *The Readers' Advisory Guide to Mystery*, second edition (Charles et al., 2012). Diana Tixier Herald's sixth edition of *Genreflecting* (2006) includes a chapter on crime fiction that divides the topic into various subcategories—the "cozy" mystery, hard-boiled, police procedurals, crime/caper stories, legal thrillers, postmodern crime novels, true crime, serial killers and psychopaths, romance/suspense, and genre blends such as historical mysteries and futuristic mysteries.

Heroic attempts have been made to patrol the borders of the detective/mystery story proper and distinguish it from the thriller, the spy story, romantic suspense, and psychological horror. But do ordinary readers make these distinctions? Where do they draw the line? Do they distinguish between the traditional mystery, where the crime threatens an individual, and the spy thriller, where the threat is against Western civilization and democracy as we know it? Some readers do, and some do not. Many readers use terms such as *mystery*, *thriller*, and *crime story* interchangeably, and genre-blending writers deliberately blur the lines. A survey-based study of mystery readers sponsored by Sisters in Crime (2010, 36) reported that female mystery readers (65% of the sample) and mystery readers over age 50 (about 65%) were the most likely to have a strong sense of how the mystery genre differs from other genres: "Close to half of those under 50 do not distinguish between mystery, thriller, espionage or suspense genres." Accordingly, creators of bibliographies, readers' guides, and criticism of the genre often take an inclusive approach and include any story where the main interest is crime.

Nevertheless, it can be useful to consider some of the basic distinctions among genres and subgenres because many readers are selective: they don't enjoy all crime fiction equally. They enjoy books in certain subgenres—say the cozy mystery in which the violence takes place offstage—but not others; not, for example, the hard-boiled stories, in which women's roles are limited to being the dead body, the seductress, or the secretary; or not stories that put children in jeopardy. Or they enjoy forensic mysteries that treat the death and the investigation seriously but not mysteries that downplay the murder and feature knitting, scrapbooking, or recipes. Or they are bored with the localized evil of an individual murderer in a country-house setting and prefer books where the murder signals a much larger social evil involving corrupt corporations, institutions, and governments—for example, a pharmaceutical company that knowingly infects people in Africa with the AIDS virus, a religious charity that is really a front for selling children to sexual predators, a hospital transplant unit that oversees an operation to kidnap orphans from Eastern Europe to harvest their organs for rich patients in the United States, or a government agency that turns a blind eye to dumping toxic radioactive waste into lakes, poisoning underground water tables and drinking water.

The story of the development of the traditional detective story has been told many times—see Sayers (1929) for a classic statement of the genre's contours and development. The genealogy usually starts with Edgar Allen Poe's three short stories, published in the 1840s, that feature C. Auguste Dupin. "The Murders in the Rue Morgue" (1841) was the first locked-room mystery. "The Murder of Marie Roget" (1843) was the first appearance of the armchair detective who solves the problem from facts in the police report and newspaper accounts. "The Purloined Letter" (1844) introduced the principle that the best way to hide something is to display it in full view. After Poe, the next key developments of the detective story happened in Europe with the novels of Emile Gaboriau in France and of Wilkie Collins and Charles Dickens in England. Then comes the watershed development: the first appearance of Arthur Conan Doyle's Sherlock Holmes in "A Study in Scarlet" (1887). Holmes explains to Watson what he means by the "study in scarlet": "There's the scarlet thread of murder running through the colourless skein of life, and our duty is to unravel it, and isolate it, and expose every inch of it."

One thing is clear: despite the highly conventionalized form of the detective story, writers have been able to achieve remarkable variety. P. D. James (2009, 10) observed, "what I find fascinating is the extraordinary variety of books and writers which this so-called formula has been able to accommodate, and how many authors have found the constraints and conventions of the detective story liberating rather than inhibiting of their creative imagination." Like a dinner menu with its categories of drinks, appetizers, entrees, and desserts, the genre's structure is fixed, but there are lots of menu options for each category, hence a satisfying variety in possible dinners and possible detective stories. Detective fiction varies:

- in the *nature of the detective*. Is the detective an amateur like Miss Marple or Lord Peter Wimsey, or is the detective a professional— a private eye, forensic specialist, or member of a police force? Does the detective work alone, as Kinsey Millhone does in Sue Grafton's alphabetic mysteries? Or does the detective work with a close partner (e.g., Tess Gerritson's Boston medical examiner Dr. Maura Isles and homicide detective Jane Rizzoli or Reginald Hill's Chief Superintendent Andy Dalziel and Detective Sergeant Peter Pascoe) or work as part of a larger team (e.g., Ed McBain's 87th Precinct)? To what extent is the personal, family, and romantic life of the detective allowed to enter into the telling of the story? In the case of amateur detectives, what special area of knowledge does the character possess that provides an edge in solving the crime—knowledge of rare books, computer searching or hacking skills, knowledge of human nature developed through a lifetime of close observation of village life, forensic anthropology, toxicology, and so on?

- in whether the story is *part of a continuing series* featuring the same detective or a one-off, stand-alone story (e.g., the novels of Minette Walters or Dick Francis).

- in the *amount of personal risk* to the detective. Does the detective use his or her "little gray cells" from a safe vantage point, or is he or she at risk of being the next victim?

- in the *nature of the crime*. Does the murder result from an individual flaw such as greed or jealousy, or does it result from the widespread corruption of social institutions, as happens in many Scandinavian crime novels.

- in the *method of murder* and the degree of special preparation, background, or physical strength required to use the method. Detectives work backward from the method used to the characteristics of the unknown murderer (e.g., the murderer who delivered this blow must be left-handed or unusually tall, the person who hefted this body down a well must be remarkably strong, the person who put this mushroom or hemlock into the casserole must be an expert in natural poisons, the serial killer who flayed the skin off the body must hate women). Possibilities include blunt force trauma with a rock or a golf club; poisoning from everyday arsenic or rare neurotoxins; shooting by gun or crossbow; stabbing; drowning; electrocution; hit-and-run car attacks; garroting with a belt, cello string, or nylon stocking; and falls from buildings, over cliffs, or down a staircase. Dorothy Sayers (1929, 42) lists half a page of highly ingenious methods of getting yourself killed: "licking poisoned stamps; shaving-brushes inoculated with dread diseases; poisoned boiled eggs . . .; poison-gas; a cat with poisoned claws; poisoned mattresses; knives dropped through the ceiling; stabbing with a sharp icicle; electrocution by telephone; . . . air-bubbles injected into the arteries."

- in the *nature of the setting*—whether a tightly circumscribed, closed setting typical of the classic detective story or the wide-open setting typical of the serial murder story and stories of international intrigue.

- in the *emphasis given to the more grisly aspects* of the crime and the forensic investigation. Is the corpse kept discreetly offstage, or are we brought into the details of the autopsy, Stryker saws, blood spatters, maggots, decomposition of the corpse, and the like, as in the forensic mysteries of Patricia Cornwell and Kathy Reichs?

- in the *tone of the book*. Is the crime treated with high seriousness, or are there elements of humor and whimsy, such as cat protagonists in Lilian Jackson Braun's *The Cat Who* series?

- in the *degree to which justice is done*. By the end, has the evil that was let loose by the murder been expelled from the community and order restored? Or is the very idea of order an illusion? Maybe the particular murderer has been identified, but the larger system of evil behind the murder will continue unabated with replacement agents continuing the dirty work.

- in the *specialized interest* provided by the setting and sometimes by the professional background of the detective. Does the reader find out specialized information on such things as Navaho culture (e.g., Tony Hillerman), rare book collecting (John Dunning), cooking and recipes (Diane Mott Davidson), archaeology (Kate Ellis), horses (Dick Francis), and so on?

- in the *narrative method*. Is the story told in the first person either by a friend of the detective (e.g., a Dr. Watson) or by the detective himself or herself, as in Kinsey Millhone's case files? Hard-boiled stories are often narrated in the first person by the detective, whose snappy, wisecracking style and jaded outlook goes a long way toward creating the *noir* world of the novel. The third-person narrative method is the best choice if the writer wants to get into the minds of more than one character or cut between different scenes going on simultaneously to increase suspense.

- in the inclusion of a *critique of contemporary social arrangements* such as gender roles, gay–straight issues, or race relations. For example, hard-boiled writers such as Sara Paretsky, Sue Grafton, Marsha Muller, and Linda Barnes have recast the conventions of male private investigator novel to explore feminist issues and questions of social justice (Walton and Jones 1999). Series such as Joseph Hansen's Brandstetter novels and Richard Stevenson's Strachey novels confront issues such as homophobia, the post-Stonewall struggle for gay rights in Los Angeles, and the ravages of AIDS (Gunn 2005). African American writers such as Chassie West and Valerie Wilson Wesley have made issues of race central to their stories of investigation.

- in the *inclusion of genre-crossing elements* such as the terror of being hunted typical of the thriller, the international intrigue typical of the spy story, the courtship and deepening relationship among characters typical of the ROMANCE, the time shifting and alternative histories typical of speculative fiction, or the strange uncanniness typical of the paranormal story.

Who Reads Detective Fiction, and What Do Readers Look For?

To find out, an association of women crime writers called Sisters in Crime sponsored a study, *The Mystery Book Consumer in the Digital Age* (2010), based on publishing industry data gathered by R. R. Bowker's book sales analysis division, PubTrack. The 1,056 subjects, who had bought at least one mystery fiction title in the past year, were drawn from a pool of 75,000 survey respondents who had bought at least one book during this period. In comparison with the general population, mystery buyers were disproportionately likely to be women (68%) and people age 60 and over (47%). Here are some findings:

- Readers over age 50 read many more mystery books a year than do readers under age 30.
- About 20 percent of all readers borrow mysteries from libraries.
- Readers under age 40 "look for dark, suspenseful stories" and "don't see mysteries as distinct from other genres as older readers do."
- The top three factors that influence a buying decision are (1) liking for the author (52%), (2) liking for the series (39%), and (3) and liking for the character (26%).
- The top three "media influencers" that encourage a buying decision are (1) a recommendation from someone I know, (2) the cover, and (3) presence on a best-seller list.
- Face-out displays of books influence choice not only because of the cover art but also because of "elements such as title, author name, blurbs by other authors, and flap copy. Covers trigger impulse buys."
- Mystery readers are more open to trying new authors than are readers in general, and they actively seek out new books.

The finding that readers under age 40 are less likely than older readers to consider mysteries a distinct genre raises interesting questions about genres; about how readers themselves, as opposed to literary theorists, define genres; and about what readers look for in a satisfying crime novel.

Detective story experts and rule makers in the 1920s and 1930s put great emphasis on playing fair with clues, thinking that readers engaged with the text primarily as puzzle solvers. But were they right? Do readers still, if they ever did, read that way? Well, some people do say that they enjoy the puzzle element. Maurice (professional engineer, age 57) doesn't actively try to solve the crime exactly but is always engaged in an interpretive effort: "I'm quite happy to wait till the end and find out who did it. But I'm always thinking about it"—"just a minute, that's suspicious" or "that means something" or "there's got to be some significance in that." Others say that they are attracted to the mystery genre because it guarantees a proper story with a definite beginning, middle, and end. But lots of other readers say that they enjoy mysteries because of the characters. Michelle says, "Mysteries mostly cruise on good characterization. If the characters are good, the mystery works." Ivor (student, age 26) says that he enjoys the psychology of Georges Simenon's fiction: "He really understands how people's minds work and that's what really interests me about them. Not so much the mystery. The mystery, the murder, whatever it is, is almost beside the point." Here's Elizabeth (PhD student, age 35), who reads a lot of mysteries but doesn't like suspense at all:

> There is no interest for me in trying to figure out who did it. I prefer to find out right away who did it, by reading the ending, and then to read the book. What interests me is the interconnection of motive and actions of various people.

Series with the same investigator have been a popular feature of the genre right from the beginning, starting with Poe's Auguste Dupin and Conan Doyle's Sherlock Holmes. Then there's Agatha Christie's Hercule Poirot and Miss Marple, Margery Allingham's Albert Campion, Dorothy L. Sayers's Peter Wimsey and Harriet Vane, Raymond Chandler's Philip Marlowe, Ross McDonald's Lew Archer, John D. MacDonald's Travis MGee, Robert Parker's Spenser, Colin Dexter's Inspector Morse, Peter Dickinson's Inspector Pibble, Ian Rankin's Inspector Rebus, Joseph Hansen's Dave Brandstetter, Mark Richard Zubro's Paul Turner, Janet Evanovich's Stephanie Plum, Donna Leon's Commissario Guido Brunetti, Tess Gerritsen's Maura Isles and Jane Rizzoli, Louise Penny's Chief Inspector Armand Gamache, Gail Bowen's Joanne Kilbourn, Henning Mankell's Kurt Wallander, Elly Griffiths's Ruth Galloway, George Pelecanos's Spero Lucas, and hundreds more. Publishers say that detective fiction is a "word-of-mouth" kind of genre, where readers hear about one book in the series and then go on to read them all. Book JACKETS and covers therefore prominently display the name of the series detective on the front. As another signal to readers, some authors use a repetitive element in their titles to emphasize the series aspect of their books. The Sue Grafton series featuring Private Investigator Kinsey Millhone have alphabetic TITLES, starting with *A Is for Alibi*, *B Is for Burglar*, and so on up to *W Is for Wasted* and, it is anticipated, *Z Is for Zero*. John D. MacDonald's Travis McGee mysteries all include a color in the title such as *The Deep Blue Goodbye*, *Nightmare in Pink*, *Dress Her in Indigo*, *The Girl in the Plain Brown Wrapper*, and *Free Fall in Crimson*.

Series are popular because they offer the promise of a repeatable pleasure within the control of the reader. They reduce the work involved in getting into the world of the book, and they offer readers the chance to reencounter old friends, following a character's development through a number of books. Sara Paretsky (2002, 77), who has written some 15 first-person novels featuring V. I. Warchawski, comments on the advantages of a series character, among which is "the pleasure in developing a set of people in detail, showing the progression of their lives, not abandoning them at one climax when we all know most lives have many pivot points." The pleasure of the series is cumulative, depending on repeated encounters with the same set of characters, settings, and plot types over time. Ina (pharmacist, age 26) says, "With those books [Ellis Peters's Brother Cadfael and the Kinsey Millhone books], it's as much an on-going character development as anything else that keeps you reading." Gilbert (teacher, age 47) agrees: "I like the idea of a series, where you follow the same character. I read mysteries for setting and for character, especially if it's in a series."

Setting has been a strong source of reader appeal from the very beginning. Think of Conan Doyle's fog-enshrouded London, the horse-drawn carriages, and the house at 221b Baker Street, where setting becomes almost another character. Ron (English teacher, age 29) reports that he read his first Sherlock Holmes when he was 14 and thereafter read every Holmes story he could find. What was the initial pleasure that attracted him to these stories, I asked. Ron answered, "Almost every story begins with a description of what happens outside the window on Baker Street. The atmosphere really got to me—especially the foggy days or the drizzly days. There's the sense of its needing some kind of action, and than some really *strange* thing would come up. I remember the first Holmes book I got had a story about a cardboard box with an ear in it." Some readers enjoy exotic settings with the appeal of a travel book. In other cases, the setting achieves its effect by intensifying the growing sense of threat to the characters. For example, in *The Crossing Places*, Elly Griffiths's debut novel featuring forensic anthropologist Ruth Galloway, much of the action takes place on a saltmarsh in North Norfolk, England. The saltmarsh is a border territory, part land and part sea, made more treacherous by flooding tides and sudden holes in which the unwary sink into sand up to their necks.

Reading Detective Stories as a Paradigm of All Reading

The detective story, some think, is a kind of primer for learning how to read in general. George N. Dove claims that it provides an exemplary case of what happens in *all* reading: the reader co-creates the text. In the detective story, says Dove (1989, 11–12), "more than any other, the reader spins his own story while the printed one unfolds in his hands. He does his own sifting of clues, his own interrogation of suspects, his own search for hidden motives and patterns of conduct." Jane Smiley (2005, 7) says that when she was writing her murder mystery, *Duplicate Keys*, she "was convinced of the idea that every novel is really some sort of mystery or whodunit because every novel is a retrospective uncovering of the real story behind the apparent story."

Detective stories, from *Nancy Drew* on, teach important lessons in reading that are never formally taught in school—for example, which details, in the myriads provided in a long text, to pay attention to and remember. The detective reads the scene of the crime, observes details, sifts evidence, pays attention to the conflicting stories that people tell, listens for the telling omissions and gaps in what people say, and at the end provides an interpretation. In short, the detective enacts the process that all readers go through as they read any novel—filling in gaps, making predictions, and paying attention to details, even those that don't seem at first glance to make sense or be connected with anything else. Readers hold it all in suspension, until by the end the true pattern emerges that unites the details into a coherent whole. In the detective story, the task of making meaning—which is also the reader's job—is foregrounded by the plot itself and modeled by the detective. A common trope in a detective novel is the double-reading: the inept police team reads the evidence wrong and arrests an innocent person, who is eventually cleared by the detective hero, who does a better job of reading the same evidence.

Readers have provided accounts of how they themselves learned lessons in reading from detective fiction. Michael Dirda (2012), Pulitzer Prize–winning literary critic, reported that reading Conan Doyle's *The Hound of the Baskervilles* (1902) was the first step on the path to his becoming a professional reader: "it changed my life" (22); "I was no longer the same ten-year-old when I reached its final pages" (16). He had been introduced to Holmes's method of "the observation of trifles," a method he later recognized in the close-reading techniques of the New Critics. Dirda said, "I soon realized that Sherlock Holmes 'read' a person or crime in the way a critic such as William Empson read poetry" (102).

The Hound of the Baskervilles had a similar life-changing effect on Jane Smiley (2005) when she read it at age 11 or 12 (see CHANGING LIVES). She read it for atmosphere and excitement, she says, but what she learned was something completely different—how stories are put together:

> Although I was an avid reader, I was not a sophisticated one, and when I took up Holmes, I had only the dimmest idea of most of the things Watson talks about in the novel—I could hardly picture a moor or a mire, I had never seen a convict or been to London. I did not understand what an "avenue of yews" was or know why the Baskerville estate passed from one distant relative to another. . . . I am sure that the first time I read *The Hound of the Baskervilles*, I had no idea what the solution to the mystery was. . . . But I can't remember, because I read the novel many times, until the details of the mystery, and even certain phrases and effects, were completely, though unconsciously, memorized. I read it because of the air of dark fascination that

hung over the setting and because of the exciting appearance of the hound itself, with his phosphorescent face and huge size. . . .

What I learned from it was not what I read it for. Each time I reread the novel, knowing the tricks and the deceptions of the plot, I learned how the tricks and the deceptions worked together logically. . . . I learned about the logical construction of plot and the clear construction of character. (31–32)

References

Bleiler, Richard J. 2004. *Reference and Research Guide to Mystery and Detective Fiction*, 2nd ed. Westport, CT: Libraries Unlimited.

Chandler, Raymond. 1946. "The Simple Art of Murder." In *The Art of the Mystery Story*, 222–37. Edited by Howard Haycraft. New York: Carroll and Graff. http://www.en.utexas.edu/amlit/amlitprivate/scans/chandlerart.html.

Chandler, Raymond. 1976. "Twelve Notes on the Mystery Novel." In *The Notebooks of Raymond Chandler and English Summer: A Gothic Romance*, 35–40. Edited by Frank MacShane. New York: The Ecco Press.

Charles, John, Candace Clark, Joanne Hamilton-Selway, and Joanna Morrison. 2012. *The Readers' Advisory Guide to Mystery*, 2nd ed. Chicago: ALA Editions.

Clark, Katherine Hensen. 2008. "What Is Cozy?" Unpublished PhD Dissertation. Case Western Reserve University.

Createc. 2005. *Reading and Buying Books for Pleasure: 2005 National Survey, Final Report*. Canadian Heritage. http://publications.gc.ca/collections/Collection/CH44-61-2005E.pdf.

Dirda, Michael. 2012. *On Conan Doyle: Or, the Whole Art of Storytelling*. Princeton, NJ, and Oxford, England: Princeton University Press.

Dove, George N. 1989. *Suspense in the Formula Story*. Bowling Green, OH: Bowling Green State University Popular Press.

Eco, Umberto. 1983. *The Name of the Rose*. Translated by William Weaver. New York and Toronto: Harcourt, Inc.

Gunn, Drewey Wayne. 2005. *The Gay Male Sleuth in Print and Film: A History and Annotated Bibliography*. Lanham, MD: Scarecrow Press.

Heilbrun, Carolyn G. 1990. "Detective Fiction." In *Hamlet's Mother and Other Women*, 231–60. New York: Columbia University Press.

Herald, Diana Tixier. 2006. *Genreflecting: A Guide to Popular Reading Interests*, 6th ed. Westport, CT, and London: Libraries Unlimited.

James, P. D. 2009. *Talking about Detective Fiction*. New York and Toronto: Alfred A. Knopf.

Kermode, Frank. 1983. *The Art of Telling: Essays on Fiction*. Cambridge, MA: Cambridge University Press.

Knox, Ronald. 1929. "Ten Commandments for Detective Fiction." In *Best Detective Stories of 1928*. London: Faber & Faber. http://www.ronaldknoxsociety.com/detective.html.

Lodge, David. 2006. "Umberto Eco: The Name of the Rose." In *The Year of Henry James: The Story of a Novel. With Other Essays on the Genesis, Composition and Reception of Literary Fiction*, 246–73. London: Penguin Books.

Paretsky, Sara. 2002. "Writing a Series Character." In *Writing Mysteries: A Handbook by the Mystery Writers of America*, 2nd ed., 72–78. Edited by Sue Grafton. Cincinnati, OH: Writer's Digest Books.

Sayers, Dorothy L. 1929. "Introduction." In *The Omnibus of Crime*, 9–47. Edited by Dorothy S. Sayers. Garden City, NY: Garden City Publishing Company.

Sisters in Crime. 2010. *The Mystery Book Consumer in the Digital Age*. http://sistersincrime.org/associations/10614/files/ConsumerBuyingBookReport.pdf.

Smiley, Jane. 2005. *Thirteen Ways of Looking at the Novel*. New York: Anchor Books.

Todorov, Tzvetan. 1977. "The Typology of Detective Fiction." In *The Poetics of Prose*, 42–52. Translated by Richard Howard. Ithaca, NY: Cornell University Press.

Van Dine, S. S. 1928. "Twenty Rules for Writing Detective Stories." *American Magazine*, September. http://gaslight.mtroyal.ca/vandine.htm.

Walton, Priscilla L., and Manina Jones. 1999. *Detective Agency: Women Rewriting the Hard-Boiled Tradition*. Berkeley and Los Angeles: University of California Press.

E-reading

Which of the following best describes you?

A   I don't read eBooks. I love the physical book—the sensuous look, feel, and smell of the book in my hands; the appeal of the book jacket; the rustle of the paper; and the ability to write in the margins. I want to be able to lend my books to my friends and pass them along to my children. Why would I want to squint at a screen?

B   I love the convenience of eBooks, especially the instant gratification of being able to download a book immediately and usually getting it cheaper than a print book. When I travel, I don't want to take a suitcase of books—just my eBook reader or tablet loaded up with eBooks, many of them free from the Gutenberg site. And eBooks are great for some of my friends, who have trouble with small type or who have arthritis. They can increase the size of the font, and they don't have to struggle to hold a heavy 500-page hardcover.

C   I read and enjoy both eBooks and print books. I usually choose the format depending on the kind of book, the intended use, and the reading occasion. I like eBooks for free Gutenberg books, for new series titles, and for travelling. eBooks are great for something that I want to read once but not keep in my permanent collection of important books. I prefer print books for nonfiction, especially for books where I want to flip back and forth quickly and compare pages. I love paperbacks for the beach and the bathtub.

D   I've never tried reading digital books, but the idea sort of scares me. I worry that it will be a case of the Beta versus VHS format wars all over again—I'll end up with a collection of unreadable books when the technology is discontinued. And I worry even more what's going to happen to book publishing, bookstores, and the whole future of books themselves.

If you said A or D, you are in good company—so far. But all bets are off for the future as dedicated e-readers and tablets make reading digital books more convenient and mobile. In a *New York Times* article, "Tablet and E-Reader Sales Soar," Julie Bosman (2012) reported some findings from a Pew Research Center survey indicating that almost one-third of Americans owned at least one tablet or dedicated e-reader, many getting them as Christmas gifts. At the same time, some readers have ongoing concerns about scary aspects of the technology. For example, what about privacy? E-reader platforms such as Google Books, Amazon Kindle, and Kobo can monitor which pages of a book you have read and can share this information with third parties (Cohn and Higgins 2012). So new questions arise. What are readers doing with these reading devices? How much e-reading are they actually doing on their new devices? How does their e-reading experience compare with the experience of reading the physical book? What is the interplay between eBook reading and physical book reading in the everyday lives of readers? Or, as Hupfeld and colleagues (2013) put it in one of the few good empirical studies of the experience and affordances of e-reading, what are the "mundane ways in which e-books are finding a place in everyday life?"

The jury is still out on these questions and others. Some people are already speculating on whether people who read eBooks on tablets rather than on dedicated e-readers are more likely to be distracted from their book by the siren call of e-mail, Google, Twitter, YouTube, and Facebook. Publishers worry that people might switch from print to tablets and then slow down on reading—as happened with consumers who bought expensive, automatic coffeemakers but then tapered off their coffee drinking when the automated coffeemakers turned out to produce an unsatisfying coffee experience. On the other hand, some in the book trade hope that eBooks will recruit new readers attracted by lower book costs and by the convenience of mobile reading on a smart phone or tablet.

If you answered B or C, you will probably be in the majority in a few more years. Once people start reading eBooks, it seems that they continue. Many read both eBooks and print books, with their choice of format depending on their reading situation (on a plane? on the beach? in bed?) and on the kind of book chosen. Some advantages of eBooks are already abundantly evident. When you travel, you can carry hundreds of books on a device that weighs 11 ounces or less. This lightness is especially appreciated by people with arthritis or other conditions that make it hard to hold heavy books. Then too, if you have trouble reading small print, you can adjust to a larger font size or use the text-to-speech feature. Fans of denigrated genres such as ROMANCE or SELF-HELP can read their favorite authors in privacy. The eBook format, by changing the method of book distribution, has opened up new niches for small indie publishers and self-published authors as well as writers of fanfiction. And eBooks are great for people who don't like to wait till the bookstore opens or who don't live in a big urban center near a well-stocked bookstore. If you want a book, you can get it immediately and be reading within minutes. Moreover, thanks to the Gutenberg project, you can choose from some 42,000 public domain books and download them for free.

Reaching a Tipping Point for E-reading?

In my long-standing project of interviewing avid readers (see QUESTIONS ABOUT READING), I added a new question in 2011 on eBook reading: "How do you feel about different formats for reading—for example, audio-books or e-books?" The timing of these 2011 interviews captured readers at a strategic moment right on the cusp of a popular take-up of the technology. Previously, e-reading had been the domain of early adopters and new technology wonks. However, by 2011, a number of convenient tablets and dedicated e-readers were available, and prices were coming down: Apple's iPad was introduced in 2010, Barnes & Noble's Color Nook appeared in 2010, Amazon's Kindle Touch appeared in 2011, Chapters's Kobo Touch appeared in 2011, and so on. The market share of eBooks in the U.S. consumer book industry has been marching upward (Owen 2013)—7 percent in 2010, 15 percent in 2011, and 20 percent in 2012. This seemed like the right moment to ask avid readers about e-reading.

So it was interesting that only 4 of the 22 avid readers who were asked the question about e-reading in 2011 had positive things to say about it. Finn (manager of an ESL academy, age 35), who was currently living in China "surrounded by everything in Chinese," said that just being able to go home at night and read English-language books downloaded from Gutenberg or torrented from btjunkie "made all the difference." Chloe (nurse instructor, age 49) said, "I bought a Kindle for my partner for his birthday, and he put some books on it and it's a process . . . I like the concept of it, I like the idea." However, for Chloe, reading has always been "a very sensuous experience, I like feeling the page, I like the smell of the book." With the Kindle, she feels as if she is "sitting in front of my computer screen." So the process of breaking old reading habits so far has been slow: "I've read probably 14 books since the one I downloaded on my Kindle, that I am on chapter seven on." Sonia (employment counselor, age 34) said, "I do read a lot of e-books. The problem is trying to find ones that I would enjoy that are free."

These comments about free eBooks and pirated books highlight a problem facing book publishers: free Gutenberg copies of popular classics compete with backlists, and pirated books displace sales and threaten the new book market. Nevertheless, publishers' efforts to protect copyrighted eBooks with digital rights management (DRM) technologies have had the effect of dampening enthusiasm for eBook reading in general. This same worry about controlling markets has led some publishers to refuse to sell eBooks to libraries or to cap the number of times the book can be borrowed. In response, a coalition of almost 300 library systems worldwide has rallied behind the ReadersFirst initiative to fight for the public's right to the same open and free access to eBooks that they have to physical books.

Five interviewees said "maybe" to eBooks, or "not sure" or "I've never tried it and I don't know how I would like it." Ko-Ko (speech pathologist, age 29) said tentatively, "I feel kind of open minded to it. I've been kind of intrigued. I think that I might like a Kindle . . . because it sort of mimics a lot of the enjoyable parts about reading with a book. Like you go page-by-page, and you can highlight and make notes. So I think that I would like a Kindle. Maybe." Pilar (student, age 24) wasn't interested in reading eBooks herself—she liked "feeling the book and holding it"—but acknowledged that eBooks could be good for older people:

> We bought my father a Kobo for Christmas and he really loves it. I think it's because he is getting old and they're moving into a condo and wanting to be able to downsize. There's just too many books in their house.

Thirteen interviewees flat-out said no to eBooks, usually just before launching into an idyllic account of the pleasures of the physical book. Concerns about eBooks included anxiety over incompatibility of eBook file formats with different reading platforms, the hassle and restrictions of reading books protected by DRM, and the fact that DRM renders eBooks worthless as commodities because you can't lend them to friends or family members and you can't resell them. Just thinking about eBook technology made Gitta feel very, very anxious: "I'm terrified of them—I have a real fear of e-readers because I think they're brand new and no one knows what they're doing with formatting. I feel like I'll buy all these books and then the formatting will change."

Screens are the problem for some pleasure readers (Jabr 2013). When the Kindle was first released in 2009, Jeff Bezos, founder and chief executive officer of Amazon.com, said, "Our top design objective was for Kindle to disappear in your hands—to get out of the way—so you can enjoy your reading. We hope you'll quickly forget you're reading on an advanced wireless device and instead be transported into that mental realm readers love, where the outside world dissolves, leaving only the author's stories, words and ideas" (Brown 2009). That effortless experience of reading where the screen drops out of awareness probably requires some practice and familiarity with the new technology. Jasmine (student, age 23) doesn't want an e-reader herself because, she said, "I get headaches from looking at a screen too long." But she thinks it's an "awesome tool"—for others: "I mean it's portable, you can read anywhere, you can download a book, there are so many advantages. I'm not a Luddite. It just hurts my eyes." Lola (student, age 25) doesn't like "reading things from a screen."

Although she expects screens to improve, she says, "they're not perfect yet. I *hate* the delay and the flash and the wait before the page turns. I hate that."

The question about other formats had the rebound effect of focusing readers' attention on what they most valued about the physical book. Noah, one of the no-sayers to eBooks, said, "I don't have an e-book, I don't want an e-book," and then described all the things he liked about the physical book, such as "I like the pages. I like writing my funny comments on the side" (see MARGINALIA). Fans of the physical book also appreciate the stability of the page and use it when they want to go back to a previously read passage. Nadia (librarian, age 29) said, "I'm quite conscious of the shape of the words on the page. I'm conscious of not just where the words are on the page, but the spaces, the margins. I may not remember a page number. But if I want to try and find something, I'll know whether it's on the right or left hand side, part way down, end of a paragraph, beginning of a paragraph or whatever."

Two themes cropped up repeatedly when avid readers considered the physical book. First, there is the sensuality of the experience of engaging with the book, which, beyond the visual appeal of JACKETS and fonts, involves the heft of the book in hand, the smell of binding and paper, and the rustle of turned pages. Nathan (English professor, age 50) says, "My first experience with books had to do with something sensual and that sense of the texture, the newness, the freshness, the crispness of books never left me. I often still associate books with the smell of pulp." Second, there is the intimacy of the reading experience, being lost in the world of the book, which eBook reading is alleged not to support, Jeff Bezos's hope to the contrary. Here's Kjell (student, age 25) who calls himself "a book snob": "I highly prefer hardcover books. There's some sort of intrinsic quality about holding a book in your hand and just being absorbed in that text. I don't expect to get that same sort of intimacy with an e-book." For some, it comes down to a question of possession, of truly taking possession of the book. One online reader posted the comment, "I can have thousands of e-books on my Kobo but it feels like I don't really own them."

Aura of Bookishness

Whenever an established technology is jeopardized by a competing technology—for example, theater threatened by movies, radio by television, television by videogames—people start paying nostalgic attention to the virtues of the endangered technology, previously taken for granted. Books with such titles as *The Gutenberg Elegies* (Birkerts 1995) and *The Edge of the Precipice* (Socken 2013) have focused on a type of "deep reading" of serious literature, thought to be under threat in a digital age. Hence, answers to the eBook question may tell us more about readers' feelings about print books than they do about eBook reading itself. For many, printed books still represent the aura of bookishness. This aura goes well beyond reading to include the physicality of the book, the book as an object of collection and display, and the book as a generational link between grandparents, parents, and children. The experience of the printed book is a sensory feast involving the smell of the book, the sounds of the pages turning, the feel of the book in hand, and the appearance of the crisp fonts and illustrated covers. Commenting on what he calls this redundancy, Andrew Piper (2012, 154) says, "The same information processed in different ways and woven together is one of the profound secrets of bookish thought." Jennifer, a student in my course on reading, shared this account of her love affair with the printed book, mentioning the various interwoven aspects of the book's appeal:

> Reading to me is an experience that is much more than the story itself. There is the physical object, the book. I love books— e-books hold no interest for me. Opening a book is a sensory experience. There is something almost visceral about the pleasure that I get. I love the smell, the heft, the aesthetic pleasure that one derives from opening a new book, the tactile sensations, the rustling of the pages, the creaking of the spine, the wonderful fonts, the contrast of the black lettering against the cream of the page. You feel a sense of continuity and of history when you read a book that someone else has owned and loved. Their inscriptions on the flyleaf, their notes in the margins are their conversations not only with the writer, but with you.

As Piper (2012, ix) points out in his excellent book on "reading in electronic times," the book was there first: "we cannot think about our electronic future without contending with its antecedent, the bookish past. . . . Books and screens are now bound up with one another whether we like it or not."

Privacy versus Display

Privacy—being able to read in public without anyone seeing and judging the book—is a virtue of e-reading that has turned readers of scorned genres into early adopters of eBooks. But some readers don't want privacy. They value books, especially hardcover books, as a form of display (see KINDRED READERS). They want to be able to see the books on their own shelves, and they want others to see them. Kjell says, "Every book I read, I like to have it on my shelf. And I like to think of that as not just something I've read, but something that's part of me that I want to stay with me. So I don't feel that I would get that from an e-format." Hunter (student, age 27) agrees, saying, "I love the sight of a bookshelf." He distinguishes among the various functions of the book—the book for reading, the book for possession and collection, and the book for display: "When I see people's bookshelves I don't assume they're reading them. That's why we separate reading out from a constellation of actions and attitudes around books. . . . [R]eading books is just one thing to do with them." Another thing to do with them is to put books on the shelf, organize the books in idiosyncratic ways, create mini-collections, and selectively show them off to others. During the interview, Hunter drew attention to the Web site *Lookshelves*:

> There's a whole aura around books and bookishness that I some-times like as much as reading them. My friend's website, *Look-shelves*, is pictures of books, people's bookshelves, but taken so that you can actually see what's on there. And it's so strangely compelling. I love it.

The originator of *Lookshelves*, Meghan Beresford, asks people to upload a photograph of their shelved books and answer a few questions about themselves, their shelf, and one book on the shelf. Shelves submitted include "A Brooklyn Beer Brewer's Lookshelf," "A Kingsley Amis Lookshelf," "A Tokyo Apartment Lookshelf," "A Tom Swift Lookshelf," and "An Unread Lookshelf." On her site, Beresford explains why she finds bookshelves so intriguing:

> When I go to someone's house, I am immediately drawn to their bookshelves. I want to know what they read (or buy), how they display their books, what's well-thumbed and what's in the darkish corners. I want to stumble into their secret interest in banjo, or ouija boards, or the Ottoman Empire. I love seeing that we've read the same thing. . . . For all of these reasons, I love bookshelves.

Somehow we have come full circle. Meghan Beresford's love of physical books "with pages and marginalia and musty smells" and "old library card pockets glued into the front covers" was the catalyst for her curating a digital collection of bookshelves available to be inspected online where she "could actually see books in their 'natural habitat' . . . on shelves, in homes."

References

Beresford, Meghan. *Lookshelves: The Site for Literary Voyeurs.* http://lookshelves.squarespace.com/about-lookshelves/.

Birkerts, Sven. 1995. *The Gutenberg Elegies: The Fate of Reading in an Electronic Age.* Winchester, MA: Faber and Faber.

Bosman, Julie. 2012. "Tablet and E-Reader Sales Soar." *New York Times*, January 22. http://mediadecoder.blogs.nytimes.com/2012/01/22/tablet-and-e-reader-sales-soar/?_php=true&_type=blogs&_r=0.

Brown, Ian. 2009. "Not Exactly Kindling His Passion." *Globe and Mail*, November 21. http://www.theglobeandmail.com/arts/not-exactly-kindling-his-passion/article4295695/.

Cohn, Cindy, and Parker Higgins. 2012. "Who's Tracking Your Reading Habits? An E-Book Buyer's Guide to Privacy, 2012 Edition." *Electronic Frontier Foundation*, November 29. https://www.eff.org/deeplinks/2012/11/e-reader-privacy-chart-2012-update.

Hupfeld, Annika, Abigail Sellen, Kenton O'Hara, and Tom Rodden. 2013. "Leisure-Based Reading and the Place of E-Books in Everyday Life." http://research .microsoft.com/en-us/people/asellen/ereading.pdf.

Jabr, Ferris. 2013. "The Reading Brain in the Digital Age: Why Paper Still Beat Screens." *Scientific American*, October 28. http://www.scientificamerican.com/ article.cfm?id=the-reading-brain-in-the-digital-age-why-paper-still-beats-screens.

Owen, Laura Hazard. 2013. "Ebooks Made Up 20% of the U.S. Consumer Book Industry in 2012, Up from 15% in 2011." *PaidContent*, May 15. http://paidcontent.org/ 2013/05/15/ebooks-made-up-20-of-the-u-s-consumer-book-industry-in-2012-up -from-15-in-2011/.

Piper, Andrew. 2012. *Book Was There: Reading in Electronic Times*. Chicago and London: The University of Chicago Press.

ReadersFirst. http://readersfirst.org/.

Socken, Paul, ed. 2013. *The Edge of the Precipice: Why Read Literature in the Digital Age?* Montreal and Kingston, Canada: McGill Queens University Press.

Further Reading

Sloan, Robin. 2012. *Mr. Penumbra's 24-Hour Bookstore*. New York: Farrar, Straus and Giroux. An exuberant quest story involving a fellowship of friends in a Google-meets-fifteenth-century-typesetting world. Sloan said, "I wrote this book because it's the one I wanted to read, and I tried to pack it full of the things I love: books and bookstores; design and typography; Silicon Valley and San Francisco; fantasy and science fiction; quests and projects."

Five-Foot Shelf of Books

The Five-Foot Shelf of Books today invites ridicule. We can imagine people buying the Five-Foot Shelf as furniture, publicly advertising their intellectual aspiration by showing off those books in a uniform, red, hardcover binding. INDISCRIMINATE readers, who read everything, high and low, classics and so-called trash, are apt to deride people who need to be reassured by experts that they are reading truly important, worthwhile books and not wasting their time on the wrong stuff. Omnivores read everything, higgledy-piggledy, directed only by their pursuit of enjoyment. They are suspicious of readers who need to follow a systematic program of self-improvement for "fifteen minutes a day." If you are one of these readers who are skeptical of systematic programs, you may find eye-opening Christopher R. Beha's *The Whole Five Feet* (2009), which describes in personal terms his YEAR OF READING of the Five-Foot Shelf, also known as the Harvard Classics.

So what is the Five-Foot Shelf? When Charles W. Eliot was president of Harvard, a post he held for some 40 years, he gave speeches in which he waxed enthusiastic about a five-foot shelf of books that would furnish a liberal education to anyone willing to devote 15 minutes a day to reading them. As he neared retirement in 1909, he was approached by publisher P. F. Collier, who proposed that Collier and Son should publish just such a collection. Eliot agreed to choose the books, write an editor's introduction, and lend his (and Harvard's) name to the project. In his introduction, he describes his reading program as a course of study that would develop in "a careful and persistent reader" "the essentials of a liberal education, even if he can devote to them but fifteen minutes a day." His goal was "to present so ample and characteristic a record of the stream of the world's thought that the observant reader's mind shall be enriched, refined, and fertilized by it."

The 51-volume set that makes up the Five-Foot Shelf contains an eclectic mix of texts judged to be touchstones of a liberal education. Apart from *Don Quixote*, novels are not included, a gap that Collier filled with a later series, "Harvard Classics Shelf of Fiction." You can find the entire Harvard Classics, together with introductions, at Bartleby.com. The following examples are illustrative of what is included but are not exhaustive:

Biography/autobiography:	Plutarch, Carlyle, Augustine, Walton, Franklin, Mill
History:	Herodotus, Froissart, American Historical Documents: 1000–1904
Philosophy:	Plato, Descartes, Mill, Hume, Hobbes, Berkeley, Locke, Adam Smith
Letters:	Pliny the Younger, Voltaire, Burke
Essays:	Cicero, Bacon, Montaigne, Emerson, Thoreau, Arnold
Plays:	Aeschylus, Sophocles, Shakespeare, Dryden, Sheridan, Corneille, Racine, Moliere
Poetry:	Homer, Virgil, Goethe, Dante, Milton, Burns, Wordsworth, Beowulf
Religious	texts: Sayings of Confucius, selections from the Old and New Testament, the Koran, the Bhagavad-Gita, and Buddhist writings
Prose fiction:	*The Thousand and One Nights*, Aesop, Grimm Brothers, Cervantes, Mallory, More
Science:	Darwin, Harvey, Jenner, Pasteur, Lyell

Fifteen Minutes a Day

During the first 20 years of publication, almost half a million sets of the Five-Foot Shelf were sold. In *The Making of Middlebrow Culture*, Joan Shelley Rubin (1992, 18, 27) argues that with the expansion of publishing the American reader felt "adrift in uncharted waters," struggling to discern "the best" when there is so much out there to be read. Accordingly, readers turned with gratitude to experts not only to accumulate prestige or set themselves apart from the masses but also "because they sought stability, insight, and pleasure in the books to which they were directed" (27). Sales of the Five-Foot Shelf, says Rubin (29–30), surpassed Collier's expectations, spurred on by advertisements in the 1920s and 1930s that linked the ownership of these volumes to business and social success.

Readers may have been reassured that this "liberal frame of mind" could be managed in "fifteen minutes a day," but soon critics ridiculed the project as infected by, as Everett Dean Martin (1926, 17) put it, "our passion for short-cuts." "Education requires time," Martin declared. "The only time wasted is that spent trying to save time. There should be no haste or crowding or cramming. Mastery of any subject requires years of familiarity with it." As an example of genuine reading, Martin describes books that came from "the small library of a New England farmer of the early years of the Republic, who read his books by his kitchen fireside . . ., who lived with them for years, and found in them a per-petual source of interest and wisdom" (14). In contrast, Martin points to the commodification of culture evident in a full-page advertisement in the Sunday papers for the Five-Foot Shelf that depicts a "gaudy dining-room" with three people seated at dinner:

> There are two men and a beautiful woman. She is talking to the man on her right, and is evidently fascinated with his brilliant con-versation. The man on the left sits dumb and miserable and unno-ticed; he cannot join in such sophisticated and scintillating discussion. We are informed that the poor man has neglected to read his fifteen minutes a day. (14)

Martin heaps scorn on anyone who would launch into a study of the world's classics to "impress people with his knowledge, appear genteel, make himself attractive to women or gain entrance to an exclusive social set" (13). But readers often *do* read difficult and demanding books in the first instance because they want to become the sort of person who reads that sort of book. The initial motivation for reading something doesn't tell us much about the actual reading experience. The interest in Christopher Beha's book is that he provides just that detailed register of his day-to-day reading experience that is usually not available to us. He comments on what bored or baffled him, what moved or delighted or strengthened him, and his year-long reading program is interwoven with events of his life. After three months of reading, he remarks, "life was teaching me about these books just as much as the books were teach-ing me about life" (73).

Christopher Beha and *The Whole Five Feet*

At the beginning of *The Whole Five Feet*, Christopher Beha is wandering lost in a dark wood. Well, actually, he is alone in the library of his parents' apartment in Manhattan in the last few minutes of the year 2006. Twenty-seven-year-old Beha has just quit his job, broken up with his girlfriend for no apparent reason, moved back home with his parents—and, a week earlier, suffered his first anxi-ety attack. So when he opens the first volume of the Harvard Classics and begins reading Benjamin Franklin's *Autobiography* (1788), he is reading to save his life. And during his year of reading, he is also dealing with the stuff that life itself brings—his aunt Mimi had a persistent sore on her foot that was diagnosed as a melanoma; she undergoes surgery, convalesces, goes back into hospital for further surgery, moves into the apartment with Beha and his parents, undergoes radiation, and in May lives out her last days.

The decision to read the whole Shelf during 2007 was not arbitrary but connected to the two sets of the Harvard Classics that "populated [his] childhood," one set belonging to his bibliophile, collector father and the other to his maternal grandmother. As a child visiting his grandmother's house in the summer, Beha frequently took down from the shelves the 50th volume, which was Eliot's introduction, reader's guide, and index to the Shelf. Beha said that the Harvard Classics appealed to him "most immediately for the reason that similar projects appeal to so many people: they suggested the existence of a discrete and relatively stable canon, one that I might eventually conquer" (7). When Beha mentioned to his mother his plan of reading the Shelf, she surprised him by saying that her own mother "used to say that she was educated by the Harvard Classics. . . . She never got past the eighth grade" (12). So here in his own family was one of the readers that Eliot had imagined for his project: a person with little formal education but with a great deal of "intellectual ambition" (16).

Beha's book is divided into 12 chapters corresponding to the 12 months of reading, plus an introduction and afterward. In January, Volume I proves to be a somewhat daunting beginning, containing as it does Franklin's *Autobiography*, John Woolman's *Journal*, and William Penn's *Fruits of Solitude*. Franklin's *Autobiography* offers a weekly calendar for mastering the 13 virtues necessary for upright living, fixing the attention "on one of them at a time" (24). Unlike Jay Gatsby (see RAGS TO RICHES), whose daily self-improvement program focused on useful accomplishments for social and economic success, Franklin emphasizes good character. Franklin's checklist for acquiring the 13 virtues begins with "temperance ('Eat not to dullness; drink not to elevation') and ends with humility ('Imitate Jesus and Socrates')." Initially, chafing under the yoke of reading texts that seem didactic and unliterary, Beha ends January having decided the first volume was "a kind of corrective. The earliest part of the Harvard Classics were trying to turn me into the person I needed to be in order to read whatever came next."

During the short, dark days of February, Beha might have been content to spend entire days in secluded reading in his parents' library, but Emerson's "The American Scholar" sent him out into the world: "Every day, men and women, conversing, beholding and beholden. The scholar is he of all men whom this spectacle most engages" (47). By June he is tormented by hives that cause swelling and redness and cover his entire body, especially his head and feet. At such a time, to be reading Allesandro Manzoni's *I Promessi Sposi* (*The Betrothed*), which is set in plague-stricken Milan of 1630, seems only appropriate. Beha reads that in seventeenth-century Milan, "Sickness and deaths began rapidly to multiply . . . with the unusual accompaniments of spasms, palpitation, lethargy, delirium, and those fatal symptoms, livid spots and sores; and these deaths were, for the most part, rapid, violent, and not unfrequently sudden, without any previous tokens of illness" (114).

By July he is drugged, numb, and in pain from what he fears is bubonic plague or possibly a recurrence of non-Hodgkins lymphoma from five years ago, but it turns out to be Lyme disease. He reads stories of recovery: Richard Henry Dana's *Two Years before the Mast* (1840) and John Stuart Mill's *Autobiography* (1873). Groomed to be a Benthamite and utilitarian reformer by his father who taught him to read Greek when he was three and Latin when he was eight, Mill experienced what in Chapter V, "Crisis in my Mental History," he calls "a dull state of nerves." In this dejected frame of mind, he asked himself whether he would be happy were he to achieve all his cherished goals in life. The answer was no. He observed, "I seemed to have nothing left to live for"—this at the age of 20. Mill had been trained as a reasoning machine, but he began to realize that "the habit of analysis has a tendency to wear away the feelings." Throughout the winter of 1826–1827, he felt numb and directionless: "I seemed to have nothing left to live for." He felt like a stranded vessel, all outfitted to begin a sea voyage but with no sail (141–43). Mill's recovery came with the cultivation of the emotions, especially with his reading of Wordsworth: "What made Wordsworth's poems a medicine for my state of mind, was that they expressed . . . states of feeling, and of thought coloured by feeling, under the excitement of beauty" (146). Ruthlessly trained in logic and rational analysis, Mill recovers through the integration of thought and feeling.

A low point comes in August when Beha wakes up unable to read. Like Howard Engel (see ALEXIA), he finds that print has turned into hieroglyphics:

> I found that I could no longer read. When I looked at a page the letters refused to cohere into words; the words refused to form sentences. The printing was a code whose key I didn't possess. The problem seemed related to my short-term memory, which had gotten worse over the preceding days. (163)

"Brain fog" is the diagnosis, apparently related to the Lyme disease. Beha remembers Thoreau's comment in his essay "Walking" that he cannot preserve his "health and spirits" unless he spends at least four hours a day "sauntering through the woods and over the hills and fields" (165). Being unable to read brings home a truth: "Reading had become my way of sauntering, my way of being *sans terre*, at home in no one place but comfortable moving about the world, and it was these walks that I missed most."

Fortunately, the brain fog passes, and Beha is able to complete his year of reading. What struck me most forcibly about Beha's account is how he read his own life into the works he was reading and then read the works back into his life. Given a treasure house of texts as rich, deep, and varied as the Five-Foot Shelf, I expect that other "careful and persistent" readers would find many texts that seem to speak directly to their own lives and concerns, but not necessarily the same ones that spoke most feelingly to Christopher Beha.

References

Beha, Christopher R. 2009. *The Whole Five Feet: What the Great Books Taught Me about Life, Death and Pretty Much Everything Else*. New York: Grove Press.

Martin, Everett Dean. 1926. *Meaning of a Liberal Education*. New York: Norton. Available in the Gutenberg Project.

Rubin, Joan Shelley. 1992. *The Making of Middlebrow Culture*. Chapel Hill and London: The University of North Carolina Press.

Gothic

Gothic fiction is a genre obsessively focused on the house. "Last night I dreamt I went to Manderley again" is the famous first sentence of Daphne du Maurier's *Rebecca* (1938). In some other kinds of stories, the house is a place of safety, a sanctuary from the world. But not in gothic fiction, where interior spaces become prisons for imperiled heroines or represent a domestic happiness from which the scarred male protagonist is excluded. Naturally, the house in question is not just any house but a very impressive architectural monument, usually a castle but sometimes a monastery, convent, prison, or insane asylum. In the female-centered gothic, the male owner of the castle is an older man with a piercing glance—aristocratic, obsessed, moody, and secretive, with qualities that mark him as a literary descendent of Satan in *Paradise Lost*. The heroine comes to the fortress as a governess, bride, or prisoner and, once there, she lives in a state of heightened emotional arousal, in terror for her life. Claiming that architecture is a repository as well as an embodiment of the past, DeLamotte (1990, 15) says, "[The gothic house] contains evidence of specific life histories: a skeleton stashed beneath the floorboards or locked in a chest, a prisoner shut away in a dungeon, a manuscript reporting a crime, an ancestral portrait revealing the hero or heroine's true lineage, the ghost of a previous occupant, an aged retainer who remembers certain sinister events of long ago." At the heart of the gothic house is a terrible, terrible secret.

Horace Walpole is credited with beginning the genre of gothic fiction with *The Castle of Otranto: A Gothic Story* (1765). This novel seems dull enough reading now, but it electrified its early readers with its medieval castle setting, its supernatural elements, its themes of inheritance and false identities, its depiction of the deranged villain Manfred chasing the beset heroine through dark passages and vaults, and the simultaneous implosion at the end of both Manfred and the castle itself, disintegrating into rubble. Elizabeth MacAndrew (1979, 13) points out, "The central device in

Otranto became the most famous of all Gothic devices: the identity of the castle or house with its owner." Between 1790 and 1820, the gothic novel was the most popular type of English fiction written and read. Many of the gothic titles were published by the William Lane's Minerva Press and made accessible through circulating libraries to a newly created class of novel readers. A large proportion of Minerva Press authors as well as readers were women. The Web site British Fiction 1800–1829 (Garside et al. n.d.) lists 522 titles published by Minerva Press.

Gothic authors drew on a repertoire of often-repeated dramatic situations, settings, character types, and themes to explore the darker emotions of melancholy, anxiety, fear, and HORROR. MacAndrew (1979, 5) argues that certain conventional features have reappeared in fiction for 250 years because these features are tried-and-true ways to convey psychological evil—evil that is not an outside force but an internal warping of the human mind. Dream materials drawn from the unconscious—mirrors, moving statues, portraits that reflect the soul, identical twins, spirals and vortices, underground vaults, live entombment, hermetically sealed worlds—are all used to intensify the reader's sense of characters in an extreme mental state. Three famous seminal gothic stories—Walpole's *Otranto*, Mary Shelley's *Frankenstein*, and Robert Louis Stevenson's *Dr. Jekyll and Mr. Hyde*—actually had their origins in a dream or nightmare.

Writing the Gothic

Before I was aware that there existed a recognizable type of fiction that featured moldering castles, impoverished governesses, and brooding heroes with piercing eyes, I encountered Victoria Holt's *The Mistress of Mellyn* (1960) when it was first published, month by month, as a serial in *The Ladies Home Journal*. I was hooked, and so were my mother and my aunts. It gave me my first experience with reading fiction in installments and waiting for a month in high suspense for the next section. What I remember most about it now was the remote Cornish landscape, the menacing house, the heroine's mixed feelings of love and fear for the owner of the house, and the sense of impending disaster. I did not know at the time that Victoria Holt was the pen name for a British author, Eleanor Hibbert, who wrote under six other pen names, including Jean Plaidy for historical romance, Eleanor Burford, and Philippa Carr (at the time of her death in 1993, Hibbert had sold some 100 million books). Nor did I know that *The Mistress of Mellyn* stood in a long line of governess novels from Charlotte Bronte's *Jane Eyre* to Daphne du Maurier's *Rebecca*, with even earlier sources in eighteenth-century gothic prototypes. Fortunately, excellent guides are now available that map out the contours of the gothic genre (Punter 1996; Pringle 1998; Hughes 2013).

Writing about these eighteenth-century gothic novels, Kate Ferguson Ellis (1989, x) asks, "Why did these books become so popular just at the time when women were becoming a significant part of the reading public? What in the culture created the demand for such fare, and what were its messages to readers?" We could ask the same question about the rebirth of the gothic in the twentieth century. Following Holt's great success in recreating *Rebecca*'s strong appeal for readers, there was a decade-long publishing boom in the 1960s in paperback gothic romances. Characteristic cover art (see JACKETS) identified the gothic romance genre: a castle in the background with a tower with one illuminated window, a fleeing young woman in a diaphanous gown, ominous clouds, and color tones of purple and blue.

Eventually, the post-Holt publishing boom in gothic romances exhausted itself through repetition, but not before many popular books were published, including parodies. My personal favorite is *A Cluster of Separate Sparks* (1972) by Joan Aitken, who has also written celebrated children's books such as *The Wolves of Willoughby Chase* and *Arabel's Raven*. You become sure that you are reading a parody when Aitken's heroine Daphne, who has been locked into a hidden passageway stuffed with poison gas, escapes through a door into a bathroom in which the hero/villain is taking a bath in a huge tub. To evade an angry swarm of killer African bees that have suddenly penetrated the room, both she and the hero have to submerge themselves together up to their noses in bath water. Fortunately, the self-possessed heroine has learned exactly what to do in such cases from her mother, who was a bee woman, and the heroine is able to calm the enraged bees by singing to them. Oh, and did I mention that there's an *oubliette*? The gothic is a genre that invites parody and has been so from its beginning—think of Jane Austen's *Northanger Abbey* in which the 17-year-old Catherine Morland fancies herself a heroine in a gothic novel. When Catherine accepts an invitation from General Tilney to visit Northanger Abbey, Henry Tilney asks her, "Have you a stout heart? Nerves fit for sliding panels and tapestry?" and reminds her to expect to be lead by an "ancient housekeeper . . . along many gloomy passages, into an apartment never used since some cousin or kin died in it about twenty years before."

Gothic Prototypes

The Mysteries of Udolpho (1794) by Ann Radcliffe is considered a founding text for the genre. A best-seller in its day, it has often been reprinted, pirated, imitated, talked about, and parodied. The governess in Henry James's *The Turn of the Screw* had read it. The very sensible Henry Tilney confessed to having read *Udolpho* in two days, "my hair standing on end the whole time." In *Udolpho*, Ann Radcliffe provides a full description of the gothic castle with frequently imitated details of labyrinthine passages, locked rooms, galleries lined with ancestral portraits, and secret staircases. Emily St. Aubert, the orphaned heroine, is separated from Valancourt, the man she loves, and carried off to Italy to live in a moldering castle in the Apennines under the power of her aunt's villainous husband, Signor Montoni. When Emily sees the castle of Udolpho for the first time, she has "one of those instantaneous and unaccountable convictions" that things are about to go badly wrong:

> Emily gazed with melancholy awe upon the castle, which she understood to be Montoni's; for, though it was now lighted up by the setting sun, the Gothic greatness of its features, and its mouldering dark grey stone, rendered it a gloomy and sublime object. . . . As the carriage-wheels rolled heavily under the portcullis, Emily's heart sunk, and she seemed, as if she was going into her prison. (Chapter 5)

Some of Emily's terrors can be attributed to the workings of her overwrought imagination. Characters in gothic fiction are always on high alert in a state of intense nervous sensibility. But feminist critics (Hoeveler 1998) have pointed out that stock elements of gothic plot machinery that give rise to the heroine's anxieties—the imprisoning house, disputed inheritance or wills, threatened incest or rape—had their real-life counterparts in contemporary English society: laws that allowed husbands to lock up disobedient wives; guardians who separated lovers and forced young women to marry older men against their will; laws that gave husbands complete control over their wives' property and bodies; social norms that punished women but not men for extramarital sex and illegitimacy; the vulnerability of working women to assault, rape, and dismissal if pregnant; and so on. In *The Mysteries of Udolpho*, Montoni has designs upon his wife's fortune. Having tried unsuccessfully to force Emily to marry one of his friends, Montoni takes her to his decaying castle in Italy where he thinks he can bend her to his will. Capping off his poor behavior, he locks up his wife and literally starves her to death in a cold room when she refuses to sign over to him her estates in Toulouse. (" 'Come, come,' said Montoni, '. . . I must be trifled with no longer. I have immediate occasion for what I demand—those estates must be given up, without further contention; or I may find a way—' "). Even in gothic romances with happy endings, the economic precariousness of the heroine is foregrounded. The first sentence of *The Mistress of Mellyn* is " 'There are two courses open to a gentlewoman when she finds herself in penurious circumstances,' my Aunt Adelaide had said. 'One is to marry, and the other is to find a post in keeping with her gentility.' "

The Monk (1796) by Matthew Lewis is a foundational text of a different sort, in which gothic conventions intensify a lurid treatment of sexual obsession and violence. Written when its author was only 20 *and* a member of parliament, *The Monk* scandalized Byron, himself no stranger to scandal, who called the novel the "ideas of a jaded voluptuary." Unlike Radcliffe's female-centered gothic about the beset heroine whose virtue defeats evil, *The Monk* is a male-centered story of a once-good man who spirals downward into a nightmarish abyss of deranged violence. Set in Spain during the Inquisition, the novel has several interconnected plots. The central one traces the fall of the monk Ambrosio, a saintly man of mysterious parentage, who has always lived in seclusion, unfamiliar with the temptations of the world. Ambrosio's problems start when his cloistered virtue is undermined by Matilda, who has entered the monastery disguised as a boy novice but turns out to be a beautiful seductress and agent of Lucifer. Once having broken his vow of chastity, Ambrosio wades deeper and deeper into sexual passion, psychopathic violence, cruelty, and tormented self-destruction. At each step into evil, he reflects in horror on what he has done but is helpless to stop himself.

The eighteenth century believed in rationality and the moderate enjoyment of God's gifts, including sexuality, but Ambrosio lurches from one extreme to its opposite. Sexual desire, which has been repressed in the monastery, is unleashed in a perverse, violent form that Ambrosio can't control. With Matilda's help, he rapes an innocent young girl, Antonia, having first strangled her mother, Elvira, to get the girl's guardian out of the way. The rape itself takes place in a subterranean vault with tombs nearby: "[Antonia's] alarm, her evident disgust, and incessant opposition, seemed only to inflame the Monk's desires, and supply his brutality with additional strength." When the crimes of Ambrosio and Matilda are discovered, the two accomplices are cast into a prison of the Inquisition. The locale of the novel shifts from cathedral and monastic cell to underground funeral vaults to an Inquisition prison, marking the downward spiral of Ambrosio's unstable personality. To escape prison, Ambrosio sells his soul to the devil, who then reveals to Ambrosio that Elvira was his mother and Antonia his sister. This over-the-top book is packed with the elements we associate with the gothic: gloomy landscapes, haunted castles, corrupt ancient monasteries, dungeons and labyrinthine passages, subterranean vaults, ghostly hauntings, fortune-telling gypsies, mysterious parentage, the double depiction of women as evil seductress and as innocent virgin, the doomed hero/villain, evil nuns, a pact with the devil, torture, rape, incest, murder, and necrophilia. The divided self—the Ambrosio character in whom goodness struggles to the death with evil—turns up again and again in gothic fiction. Think of Robert Louis Stevenson's *Strange Case of Dr. Jekyll and Mr. Hyde* (1886) or Oscar Wilde's *The Picture of Dorian Gray* (1890).

Gothic Conventions

Once these conventions were introduced in eighteenth century, the gothic became a treasure box of available motifs, tropes, images, and plot elements that individual authors could dip into, select from, and recombine to heighten the emotional impact of their fictional work. The gothic has been a parent genre for the DETECTIVE story, the ghost story, HORROR, and romantic suspense genres, and its influence is felt in film as well as in fiction. In novels such as *Jane Eyre*, Nathaniel Hawthorne's *The House of Seven Gables* (1851), and modern gothic romance, there are strong elements of suspense and fear, but love wins out. In such fiction as *Frankenstein*, Edgar Allan Poe's "The Fall of the House of Usher" (1839), and Bram Stoker's *Dracula* (1897), sexuality and desire are undercurrents in texts primarily designed to evoke horror and fear in the reader. Then, too, gothic elements can wander into literary fiction such as Umberto Eco's *The Name of the Rose* (1983). Usually considered a detective story, this internationally best-selling novel is set in a medieval abbey, complete with its hidden locked rooms and passages, the terrible secret, and the fire that consumes everything at the end. Sarah Waters's Booker-nominated *The Little Stranger* (2008), which highlights the house in its opening sentence, "I first saw Hundreds Hall when I was ten years old," tells a chilling ghost story set in a crumbling manor house post–World War II. Jennifer Crusie's *Maybe This Time* (2010) is a retelling of Henry James's *The Turn of the Screw* in which the heroine Andie is sent by her ex-husband to a creepy mansion where she must protect two orphaned kids from a danger related to the house's past occupants (it goes without saying that previous governesses have either left or died).

We know that we are in gothic territory when we find evidence of the following conventions:

• *Setting*

The gothic setting pushes any geographic feature to its extreme. Outside the gothic house may be a glacial polar waste, desolate windswept heath, dark forest, or rugged range of mountains. In the frame narrative that begins *Frankenstein*, Captain Walton is trapped in his ship "surrounded by mountains of ice" in the frozen arctic ocean when he sees "a being which had the shape of a man, but apparently of gigantic stature" in a dogsled being chased across the ice. A castle on a cliff top near the sea is a popular setting for the female-centered gothic, providing elements from the natural world that amplify fear: crashing waves that seem to whisper a menacing name, boulders that hurtle down the cliff face and almost kill the heroine, slippery coastal paths that suddenly give way, and fogs that turn trees and figures into wavering outlines. Ruined buildings on the castle grounds are assets because they evoke melancholy reflection on the *momento mori* theme of it's-later-than-you-think. Aspects of setting, such as a violent thunderstorm or a tranquil lake, convey the mood or emotions of the characters.

The interior of the castle is provided with special architectural features: hidden passages, peep holes available for a hidden observer, a secret room or priest's hole, an underground crypt, a dungeon, or an oubliette. In more realistic fiction, the castle may be displaced into a more everyday setting such as Bates's hotel in *Psycho* or the plantation in southern gothic. Atmospheric effects of light and dark are common: candles gutter or flashlights expire just when the heroine is in a dark passage, moonlight creates a phantasmagoric interplay of light and shadow, and flashes of lightning reveal hidden presences. Borders are breached between things that ought to be distinct and separate such as inside and outside, life and death, and platonic love and erotic love. Hence a secret sliding panel opens in a solid wall; things dead come to life; statues and people in portraits or on wallpaper start to move; love for a sister turns into sexual love. Though made of stone, the gothic castle is very apt to be consumed in flames as happens in *Jane Eyre* and *Rebecca*. Or it may collapse in upon itself as happens in Walpole's *The Castle of Otranto* and Poe's "The Fall of the House of Usher." In such cases, settings are part of characterization, in which the house is identified with its owner.

• *Plot*

Like the DETECTIVE story, the gothic is all about uncovering a secret that has happened before the story began. Often the mysterious crime at the heart of the plot involves the breaking of a strong taboo—for example, incest, the murder of a parent or sibling, or the pursuit of scientific knowledge into forbidden areas such as creating or prolonging life itself. In the governess plots, a gentlewoman with no family and little money takes a job as a governess for an emotionally scarred, older man. The heroine is attracted to him but fears she can't trust him: is he the one who is trying to kill her? "Someone's trying to kill me and I think it's my husband" is how Joanna Russ (1973) summarizes the modern gothic. Old family retainers or housekeepers heighten the menace by making cryptic references to sinister past events. The secret at the heart of the story needs to be something with big shock value: live burial, necrophilia, murder, a mad wife in the attic, incest, rape, an uneasy ghost, diabolism, torture at the hands of the Spanish Inquisition, and so on. In the southern gothic of William Faulkner, Flannery O'Connor, and Carson McCullers, with its grotesque and damaged characters, the terrible secret is ultimately connected to slavery.

• *Narrative Method*

The manner of telling the gothic story is striking. It is not coincidental that so many of its authors use narrative framing devices that put the strange world of the gothic story at several removes from the reader, distanced by narrators who are reporting a story that they have learned about through letters or ancient manuscripts. In *Otranto*, Walpole uses the device of the "editor," who presents a discovered manuscript containing a story from a distant time and place. In *Frankenstein*, Captain Walton in the frozen arctic sends letters to his sister that report the strange story told him by a fellow scientist, Dr. Frankenstein, a story that itself includes an even stranger inset story narrated by Frankenstein's Being. In these nested narratives, the reader starts off with an ordinary narrator who resembles the reader and then, through a series of regressions of stories within stories, is led into a world very far from everyday reality. In Henry James's *The Turn of the Screw*, the first narrator sets the scene as he and others are gathered around a fire on Christmas Eve in an old house listening to ghost stories. One person in the group, Douglas, promises a humdinger of a story involving two children, a story that is "beyond every-thing," unparalleled "[f]or dreadful—dreadfulness!" But he can't tell the story right away—the story, in manuscript form, is elsewhere "in a locked drawer—it has not been out for years." After a long postponement, the manuscript arrives, written "in old, faded ink" by a charming governess who "has been dead these twenty years." Finally, mediated by two previous narrators who stand between the reader and the story, we get the beginning of the govern-ess's first-person narration: "I remember the whole beginning as a succession of flights and drops."

• Characters

Quintessentially, the gothic is about the exploration of psychological evil. There is often a doubling of characters into good and bad versions—heroes and vil-lains, heroines and witches—although sometimes it can be hard initially to tell the two apart. In *Rebecca*, the second Mrs. de Winter wrongly thinks at first that her predecessor Rebecca was a wifely paragon. Sometimes the good and bad are split into separate characters, but often the human capacity for good and evil is explored within a single individual as in Robert Louis Stevenson's *Dr Jekyll and Mr. Hyde* (1886). A common gothic motif is transformation, as a good char-acter like Ambrosio in *The Monk* turns into a monster. *Frankenstein: The Modern Prometheus* is about a creator who creates a rational Being out of love "in a fit of enthusiastic madness" but loses control of his creation and begins to hate and reject him. Reviled by humankind and cut off from all social ties, the unnamed Being who has started off as an innocent Adam becomes, like Mil-ton's Satan, a creature who says, "all good to me is lost. Evil, be thou my good." In grief after he has killed his creator, the Being says to Walton, who is the nar-rator of the frame narrative: "My heart was fashioned to be susceptible of love and sympathy. . . . I cannot believe that I am the same creature whose thoughts were once filled with sublime and transcendent visions of the beauty and the majesty of goodness. But it is even so; the fallen angel becomes a malignant devil. Yet even that enemy of God and man had friends and associates in his desolation; I am alone."

With their dark gloomy power and sexual energy, gothic villains take center stage in the books in which they appear. The hallmark of the villain is his isolation. He may have ruptured his ties to society in a Faustian pursuit of forbidden knowledge—the creation or prolongation of life. Cut off from domestic happiness, the hero or hero/villain is often doomed to exiled wander-ing, like Melmoth in Charles Maturin's *Melmoth the Wanderer* (1820). In gothic fiction, it can be hard to make the good characters as interesting. For that reason, many of the most memorable gothic heroes are charged with some of the villain's power—think of Heathcliffe, Rochester, and *Rebecca*'s Maxim de Winter.

Female villains have been in short supply in a genre that has specialized in beset and virtuous heroines. But those who do exist have been unscrupulous virtuosos in craft, deception, manipulation, and selfishness. Examples of the evil enchantress include Walpole's Matilda, du Maurier's Rebecca, Lady Audley in Mary Elizabeth Braddon's *Lady Audley's Secret* (1862), the robber bride Zenia in Margaret Atwood's *The Robber Bride* (1993), and the amazing Amy in Gillian Flynn's *Gone Girl* (2012).

• *Supernatural Elements*

The beleaguered heroine may hear the tapping of bony fingers on window panes, feel a sudden wintery chill in the air as if in the presence of an unseen visitor, or experience ghostly presences—all of which heighten the sense of peril. Sometimes the supernatural elements are explained away at the end as counterfeit (the Scooby-Doo hoax) and sometimes not. A work that retains its ties to the ordinary rational world may yet include elements of the uncanny by means of guilt and fear projected in dreams, ancestral curses, prophetic utterances of gypsies and fortunetellers, and the presence of characters who are fey, simpleminded, or mad.

• *Emotional Effect*

DeLamotte (1990, 22–23) says, "Two fears dominate this Gothic world, the fear of terrible separateness and the fear of unity with some terrible Other. They are embodied in two classic formulas of the ghost story: the heroine's terrifying discovery that she is all alone and her subsequent discovery that—horror of horrors—she is not alone."

References

DeLamotte, Eugenia C. 1990. *Perils of the Night: A Feminist Study of Nineteenth-Century Gothic*. New York: Oxford University Press.

Ellis, Kate Ferguson. 1989. *The Contested Castle: Gothic Novels and the Subversion of Domestic Ideology*. Urbana and Chicago: University of Illinois Press.

Garside, Peter, et al. "Publisher Index: Titles Published by 'Minerva Press.' " British Fiction 1800–1829: A Database of Production, Circulation & Reception. http://www.british-fiction.cf.ac.uk/publisherTitles.asp?publisher=Minerva+Press&order=author.

Hoeveler, Diane Long. 1998. *Gothic Feminism: The Professionalization of Gender from Charlotte Smith to the Brontes*. University Park: Pennsylvania State Press.

Hughes, William. 2013. *The Encyclopedia of the Gothic*. Malden, MA: Wiley-Blackwell.

MacAndrew, Elizabeth. 1979. *The Gothic Tradition in Fiction*. New York: Columbia University Press.

Pringle, David. 1998. *The St. James Guide to Horror, Ghost and Gothic Writers*. Detroit, MI: Gale.

Punter, David. 1996. *The Literature of Terror: The History of Gothic Fiction from 1765 to the Present Day*. New York: Longman.

Russ, Joanna. 1973. "Somebody's Trying to Kill Me and I Think It's My Husband: The Modern Gothic." *Journal of Popular Culture* 6, no. 4: 666–91.

Horror

Major inspirations of the horror genre have been nightmares, bad weather, and the apocalyptic imagination of the end of things. Admittedly, scary stories have probably been told around fires from time immemorial, but the origin of two founding horror stories can be dated to "the year without a summer," when the weather was in turmoil. In the summer of 1816, the poet Percy Bysshe Shelley scandalously travelled from London to Switzerland with two unmarried women, Mary Godwin and Mary's step-sister Claire Clairmont, plus a baby. The draw was the famous, and even more scandalous, Lord Byron, who had rented the Villa Diodati on the shore of Lake Geneva and was staying there with his personal physician, John William Polidori. To pass the time during that "wet, ungenial summer," the five friends "crowded around a blazing wood fire" in the Villa Diodati and read aloud to each other from books of ghost stories translated from the German, including *Tales of the Dead* (1813).

Rain kept the friends in the house for days at a time. In a July 12 letter to Thomas Love Peacock (Rhys 1887, 188), Percy Bysshe Shelley described the volatile weather on the lake: "[It] involved more rapid changes of atmosphere than I ever recollect to have observed before. . . . The morning was cold and wet; then an easterly wind, and the clouds hard and high; then thunder showers, and wind shifting to every quarter; then a warm blast from the south, and summer clouds hanging over the peaks, with bright blue sky between." What the group of friends didn't know was that in 1815 a massive volcanic eruption from the Tambora volcano in southwest Asia had drastically changed the climate in the Northern Hemisphere, turning 1816 into "the year without a summer." The English tourists on Lake Geneva were surrounded by famine as the price of grain and potatoes tripled in Europe, the poor ate nettles and rioted in the streets, and apocalyptic prophecies were in the air (Fagan 2000, 171–72).

In the midst of this global atmospheric disruption, Lord Byron proposed, "We will each write a ghost story." The friends at the Villa Diodati had impressive literary qualifications for the challenge. Byron and Shelley were well-known romantic poets. The 19-year-old Mary Godwin was the daughter of William Godwin and Mary Wollstonecraft, who had written respectively the first mystery novel, *Caleb Williams* (1794), and the influential feminist tract, *A Vindication of the Rights of Women* (1792). In fact, two stories produced for the competitive storytelling game were long-term horror-story winners. One, by Mary Godwin (later Mary Shelley), was about an overreaching scientist, Dr. Frankenstein, who brings into existence a living creature and then abandons it. The other was an uncompleted fragment by Byron about a rich, charismatic, aristocrat Darvell, who travels with a younger man to Ephesus, where the spooky trappings surrounding Darvell's mysterious death involve a sacred oath and a ritual (of reawakening?) to be enacted on the ninth day of the month. Byron lost interest in his uncompleted story, but Polidori later took the kernel of Byron's tale and transformed it into the first literary vampire story, titled *The Vampyre*. Mary Shelley's *Frankenstein* (1818) and Polidori's *The Vampyre* (1819) each became the originating story of two distinctive horror subgenres: the story of the mad scientist who becomes captive of his own creature (see GOTHIC) and the VAMPIRE story of the undead creature who walks the night and sucks the vitality from human victims.

According to Mary Shelley's preface to the 1831 edition of *Frankenstein*, "Poor Polidori had some terrible idea about a skull-headed lady, who was . . . punished for peeping through a keyhole." Byron began a story, later published as "Fragment of a Story" at the end of his poem of Mazeppa. But Mary Shelley herself suffered a "blank incapability of invention." She described how she tried in vain to think of a story "that would speak to the mysterious fears of our nature, and awaken thrilling horror—one to make the reader dread to look round, to curdle the blood and quicken the beatings of the heart." Then after an evening of hearing the others talk of Darwin's experiments, galvanism, and ideas about the origins of life, she went to bed and had an "acute mental vision" of the "pale student of unhallowed arts kneeling beside the thing he had put together—I saw the hideous phantasm of a man stretched out, and then, on the working of some powerful engine, show signs of life, and stir with an uneasy, half vital motion." She imagines that the presumptuous creator would "rush away from his odious handiwork, horror-stricken," would fall asleep hoping that "the slight spark of life would fade," but would awaken to see the "horrid thing" standing beside his bedside, "looking on him with yellow, watery, but speculative eyes!"

> I opened mine in terror. The idea so possessed my mind, that a thrill of fear ran through me. . . . I could not so easily get rid of my hideous phantom; still it haunted me. . . . O! if I could only contrive one which would frighten my reader as I myself had been

frightened that night! ... [T]he idea ... broke in upon me. "I have found it! What terrified me will terrify others; and I need only describe the spectre which had haunted my midnight pillow." On the morrow I announced that I had thought of a story. I began that day with the words, "It was on a dreary night of November," making only a transcript of the grim terrors of my waking dream.

Notably, Mary Shelley's famous origin story emphasizes the visceral effect she wanted to achieve: "to make the reader dread to look round, to curdle the blood and quicken the beatings of the heart." As Stephen King says in *Danse Macabre* (1981, 17–18), "[T]he work of horror is really a dance—a moving rhythmic search. And what it's looking for is the place where you, the viewer or the reader, live at your most primitive level. ... The good horror tale will dance its way to the center of your life and find the secret door to the room you believed no one but you knew of." The real *danse macabre* happens, King says, in "those remarkable moments when the creator of a horror story is able to unite the conscious and subconscious mind with one potent idea" (20).

Horror Is What Scares You

When Kim Kofmel interviewed 32 avid readers of science fiction and fantasy for her doctoral research, she wanted to learn about readers' experiences, including how readers themselves defined science fiction, fantasy, and horror. Although there exists an extensive literature that uses a more or less consistent vocabulary to discuss these story types, Kofmel (2004) found that "Not only do [ordinary readers] not all use the same terms as the critical and professional material, they don't all use the same terms as one another. Even worse, they use the same words to mean slightly different things." Some interviewees in her study viewed horror as a separate genre in itself, and others saw it as an element that can be more or less present in a range of genres, including science fiction and crime stories about serial murderers. However, these readers did agree on one thing: horror is what scares you. More than any other genre, it is defined by the visceral effect it produces on its readers. It is a genre of extreme states. Kofmel's readers said that horror is what makes your "skin crawl," makes your "hair stand on end," and sends a "chill up and down ... your spine" (2002, 87).

Kofmel asked her interviewees questions designed to map the boundaries of the horror genre: "What makes horror different?" "What kind of experience are you looking for from horror?" and "What do you like about horror that doesn't occur in other genres?" Of the three genres—science fiction, fantasy, and horror—horror was the one most likely to be avoided by these readers. When they didn't like it, they were apt to say that they were scared enough already by everyday news events. Kofmel's readers often commented on gore and violence, some to say that they disliked it and others to say that the gore and violence exerted a fascinated attraction–repulsion that heightened the genre's visceral impact. James, who doesn't like horror and finds it pointless, defines horror as "anything that titillates . . . with feelings of dread and fear" and has supernatural evil in it. When choosing books (see BEFORE READING), he knows what to avoid: "Black colors. Black covers and red letters. Avoid anything by Clive Barker with the word blood in the title."

Unlike nonreaders of horror who had a simple account of the genre—"it scares you and I avoid it"—fans of horror usually had a detailed and well-populated schema to explain horror and its appeal. Different readers drew the boundaries differently between horror and fantasy but generally agreed that the horror genre plays to intense emotions: it has to evoke fear. Here are some of the answers provided by readers interviewed by Kim Kofmel who enjoyed reading horror at least sometimes.

- *Horror is that part of fantasy that touches on our deepest fears.* Heather (office coordinator at a museum, age 33) explains, "If the aim of the story is to touch on your fears, it is horror. If the aim is not to touch on your fears, but to touch on something else—the sense of wonder or sense of adventure—then it's more fantasy." What Heather looks for in a good horror book is "something twisted," which "takes a fear, probably which I sort of know I have." When you finish the book, your "hair stands up on your head, but you're not sure why." Whatever that undefinable something is causing the fear, it is malevolent and "intentional."

- *Horror taps into childhood fears.* Morag (publishing company employee, age 35) says, "Horror is stuff that scares me." Her example: "I've just finished reading Dan Simmons's *Summer of Night*, which tapped into childhood fears. When I was little, living on the farm, there was a rendering truck, and I was scared stiff of this thing because every so often you'd see it drive by with four legs sticking out of the back and the smell that accompanied it. And so as soon as I read 'rendering truck,' I'm sitting on my couch, I'm shaking. You want an intense emotion, but you don't necessarily want to go out and live that emotion. You sort of want to live vicariously through something else, and you need this jolt."

- *Horror puts you inside the book.* Fiona (information specialist, medical genetics, age 31) said that the key to horror is the way that it's written "to hit you at gut level" and put you "inside the book": "That's where the feeling of transportation [comes in]. If you're really inside the book, then you're inside the scene, and what's frightening to the characters in the scene is frightening to you. If you're really seeing the words on the page, you're not really inside the book. It's got to be going on in your head."

- *In the horror genre, more bad things happen.* Jules (senior computer programmer, age 33) says, "More people get dismembered. ... There is a part of you that has an impulse to do the stupidest things possible and that's what horror caters to. To do the stupidest and the most destructive and the most painful things possible. There's always a part of you says, 'Yeah, do that!' [When I read horror], I want to be afraid to turn the lights off. I want to be appalled and shocked. I want to be made uneasy and unsettled by it. That's what I want from horror—it's a case of a particular emotion. ... I want to be going, 'Oh my God, no.' "

- *Traditional horror provides an emotional catharsis.* Michelle (library collection specialist, age 42) says, "Horror always involves intrusion from outside the normal space and time, with the intent of destroying, or harming, the culture as we know it, the situation as the book portrays it. The function of [traditional] horror is usually catharsis. The menace is seen, realized, intensified, and then dissipated." Michelle contrasts traditional horror, which is the cathartic sort she enjoys, with other types of horror that she does not enjoy: those that feature "excessive amounts of blood and gore" and "post-modern horror, where the whole horror of it is that there's nothing there." She says, "I like the good guys to get away. I like a certain element of risk, but it's a very safe sort of danger. And sometimes you learn something about yourself—it's like a funhouse mirror."

- *The fantastic element that intrudes is always a bad thing.* Max (operations manager for an insurance broker, age 33) says that horror does not offer "an even-handed treatment": "If you want an exploration that zombies might be a good thing, don't look for it in horror." Horror has to have an aura and "make your skin crawl," whether it's "outright gross-out or that quiet, creeping dread, almost in the Poe tradition." Horror is "visceral"—"grabbing you by the guts and squeezing a little bit."

- *Horror projects a universe that is fundamentally malevolent.* Mitch (PhD student in philosophy, age 29) defines horror as "the genre of popular literature that pertains to the malevolent sense of life," where "joy is impossible," "death and tragedy are not just the norm, but unavoidable," and "any sort of struggle of good against evil is futile." He says that horror writers highlight the unpredictability and irrationality of the horrifying events that erupt into the everyday world from "another dark, supernatural dimension." "It's like there's another world that's overlapping and coming into our world." For Mitch, the key is that the reader needs "to relate to the character who is going through the horror so that it's like—it could be you. The horror author needs to capitalize on fears that are derived from this world."

- *Horror makes you face up to reality.* Jack (computer support supervisor, age 36) says that it takes courage to face up to the difficult situations that everyone experiences: "Horror, for me, points the way to courage in every day life." What makes horror different from other genres for Jack "is the starkness of the reality. Veneer is stripped away. You're basically down to the roots of what makes people tick the way they do."

- *Horror gives you permission to work out your darker fantasies.* Ian (engraver at a trophy company, age 33) says, "There's a part of me that can sort of get off on the serious violence and the serious gore, and that part scares me. The reasons why I don't like horror are part and parcel with the reasons that I do like it—the visceral descriptions of something really awful and bloody. It's like the car accident, you want to look away and you can't. That's what horror is all about, is giving people a chance to experience what they want to look away from. And often in horror, there's a certain amount of permission to commit this mayhem. So horror gives you permission to work out your darker fantasies."

In short, an effective work of horror speaks to our deepest, subconscious fears. When the book succeeds in its magic trick of transport, the reader experiences the kind of dread he or she may have felt in childhood in connection with some unnamed threat. Horror fans look for atmospheric writing that creates a nightmarish sense of menace and foreboding right from the first page. Readers enjoy the buildup and anticipation that something horrible is about to happen, but they differ on how soon in the book they want the horrible element—the monster—to appear (see Saricks 2009, 121). They distinguish between the gross-out and the chill of existential evil, and they differ in how much intensity of creepiness and gore they are able to enjoy.

Why Do We Want To Be Scared?

Well, of course many readers *don't* want to be scared. These are the ones who don't read horror, explaining that they find real life scary enough without reading books that amplify their deepest fears. But horror fans say that there is something valuable, even reassuring, about a story that articulates and gives shape to our primal, subconscious fears. Horror, they say, is valuable because it tells the truth: you are *right* to be scared. Like fairy tales for children about a step-mother who abandons her children in the woods, horror novels allow readers to acknowledge, explore, and confront primitive emotions and the dark side of human experience. Joanna Russ (1995, 61–62) has argued that the horror genre can be actually reassuring in a society that denies the shadow side of things. The thing that scares people—marrying a vampire, the house haunted by an evil presence, the whole world being made of fungus—is something that they feel is "an expression of something real about the world." She says:

> [T]hese images of basic human concerns are, as one would expect, very concrete, very bodily, very "extreme," and although grotesque and frightening, in some sense also reassuring. They validate perceptions that need validating, especially in adolescence—i.e., under the bland, forced optimism of American life terrible forces are at work, things are not what they seem, and if you feel lonely, persecuted, a misfit, and in terror, you aren't crazy. You're right.

References

Fagan, Brian M. 2000. *The Little Ice Age: How Climate Made History, 1300–1850.* New York: Basic Books.

King, Stephen. 1981. *Danse Macabre.* New York: Everest House.

Kofmel, Kim G. 2002. "Adult Readers of Science Fiction and Fantasy: A Qualitative Study of Reading Preference and Genre Perception." Doctoral dissertation. London, Ontario: The University of Western Ontario.

Kofmel, Kim G. 2004. "Sci-Fi 101." *Library Journal* archive, 01/09/2004. http:// lj.libraryjournal.com/2004/09/genre-fiction/sci-fi-101/.

Rhys, Ernest, ed. 1887. "Letter to T.L. Peacock, July 12." In *Shelley's Essays and Letters.* London: W. Scott.

Russ, Joanna. 1995. "On the Fascination of Horror Stories, Including Lovecraft's." In *To Write Like a Woman: Essays in Feminism and Science Fiction*, 60–64. Bloomington and Indianapolis: Indiana Press.

Saricks, Joyce G. 2009. "Horror." In *The Readers' Advisory Guide to Genre Fiction*, 2nd ed., 112–30. Chicago: American Library Association.

Further Readings

Castle, Mort, ed., 2007. *On Writing Horror: A Handbook by the Horror Writers Association*, rev. ed. Cincinnati, OH: Writer's Digest Books. Written as a guide for horror writers, this collection of 43 articles in eight sections includes tips on how to write and sell horror stories as well as discussions of horror subgenres.

Fonseca, Anthony J., and June M. Pulliam. 2009. *Hooked on Horror III: A Guide to Reading Interests in Horror Fiction*, 3rd ed. Westport, CT: Libraries Unlimited. Horror titles are described in terms of reader appeal and organized into subgenres, including vampires and werewolves, techno horror, ghosts and haunted houses, ecological horror, and small-town horror. The authors define horror as a text that "contains a monster," real or imaginary.

Spratford, Becky Siegel. 2012. *The Readers' Advisory Guide to Horror*, 2nd ed. Chicago: American Library Association. Written for readers' advisory librarians but also of interest to horror readers, this book provides cross-referenced lists of recommended authors and titles in chapters on ghosts and haunted houses, vampires, zombies, shape-shifters, witches, demonic possession, and so on. It also provides guidance in how to find genuinely scary horror amid the burgeoning publication of dark fantasy, which features supernatural elements but lacks fear as its main appeal. "[I]n dark fantasy, the monsters are often the heroes, while in horror, monsters remain monsters" (9). Check out Spratford's blog associated with the *Guide*, "RA for All: Horror," at http://raforallhorror.blogspot.ca/.

Important Books versus
Indiscriminate Reading

When you hear that "there are two kinds of readers," you might think fiction and nonfiction readers, male and female readers, or fast readers who skim and slow readers who savor detail. But here's a distinction you may not have thought of: readers who try to read only "important books" and omnivores who read "indiscriminately." In a nutshell, these two kinds of readers have distinctly different understandings of *what* materials to read and *how* to read them. When my students and I examined transcripts from interviews with avid readers (see QUESTIONS ABOUT READING), this difference between selectivity and omnivorousness struck us as one of the most surprising of all the many differences among readers.

The selective readers say that life is too short to waste time on an unimportant book. Nathan (professor of English, age 50) said, "I don't read popular literature that is not good literature. I always found the time for reading was precious—it had to be put to good use. If you wasted it, that's one fewer book that you could read at the end of your life." If pressed, these discriminating readers might say that there are certain books that they "should" read: more classics, more nonfiction, a better grade of fiction, books on "best 100" booklists, award-winning books—in short, books that are considered important in one way or another by cultural authorities. Marsha (student, age 26) said, "After I finished high school and before I started university, I always thought that I should read important books. And I had an idea of what I thought was an important book, because of the books we took in high school English classes. I decided that Penguins—because we had a lot of Penguins at home—Penguins were important books. So I used to go to the bookstore and look for Penguins."

Selective readers sometimes set up for themselves structured reading programs (see YEAR OF READING). They may talk about reading important books as a way of bettering themselves. For them, a key element of pleasurable reading is in learning something worth knowing. When it comes to fiction, "important books" are those written by respected, canonical authors that well-read people are supposed to know about. These selective readers can't fathom why anyone would spend valuable time reading and then say later that they can't remember authors, titles, or key themes of the books they have just read. Neil (chemical technician, age 26) recalled that as a child he read science books on space and astronomy because he "read for knowledge" and "really liked knowing things." As an adult, he requires a significant payoff for the effort involved in reading. If he is going to put the work into it, he needs to get something out in the form of knowledge worth having: "To me a popular novel is just a harder-working version of TV. If all I want is to get enjoyment out of a popular novel, I can just watch TV and get the same enjoyment. . . . I enjoy getting something out of reading. I think that's what it is. I can never understand the people who say, 'Yeah, I read the book, but I can't remember it.' "

Omnivores, on the other hand, say that they "read absolutely anything" they can get their hands on. Doreen (business consultant, age 38) says, "I will read anything. My panic is to be in the house without anything to read. That makes me just absolutely, totally panic-stricken." They often report that as children they read "everything and anything" and that they still do. Dorothy (public affairs/freelance writer, age 30) recalled, "I really was an omnivore. I read almost everything that was available. And I read a lot, so I exhausted the supply of books around me quite quickly. I would read through almost everything that was in my age group in the library." Recalling childhood reading, omnivores often describe a greedy voraciousness for reading materials of all kinds that persisted into adulthood. Robert (professor of English, age 57) said, "I know I began indiscriminately reading. It was never guided reading. . . . I read indiscriminately, always indiscriminately, and I still do. Things thrown in at the front door like that *Homemakers* magazine and the most convoluted post-structuralist criticism and recent novels I read indiscriminately."

For these readers, the pleasure of reading is the experience itself at the time of reading, not necessarily some residue afterward in the form of a permanent addition to their intellectual capital (although there is also that). They enjoy books at all levels of prestige and difficulty, and they often have several on the go at the same time. Patricia (teacher, age 48) said, "I'm too eclectic a reader [to read a book within the library's borrowing period]. I might read two chapters from a book and then not go back to it for another two months. I've been known to be reading twelve books all at the same time." The determining factor for which book is read at any given time is the reader's mood. Lorraine (elementary school teacher, age 27) said, "A lot of the time when you're reading, especially a book that's a little different from your favorite genre, you've got to be in the right mood. Maybe that's why I read two or three books at a time. I have to be in a certain mood to read a certain book."

A Surfeit of Choices

These two approaches to reading—careful selectivity and greedy omnivorousness—are divergent responses to the recent luxury of having so much choice. From Gutenberg to the early nineteenth century, books were scarce and expensive. For the most part, literate people had only a few devotional books, which they read over and over. In his detailed case study of literacy and print culture in Windsor township, Vermont, in 1760–1830, William Gilmore (1989, 275) reported that in the Windsor district 62 percent of families had "family libraries" in the 1787–1830 period. Some of these libraries contained only one book—the family Bible, which was inscribed with a list of family births and deaths. Through to 1815, the median number of volumes in family libraries was three, increasing to five volumes in 1816–1830 (264, cited in Kaestle 1991, 55). However, in the nineteenth century, an accelerating cascade of changes in the technology of printing and distribution was introducing a new kind of engagement with reading. In addition to the book as rare, cherished object, such as the family Bible, new kinds of more ephemeral reading materials were becoming available—newspapers, periodicals, pamphlets, travel accounts, political tracts, sermons, and fiction, all of which catered to readers' "craving for novelty" (Gilmore 1989, 268).

With the explosion of reading choices, from the three books in the personal libraries of early Vermont to the nineteenth- and twentieth-century flood of newspapers, magazines, dime novels, series books, cheap novels, mass-market paperbacks, and now eBooks, choosing books to read has become increasingly a challenge. Especially if one believes that books exist in a natural hierarchy with "important books" and "good literature" at the top and "trash" and "cheap novels" at the bottom, then great care must be taken in selection (see ONLY THE BEST). In *The Making of Middlebrow Culture*, Joan Shelley Rubin (1992, 17) argues that "the spread of print also carried an attendant risk": that readers "would seize on cheap novels rather than serious literature." The mountains of new materials being published made it hard for readers to discern "the best." Feeling "adrift in uncharted waters," the American reader turned for "comfort and guidance" to cultural authorities (27).

In the twentieth century, with its escalating publishing output, new programs and guides appeared to help the swamped reader select "the best," chief among which were the Harvard Classics, the Great Books program, and Mortimer Adler's *How to Read a Book* (1940) (see FIVE-FOOT SHELF OF BOOKS). Neil (chemical technician, age 26) connects the dots between the desire for "important books" and the need for a cultural authority who charts the waters:

> I only wanted important books. I hated novels. I didn't like novels, unless they were important in some respect, unless they were famous. . . . I read to gain knowledge—to gain the insights of the western world and what literature had to offer. . . . Mortimer Alder wrote a book called *How to Read a Book*. One of the things that

he pointed out is that a lot of people don't know how to read a book, and that to really understand a book you have to read it at least twice, if not more times. He also provided an excellent bibliography of what he called the "Great Books," and that's where I got a lot of my information on which books to read.

Increasingly, online and print lists of best 50, best 100, and best 1,000 books are available for readers who enjoy looking for suggestions on overlooked masterpieces or who want to rate themselves on the percentage of books on the list they have read. For example, a *Flavorwire* listing (Temple 2013) of "The 50 Books Everyone Needs to Read, 1963–2013" suggests "a single must-read book" from each of the last 50 years plus three or four "also recommended" books. The 50 must-reads are a sumptuous and varied list that includes translated fiction (Mikhail Bulgakov's *The Master and Margarita*, 1967), nonfiction (Paul Theroux's *The Great Railway Bazaar*, 1975), picture books (Maurice Sendak's *Outside over There*, 1981), short stories (Kelly Link's *Magic for Beginners*, 2005), essays (John Jeremiah Sullivan's *Pulphead*, 2011), and lots and lots of novels from Sylvia Plath's *The Bell Jar* (1963) to Renata Adler's *Speedboat* (1976) to Toni Morrison's *Beloved* (1987), to David Foster Wallace's *Infinite Jest* (1996) to Rachel Kushner's *The Flame Throwers* (2013). Such lists lend themselves to categories: Books-I-Have-Already-Read, Books-I-Have-Heard-So-Much-about-That-I-Don't-Need-to Read, Books-I-Have-Already-Read-but-Would-Like-to-Read-Again, Books-I-Have-Heard-of-and-Would-Like-to-Read, and Books-I-Have-Never-Heard-of-but-Are-Now-on-My-To-Read-List.

Important Books

Some readers are never tempted by unimportant books. David Shields in *How Literature Saved My Life* (2013, 140) quotes D. H. Lawrence as saying "it's better to know a dozen books extraordinarily well than innumerable books passably." Shields offers a list of 55 books he "swear[s] by," among which is Renata Adler's novel *Speedboat*, which he has read "easily two dozen times": "It's one book I've read so many times I feel, absurdly, as if I've written it." Inevitably, if you believe in investing a great deal of time in a single book through close reading and prolonged engagement, then it helps if you think there are only a very few books that really matter and are worth reading. Such readers often enjoy taking on the challenge of 1,000-page masterpieces such as William Gaddis's *The Recognitions*, David Foster Wallace's *Infinite Jest*, or Roberto Bolaño's *2666*. They are apt to say that the real question is not whether challenging books are worth the time spent but whether unchallenging books are worth the time wasted on them.

Other readers, especially students whose reading tastes are still developing, say that they feel the need to remake themselves as more disciplined and selective readers. They push themselves to read challenging books that are just beyond their comfort zone. In some cases, the motivation for reading Dostoevsky or Dickens is to become the sort of person who would read and enjoy a universally recognized work of literature. When she was 16 or 17, Leona (student, age 23) was an avid reader of Harlequin romances, moving on to "the more heavy type romances, the ones with lots of sex in them." Then at age 18 or 19, as she reported it, "I thought to myself, you shouldn't read this trash. You should be reading something better than this. You should read good fiction. So I started reading the classics." David (student, age 26) made the same distinction between "trash" and "the classics." He said he still reads "a lot of stuff that I know is schlock, books you can read on the bus." But one summer after his first year of university, he decided to read "great literature": "I read Tolstoy, Chekhov, I read an entire book of Chekhov's short stories, three or four Thomas Hardy." He distinguishes between books that are enjoyable and books that are good or good for you: "I still set aside time to read something that is supposed to be good for me. I maintain a distinction between books I like and books that are good."

Dickens is often the go-to author for self-improving readers who decide to "read the classics." Valery (ESL teacher, age 47) views nineteenth-century fiction as a tough slog that will be good for her. She said, "About once a year, I'll feel that I should read Charles Dickens just because: Are we a complete person if we haven't read the classics? I find them a bit hard-going. I find anything actually written before 1900 sort of hard-going." When Andrew (graduate student, age 28) wanted to bolster his claim to being a well-read person, he launched into a "catchup period" of reading Dickens: "I figure it's important if I claim to be a well-read person that I should have a background in what Dickens wrote. He's a well-known author." Nathan (professor of English, age 50) is a lifelong reader of important books, who got his start when he was 10 years old: "The first important book, really important book, that I read was a Dickens novel—*The Old Curiosity Shop*—and I remember very, very clearly knowing it was a significant book." He found it an "agonizing journey," "probably the dullest of all Dickens's novels," but continued because reading such a book "marked you as a serious person":

> I was *determined* to read this book. It took me 4-5 months. It was just an absolutely, unbelievably long, agonizing journey through this book. [Interviewer: And you stayed with it?] I stayed with it. I had this tenacity that I cannot explain. In fact, I don't think I've ever begun a book that I didn't finish, no matter how much I didn't like it. I have this tenacity to honor the artist, no matter what.

However, other readers who resolve to read important books sometimes fall by the wayside if too big a gap exists between books they think are good for them and books they like. Anita (student, age 25) is a good example. A science student in university, Anita compared herself with friends in an English program who were "reading all these classics." She said, "I had this feeling of inadequacy that I wasn't reading the right things": "I suddenly decided that I hadn't read any of the classics at all. So I made this big project that I was going to read the classics. That didn't work out very well." Anita has a strong sense of the "shoulds" of reading: she should read the classics; she should read more nonfiction. But she says, "I can't read unless I enjoy it. I really can't force myself to read a book no matter how much I think, 'I really should read this because it's good for me.' I feel like I'm not a very good reader."

Shelley (student, age 26) also worries that she doesn't read as well as other people and isn't getting the right meaning from her reading. She said, "I was always such a poor reader that I still have this really bad fear that when I read something I don't understand it as much as other people." This sense of inadequacy as a reader started in childhood. She grew up in a military family, moving every few years and constantly changing schools:

> When I was younger, I had to be put in a special class to read better. I had a really hard time. I remember having to read *The Heart of Darkness* and starting that stupid book eight times. The first sentence of that book is: "The Nellie, a cruising yawl, swung to her anchor. . . ." I didn't know what "Nellie" he was talking about. I didn't know what "yawl" was. So, there were about six words on the first page of that book that I didn't know. That was just so frustrating, because I never knew: should I look up these words now? Or should I go through it and skip over them? So I just didn't read them. So one of the reasons I read is to make up for things I've missed. I do read for that whole "bettering yourself" thing.

Indiscriminate Reading

In comparison with these readers of important books, indiscriminate readers are much less concerned with the "shoulds" of reading. Madeline (student, age 22) said, "I don't read for 'self-improvement.' I don't make an effort to read in the interests of expanding my mind." Omnivores have their own version of the Life's-Too-Short theme—life's too short to read a book that you are not enjoying. They say, if you are not enjoying the book, put it down; you may enjoy the book later, but it's the wrong book for you now. British novelist Nick Hornby agrees. He has documented a decade's worth of omnivorous reading in monthly columns written for the magazine *The Believer*. Hornby (2006, 14) complains, "One of the problems . . . is that we have got it into our heads that books should be hard work, and that unless they're hard work, they're not doing us any good. . . . Please, please, put it down." Omnivores do put it down. They abandon a book if they are not enjoying it, and they often have a number of books on the go at the same time at varying levels of seriousness and difficulty. They don't feel at all guilty, because putting down a dull book frees up time for another book that they can read with gusto.

With the one proviso that the book must be enjoyable, indiscriminate readers say they are willing to try almost anything. Victor (actor, age 68) said, "I read just about anything from the comics to Shakespeare." After declaring that she is "just willing to read almost anything" (except romance), Ruth (student, age 22) remarks ruefully, "I am coming across as a very undiscerning reader." These readers celebrate the breadth and variety of their reading, from high to low, from series books to George Eliot. Describing her childhood reading, Elizabeth (PhD candidate in English, age 35) said, "My reading was always indiscriminate. I just read what I laid my hands on. . . . At ten, I read omnivorously, so that I was reading with great glee things like *The Bobbsey Twins* and Nancy Drew and even Elsie Dinsmore, which my grandmother gave me. I was also reading all these other books we had around the house. Standard nineteenth century fiction—things like *Silas Marner* and Jane Austen's novels over and over again."

Indiscriminate readers often choose metaphors of eating to characterize their reading. They read with "gusto" (from *gustus*, Latin—taste) or with relish. They say they are "omnivorous," "voracious" (from *vorare*, Latin—to swallow), or "avid" (from *avere*, Latin—to crave). They describe themselves as "greedy" or "hungry" or "gluttons" (from *gluttire*, Latin—to gulp down) for books. They are looking forward to getting their teeth into a book. The Reading-Is-Eating metaphor (Ross 1987) draws on a particularly rich domain of common everyday experience, capable of considerable elaboration: there are different kinds of foods, various cooking styles, and many kinds of eaters and ways of eating. Some readers—the selective readers of important books—have refined, discriminating palates. In contrast, indiscriminate readers describe themselves as having a robust appetite—they are not picky readers. Phillip (student, age 20) insisted, "I'm not a fussy, fussy reader. I can read just about everything." Asked to select some terms to describe herself as a reader, Daphne (student, age 29) said, "Voracious. I read a lot. I read a lot and I really like variety too. I think some people get stuck on the one-author track, but I really like to try and look for a huge variety in the fiction that I read." Elizabeth (PhD candidate in English, age 35) explicitly rejected the notion of a very refined palate for books.

> I suppose my own attitude is grounded in my own experience, and that is that it's like eating food. I think the people who are the best judges of food are those who like a great variety of foods from very hearty, peasant kinds of various cultures to quite highly refined meals. Those who say they only like *haute cuisine* I have my doubts about. And I feel that way about books. I could quite easily read say, a Harlequin Romance and *War and Peace* and a complicated history of the Wars of the Roses at the same time and not feel that there was anything particularly jarring about that juxtaposition. They're just books—stories.

These omnivorous readers may sometimes describe their reading choices "trash" or "schlock," but they are unapologetic. In fact, they regard the variety of their reading as a major strength. Heather (manager, age 51) says, "I read *anything*. Books are part of me—if anyone visited my small collection of books, they would probably think there must be a whole lot of people here who read, because I'm a totally indiscriminate reader." Indiscriminate readers may in fact read many of the same books as the selective readers do, but they talk about their reading differently. Heather says, "Reading is a great passion of my life. I never thought it was to acquire knowledge." Adam (librarian, age 24) says:

> It's not just to better my mind—because I don't think of it in those terms. It's not like I sit down and go, "Oh, I'm going to better my mind by reading this." But that's the result. I think that when you devote a lot of time to reading anything, you're presented with a number of new ideas you'd never thought of before and those ideas help you in your life—in handling all kinds of human situations.

For Adam and other omnivorous readers, expanding their knowledge and ideas is an indirect by-product of the pleasurable reading experience, not the main goal.

"All over the place" is how Hunter (student, age 27) describes his reading. He emphasizes that he is not a systematic reader, reading with a purpose. His reading choices are promiscuously mixed—new weird stories, Buddhism, comics, a Chilean novel, a nonfiction best-seller. He does not feel obliged to finish a book, even a comic book. He says he has "pretty catholic reading tastes" and is "more of a dabbler than anything." Books he's read recently include "a novel that is 'new weird,' which is an off-shoot of science fiction based on weird fiction of the type by Edgar Allen Poe and H. P. Lovecraft," "an introductory text on Buddhism called *What the Buddha Taught*," and several anthologies of *Swamp Thing* comic books. Plus, Hunter says, "I started reading Roberto Bolaño's *The Savage Detectives*. So it's really all over the place. Oh, and I just bought Michael Pollan's *In Defense of Food: An Eater's Manifesto*. That's just a pretty small cross-section of the kinds of things that I read, but all over the place."

References

Adler, Mortimer Jerome. 1940. *How to Read a Book*. New York: Simon and Schuster.

Gilmore, William. 1989. *Reading Becomes a Necessity of Life: Material and Cultural Life in Rural New England, 1790–1835*. Knoxville: University of Tennessee Press. http://www.newfoundpress.utk.edu/pubs/gilmore/.

Hornby, Nick. 2006. *Housekeeping vs. the Dirt*. San Francisco: Believer Books.

Kaestle, Carl F., et al. 1991. *Literacy in the United States: Readers and Reading since 1880*. New Haven, CT, and London: Yale University Press.

Ross, Catherine Sheldrick. 1987. "Metaphors of Reading." *Journal of Library History, Philosophy, and Comparative Librarianship* 22, no. 2: 147–63.

Rubin, Joan Shelley. 1992. *The Making of Middlebrow Culture.* Chapel Hill and London: The University of North Carolina Press.

Shields, David. 2013. *How Literature Saved My Life.* New York: Alfred A. Knopf.

Temple, Emily. 2013. "The 50 Books Everyone Needs to Read, 1963–2013." *Flavorwire,* June 18. http://flavorwire.com/398812/the-50-books-everyone-needs-to-read-1963-2013/.

Further Readings

If you are curious about which books have been considered important (and how many of them you have already read), check out:

The Guardian. 2003. "The 100 Greatest Novels of All Time: The List." http://www.theguardian.com/books/2003/oct/12/features.fiction.

Modern Library. 1998. "100 Best Novels." http://www.modernlibrary.com/top-100/100-best-novels/.

Jackets and Book Covers

I am looking at Chip Kidd's jacket for a hardcover book that I have just finished reading. The book jacket—front, back, and spine—is black, the color of horror books, with white lettering. On the front, the title *Spillover* is etched out in white capitals that seem to have been eaten away by something. The author's name, David Quammen, appears in smaller block capitals at the bottom, together with a much smaller line in lowercase lettering: "author of *The Song of the Dodo*." Framed by the lettering and taking up most of the front cover is a blurred, out-of-focus image of a baboon's rage face in blue and orange, with a prominently displayed open mouth, tinged in red, and sharp menacing teeth. In smaller capital letters, the book's subtitle, *Animal Infections and the Next Human Pandemic*, is placed right across that threatening mouth. Or wait, could this menacing creature be some kind of bat, I wondered, once I started reading this fascinating but scary book.

Spillover is about the animal origins of deadly diseases that spill over to infect humans, and both primates and bats turn out to be key disease vectors. Quammen begins his book with the Hendra virus that first made the jump from fruit bats to racehorses to humans near Brisbane, Australia, and he ends with the disease sleuthing that traced the origins of AIDS back to a single chimpanzee in southeast Cameroon around 1908. The blurb on the back cover highlights the book's appeal to readers: the urgency of the threat of the next pandemic and the credentials of the author, who tracked chimpanzees in the Congo, netted bats in China, and trapped monkeys in Bangladesh in the company of disease scientists, all described in laudatory quotations from other authors (see LITERARY LOGROLLING). Elizabeth Kolbert, author of *Field Notes from a Catastrophe*, calls *Spillover* "a real-life thriller with an outcome that affects us all." Carl Zimmer, author of *A Planet of Viruses and Evolution*, praises Quammen as a science writer "always ready to travel to remote, dangerous places to get to the bottom of nature's mysteries." In short, this book jacket does a terrific job of doing what book covers are now expected to do: attract eyes to the book; convey the aura of the book through the felicitous patterning of image, textual elements, color, and typeface; and offer something new to be understood more fully once the reader has finished the book. A good jacket tells you what kind of book it is without giving way too much.

The Evolution of the Book Jacke

We now think of the book jacket as a form   advertising, a poster for the book designed to attract an intended readership— children, teens, or adults—with an interest in a particular kind of book, whether it's a picture book, a genre book, nonfiction, or literary fiction. As Alan Powers put it in his excellent book *Front Cover* (2001), "A book jacket or cover is a selling device, close to advertising in its form and purpose, but also specific to a product that plays a teasing game of hide and seek with commerce." Powers's comment reminds us of the special Janus-faced identity of books: both a cultural product with a special aura and a consumer good that needs to be marketed. But book jackets evolved only gradually into their current form, where every element—front, back, flaps, and spine—has a role in enticing the reader. The book jacket began in the 1830s as a plain paper wrapper intended to protect from soil the book that was expensively bound in cloth, silk, or leather; hence the alternate names *dust cover* and *dust jacket*. The wrapper kept dirt and dust off the book until it reached the buyer's home, at which point the wrapper was discarded. Powers (2001, 6) observes, "Keeping the jacket on a book would be like storing clothes in the carrier bag from the shop where they had been bought."

Before the 1820s, customers bought unbound sheets and then had the books bound in custom bindings. When publishers began to bind books in uniform house bindings, they protected the bound book in a paper wrapper completely covering it that was sealed with wax or glue. Book jackets with flaps came later, possibly in the 1850s. Scholars aren't sure when they became standard because so few book jackets have survived. And why would they, given that book jackets were regarded as temporary and disposable? Decorative book bindings were the thing that interested bibliophiles and bibliographers, not the plain paper wrappers that by the late nineteenth century had evolved to display the book title, the author's name, and possibly a printed illustration. Steven Heller and Seymour Chwast in *Jackets Required* (1995, 12) quote pioneer jacket designer George Salter as saying that by the early 1900s "the metamorphosis of the wrapper into the jacket finally took place."

The key to this transformation, claim Heller and Chwast (12), was the introduction of "a new promotional gimmick called a 'blurb,' " which has been "traced back to around 1910 and has been a fixture on jackets (and paperback covers) ever since." Book jackets had made the jump from protective casing to advertising display. Decorative elements moved from the book's binding to the book jacket. The front became an area of graphic design, the flaps became spaces for advertising copy describing and praising the book's contents, and the back was often used to list other books from the publisher's list. By the 1920s, publishers were using illustrated jackets as a promotional tool to market books. With the expansion of paperback publishing, these advertising elements became part of the cover itself, not the detachable wrapper. All along, jacket design has gone hand in hand with new technologies in printing, the production of images, and distribution, including four-color printing, digital images, and computer-assisted design. It remains to be seen what form the book jacket or cover will eventually take in the era of the eBook.

Various studies of book jackets and covers have carved out different areas for specialization, dividing the terrain by geographical area, time period, or different segments of the book market. They have examined American book jackets (Drew and Sternberger 2005; Heller and Chwast 1995), children's book jackets (Powers 2003), and American mass-market paperback covers (Bonn 1982). Some studies focus on covers produced by individual publishers (Baines 2005; Connolly 2009) or individual designers (Hansen 2005; Kidd 2005). Web sites are making it easier for readers and book historians to examine book jackets—for example, the Art of Penguin Science Fiction Web site (Pardey 2009–2011), Pieratt and Jacobsen's Book Cover Archive, or designer Peter Mendelsund's Web site featuring his design work and accompanying blog, Jacket Mechanical. The Design Observer Web site showcases the winners of the "50 Books, 50 Covers" annual competition, which selects the best cover for an English-language book published anywhere. In an interesting twist, the New York Public Library's (NYPL) practice of discarding jackets became the impetus for a digital collection of book jackets. Between 1926 and 1947, anonymous librarians rescued some 2,000 specimen book jackets from trade books and preserved them in 22 scrapbooks. Digitized, these jackets can be viewed—front, back, spine, and flaps—in the NYPL digital collection, "Dust Jackets from American and European Books, 1926–1947."

The Modern Jacket

Book jackets have become an object of controversy, serious study, and avid collection. Some readers don't like them. They remove the jacket when they read, explaining that they dislike its slidey, slippery feel. Craig Mod (2013) declared, "I take them all off, the covers. As soon as I've paid—swoosh! Gone! ... Without covers, hardcover books become confident blocks of wood—they don't shimmy or slide in your hands or atop tables. Try it. You'll love it. You'll never go back." Others take the jacket off for reading to preserve it in unrumpled condition for display when the book is back on the shelf. Book collectors of first editions sharply discount a book lacking its jacket. A first edition of *The Great Gatsby* might sell for $2,000 without a jacket. With its jacket, a first edition of *Gatsby* sold for $180,000 in 2009 (Rothman 2013). Charlie Jones of the United Kingdom–based online rare book-seller Jones Brothers estimates that there may exist in the world only five *Gatsby* first editions with intact jackets. Why so rare? Apart from a small initial print run, the normal wear and tear, and readers who throw away the covers, Jones explains that many first editions went to libraries, "where they get ruined straight away" by librarians who take off the dust jackets and put on spine stickers (Rothman 2013). Libraries that for years routinely discarded jackets are now being taken to task for destroying book history. G. Thomas Tanselle, the renowned bibliographer, entered the fray with his magisterial study *Book-Jackets* (2011), in which he argues that the jacket is an integral part of the book that should be catalogued and preserved as a resource for book history and cultural heritage.

The cover or jacket that you see on the finished book is the survivor of a long process of give and take, design, and reworking, which involves the publisher's art director, the designer, the book's editor, sometimes the author, and of course the marketing department. A book cover, says Knopf senior designer Peter Mendelsund (2013), "should be a book's true face. . . . It should work to entice a browser, and serve as a lasting emblem of the experience of having read a given text." But that's easier said than done. When working on the front cover for Stieg Larsson's *The Girl with the Dragon Tattoo*, Mendelsund mocked up 50 designs before the yellow cover with the swirling dragon was chosen. In an interview with Stewart Kuhlo (2010), John Gall, then art director at Vintage/ Anchor Books, describes the fraught process of getting a cover approved, including such ups and downs as the publisher's coming back and saying, "This needs really big type with a chicken on it." Gall says, "The re-working, dealing with all the feedback (some warranted, some moronic) 'make this bigger', 'make this smaller', 'my psychic thinks it should be blue'—that is what separates the men from the boys."

Gall should know. By the time of his interview with Kuhlo, he had overseen the production of more than 3,000 book covers, including a "dream project" of a complete redesign of the jackets for all 21 Vladimir Nabokov backlist titles that Vintage publishes. The "dream team" of top designers, which included among others Chip Kidd, Peter Mendelsund, Carol Carson, Dave Eggers, Paul Sahre, and Carin Goldberg, was given only one constraint (Gall 2009). In homage to Nabokov's passion for butterfly collecting, each cover had to use the tools of the entomologist—insect pins and paper—and be framed in a black specimen box. Gall's design motto (Bertram 2013): "A question I like to ask myself when designing a cover is: 'Can this be the cover for any other book?' The closer you get to a 'yes,' the worse off you are."

Chip Kidd's cover for Michael Crichton's *Jurassic Park* (1992) achieved the ultimate mark of success: the iconic silhouette of a tyrannosaurus skeleton became the basis of the movie poster, the logo in the film for the park itself, and an element on all Jurassic Park–licensed sale items. The whole trick was to represent a dinosaur without showing a dinosaur. Kidd (2005, 69) quotes from author Michael Crichton's account of the process of arriving at the final design:

The first cover consisted of a background of pebbled brown texture, meant to be dinosaur skin. To me it looked like a close-up of a football, or a woman's handbag. I was cranky. My editor, Sonny Mehta, said not to worry, because Chip was now stepping in to do the cover. We moved on to dinosaur shadows and dinosaur footprints, scales and tails, silhouettes and reptilian eyes peering through jungle fronds. Nothing worked. As the days passed, we began to understand that finding a menacing image that also suggested genetically recreated dinosaurs was probably impossible. We were asking too much of a single image. . . . [Finally Sonny called to say he was sending some new cover art.] I asked how many covers. "Just one . . . I think you might like it."

What about Readers?

Publishers spend a lot of money on jackets, hoping to seduce the reader. Does it work? The evidence suggests that it does, but it works best when a great cover design is accompanied by a great book. In her contribution to the edited collection *The Book That Changed My Life* (Coady and Johannessen 2006, 84), Alice Hoffman starts off by describing what attracted her to her life-changing book—its cover:

> I found *The Catcher in the Rye* on my mother's bookshelf. It was the cover that drew me to it. I was in eighth grade, I knew nothing, and I had certainly never heard of J.D. Salinger. So it was the cover—that somber unadorned maroon paperback . . .— that made me feel as though I'd stumbled onto a secret.

The Web site BookBrowse confirmed the drawing power of covers. Book-Browse (2007) surveyed its readers to get answers to the question, "What most influences you when buying a book?" Able to check off multiple influences, many of the 1,155 respondents mentioned as influences the jacket or elements that are featured on the cover: Book jacket—35 percent; I like this author—65 percent. Other influences included the following: It has good reviews—41 percent; Recommended by a friend—43 percent.

Readers say that the cover gets them to pick the book up, but then they put it through a series of other tests (see Before Reading). "You're not supposed to judge a book by its cover, but I do, I do!" confessed Zoe (student, age 24). She says, "The first thing I look at is the cover. And if the cover isn't really nice looking, I don't generally take the book out any further. But then I read the first page and I read the last page, and then I read a couple of in-between pages." Similarly, Madeline (student, age 22) says that in choosing books she goes a lot by cover but actually is taking into account a whole interplay of factors: "Color. And if it's got a sort of catchy TITLE—not a jingle-catchy—but words that are interesting. I buy by author and I buy by books I've heard of or by reviews."

Jackets—front, back, and spines—speak a coded language that experienced readers have learned to interpret through their prolonged engagement with books. Scarlet (commercial credit analyst, age 26) says, "I choose books by the cover. I like bright covers—I don't like dark and a lot of bad things happening. I try and pick books that look happy by the cover, so bright colors on the front and happy pictures." Author Francis Spufford (2003, 3) describes how he negotiates a big science fiction bookstore: "I'm a really skilled browser, believe me, finely attuned to the obscure signals sent out by the spines of paperbacks, able to detect at speed the four or five titles in a bay that pull at me in different ways." Experienced readers know that a genre book announces itself by particular colors and iconic graphics—chick lit by a hot pink cover, a squiggly font, and an illustration that might include a shoe, a handbag, a red dress, or a martini glass; crime fiction directed at men by tea-stained covers of black, dark blue, or dark green, with block sans serif lettering, and possibly a weapon; westerns by sand-colored covers and a horse and/or a man with a rifle; and so on.

Allen Lane popularized color-coded covers when he began Penguin paperbacks in 1935. The books were instantly recognizable for their two iconic horizontal bands of color—orange for fiction, green for crime, and blue for biography—separated by white band containing the author and title. (As a mark of their iconic status, Penguin covers are available for sale as postcards—*Postcards from Penguin: One Hundred Book Covers in a Box*.) Generally, the size of the lettering for the writer's name relative to the book title is another clue. The more successful the writer, the bigger the name and the smaller the title. Readers use this coded visual grammar of the cover as a way of both choosing and rejecting books. Louise (student, age 32) says, "I'm not too affected by the cover of a book, unless the cover suggests—you know, those gold things with women with their shirts half ripped off, that kind of thing, is a definite turnoff." A feature that attracts one reader is taken as a warning by another. A diecut mauve cover with a title in cursive, ornate lettering or a black cover spattered with gore each advertise themselves to their respective genre readers, while at the same time warning off others who dislike ROMANCE or HORROR.

Beginning readers and nonreaders have more trouble than old hands do in gauging a book by its cover, and they make more mistakes. Experienced readers, on the other hand, report a careful weighing of claims and a sophisticated balance of skepticism and willingness to be seduced by jacket inducements that call out, "Read me!" Commenting on cover blurbs, Lily (student, age 30) says, "Sometimes you can read those dust jackets and think, 'Oh, it sounds great,' and then you just open it up and it's just atrocious. And I'm prepared to spend hours, when I go to the library, looking around." Covers offer compressed information about the kind of reading experience to expect, but experienced readers have learned caution. Covers can be deceptive. Many readers say, "I'm suspicious of covers"; "covers are so misleading sometimes that they have no real connection with what's inside. . . . I've learned that very good books can be hidden behind lousy covers." Max (operations manager, age 33) says that "covers can have a huge impact" but then warns that with certain genres there is little connection between the quality of the cover and the quality of the book: "The number one problem with horror books is that you can't tell from the cover whether it's going to be a truly awful book of not. Most of the covers are truly awful, but that's pretty standard for the genre unfortunately. On the other hand, science fiction or fantasy have much nicer covers that sometimes disguise a truly dreadful book." Fiona (information specialist, age 31) complains that science fiction and fantasy covers often seem geared to attracting 14-year-old boys: "Covers have turned me away from more potentially good books than anything else, because they've decided that they have to put the half-naked woman, the woman in the fur bikini or the chainmail bikini on the cover."

And finally there are cover connoisseurs, some of whom buy multiple copies of the same book in different jackets. Angus (graduate student, age 26) recalls being in a Los Angeles bus station deliberating over John Irving's *The Hotel New Hampshire*: "They had six different covers available for it, and I stood there for half an hour trying to decide which one I wanted. And I finally chose the one with the bear. I almost missed my bus, but it was worth it because it was a nice cover." For many avid readers, the physicality of the book is an important part of the aura of reading (and they are most apt to start talking about this when the subject of eBooks arises—see E-READING). One such reader said, "I love the look and feel of a book on my shelf and in my hands, and I care about font and paper choices and about the cover art, which—when handled well—can express important things about the content." Ideally, a great cover is in dialogue with the book, achieving its full potential *after* the reader has read the book. This is why the most passionate discussions of jackets and covers are about books that people have read and love. Ready for a fight? Which is the best cover for *Lolita*? Which covers do you like best for the Harry Potter books? And who would buy the art deco cover based on the Baz Luhrmann movie of *The Great Gatsby* when they could have the original blue cover with the glowing cityscape and the floating mysterious eyes and lips?

References

Baines, Phil. 2005. *Penguin by Design*. London: Allen Lane.

Bertram, John. 2013. "The Land of Metaphor: John Gall on Designing the Cover of Lolita." *The Millions*, August 13. http://www.themillions.com/2013/08/the-land-of-metaphor-john-gall-on-designing-the-cover-of-lolita.html.

Bonn, Thomas L. 1982. *UnderCover: An Illustrated History of American Mass Market Paperbacks*. New York: Penguin.

BookBrowse Polls. 2007. "What Most Influences You When Buying a Book?" March 12. http://www.bookbrowse.com/bb_poll/index.cfm/question_id/index.cfm.

Coady, Roxanne J., and Joy Johannessen, eds. 2006. *The Book That Changed My Life: 71 Remarkable Writers Celebrate the Books That Matter Most to Them*. New York: Gotham Books/Penguin Group.

Connolly, Joseph. 2009. *Faber and Faber: Eighty Years of Book Cover Design.* London: Faber and Faber.

Design Observer. "50 Books, 50 Covers: Celebrating Book Design: 2012 Winners." http://designobserver.com/50Books50Covers/2012winners.html.

Drew, Ned, and Paul Sternberger. 2005. *By Its Cover: Modern American Book Cover Design.* New York: Princeton Architectural Press.

Gall, John. 2009. "The Nabokov Collection." *Design Observer*, October 29. http://observatory.designobserver.com/entry.html?entry=11597.

Hansen, Thomas S. 2005. *Classic Book Jackets: The Design Legacy of George Salter.* New York: Princeton Architectural Press.

Heller, Steven, and Seymour Chwast. 1995. *Jackets Required: An Illustrated History of American Book Jacket Design, 1920–1950.* San Francisco: Chronicle Books.

Kidd, Chip. 2005. *Book 1: Work 1986–2006.* New York: Rizzoli.

Kuhlo, Stewart. 2010. "John Gall." Saturday, July 31. *Quattro.* http://www.weare designbureau.com/projects/704/.

Mendelsund, Peter. "Design Work." http://mendelsund.blogspot.ca/.

Mendelsund, Peter. 2013. "An Interview with Peter Mendelsund." *Porter Square Books* (blog). Thursday, May 2. http://portersquarebooksblog.blogspot.ca/2013/05/interview-with-peter-mendelsund.html.

Mod, Craig. 2013. "By Its Cover." *Virginia Quarterly Review* 89, no. 2 (April 1): 122. http://www.vqronline.org/articles/its-cover

New York Public Library Digital Gallery. "Dust Jackets from American and European Books, 1926–1947." http://digitalgallery.nypl.org/nypldigital/explore/?col_id=157.

Pardey, James. 2009–2011. "The Art of Penguin Science Fiction." http://www.penguinsciencefiction.org/.

Pieratt, Ben, and Eric Jacobsen. "An Archive of Book Cover Designs and Designers." The Book Cover Archive. http://bookcoverarchive.com/.

Powers, Alan. 2001. *Front Cover: Great Book Jacket and Cover Design.* London: Mitchell Beazley.

Powers, Alan. 2003. *Children's Book Covers: Great Book Jacket and Cover Design.* London: Mitchell Beazley.

Rothman, Lily. 2013. "What Makes This First-Edition of *The Great Gatsby* So Valuable?" *Time Entertainment*, May 2. http://entertainment.time.com/2013/05/02/what-makes-this-first-edition-of-the-great-gatsby-so-valuable/.

Spufford, Francis. 2002. *The Child That Books Built.* London: Faber and Faber.

Tanselle, G. Thomas. 2011. *Book-Jackets: Their History, Form, and Use.* Charlottesville: Bibliographical Society of the University of Virginia.

Kindred Readers

I was talking to a friend about some of the advantages of reading on a tablet or e-reader—free downloads from the Gutenberg project, the advantage of having 300 books to choose from on your tablet when travelling, and so on. And finally, I said, ROMANCE readers and others who feel their tastes are denigrated can read privately in public without being judged. Yes, she said, but what about the downside of secret reading? She herself had struck up many a conversation with like-minded strangers as a result of noticing what they were reading. She is the kind of person who pays attention to what books people are reading in airports, waiting rooms, and coffee shops. And books, like dogs, are good icebreakers. However, with the privacy of on-screen reading, the serendipitous connection with a kindred reader is prevented.

Of course avid readers do use reading preferences as a kind of litmus test to suss out kindred spirits. On online dating sites, people are apt to say that they like candlelit dinners and long walks on the beach. But a better way to filter out unlikely prospects and attract the likely ones would be to declare a favorite book or movie. People say, for example, that they just *knew* there was something incompatible and undesirable (or, less frequently, congenial) about a person whose favorite book is Ayn Rand's *The Fountainhead*. On one Australian reading forum, one person said, "I knew a guy whose favorite books were: (1) *Mein Kampf* and (2) *American Psycho*." Another contributor responded, "Please don't introduce us." On the other hand, liking the same books can initiate a relationship. Noah, a 28-year-old student, said that having a favorite book in common can jump-start a conversation: "you'd be amazed that with most readers—if you've read the same book, they get pretty excited and they'll tell you anything after that. Once you're able to talk about a single book, they'll talk about anything you want. So it really can kind of allow you to get to know someone quickly. It's a pretty effective icebreaker." Morag (publishing company employee, age 35) recalled that when she was a teenager going to summer camp reading the Tolkien trilogy worked as an entrée to a crowd of kids: "A lot of people were reading the trilogy, so you were part of a group of people. You had friends that even though you might not know them, as soon as you mentioned 'Oh, yeah, you know Tolkien.' 'Tolkien, oh yes!' And all of a sudden you had this bonding mechanism happening."

In some cases, the shared book becomes the basis for a courtship or the beginning of an important friendship. In one of the offerings of my genres of fiction course, a graduate student gave an outstanding booktalk on A. S. Byatt's *Possession.* She began by saying that she chose to talk about this book because it had made a big difference to her personally—it was the book that had introduced her to her future husband. She got to know the person she later married because they were both in the same literature class at university and they had both chosen *Possession* for an essay topic. Starting out by discussing the evolving love relationship of the pairs of characters in the book, their relationship deepened into a courtship of their own. Similarly, Harry (magazine editor, age 37) said that *The Lord of the Rings,* which was the "very first adult fantasy novel" he ever read, had a big impact on both his reading life and his social life. At the time of the interview, he had read it eight times, most recently for "comfort" reading when he was in hospital for surgery. He read it first at age 13 and was "absolutely enthralled":

> I wanted to lose myself in that world. Probably because that was the very month in which my mother was finally dying when I started to read it. Maybe that was one of the reasons I'm still very attached to that book. It helped me through a very bad period. . . .
> It was a world in which I could get lost—which had adventures in it, which had peril in it, but a peril that I wasn't going to face personally.

A special series that helped Harry through the terrible days when his mother was dying, *The Lord of the Rings* became a bridge to new social bonds: "I ran into other people who had read *Lord of the Rings* and became friends with them because of that. In fact, my best friend in high school—we became friends because we both did book reviews of *Lord of the Rings.* We both ended up reading them out to the class."

In this litmus test to discover kindred readers, some books work better than others. *The Little Prince* by Antoine de Saint-Exupéry seems to be a favorite test book. One reader said, "In my salad days, whenever I dated anyone I thought might make a promising husband, I would read him *The Little Prince.* If he did not respond enthusiastically, he was *out* (much to my mother's horror). I also thought I was Isabel Archer (from *Portrait of a Lady*)—Sometimes I still think so." Sara reported a similar experience:

> Several of my friends swear by *The Little Prince,* by Antoine de St. Exupéry. One says she knew her fiancé was "the one," when they

got to talking early in their relationship and she realized he worships that book as much as she does.

Marcia (library science student, age 25) describes how a book that was taken to a nightclub as a barrier against other people ended up attracting social interaction:

> I'm not a night-club type of person, and my friend is. She wanted to take me to her favorite dance spot in Toronto, and so a bunch of us went. I sat down with a nice drink and read Woody Allen— which was great because it was the kind of off-beat kind of book that somebody who did like the nightclub kind of scene would read anyway. I had these guys come down and try to pick me up, because I was reading something interesting, when I was reading for the sole purpose of not wanting to be there in the first place. But sort of humoring my friends so they could go and dance and I wouldn't be seen as being not fun, even though I was not fun.

Literary Logrolling

The Canadian writer of children's books, Jean Little once told me that in her stories she deliberately includes references to other writers, preferably to living authors who could benefit from royalties. Novelists have to stick together, she thought. Similarly, in *Northanger Abbey* (1817), Jane Austen defends her depiction of novel reading by her characters Catherine and Isabella: "for I will not adopt that ungenerous and impolitic custom so common with novel-writers ... of scarcely ever permitting [novels] to be read by their own heroine. ... If the heroine of one novel be not patronized by the heroine of another, from whom can she expect protection and regard?"

Apparently it works. Many readers in my avid readers study have said that they pick books by following up recommendations from authors, either within the recommending author's book or in a blurb on the JACKET of the recommended book. "Pyncheon writes jacket blurbs for DeLillo," noted one reader when describing how he follows threads that link one author to another and one book to another. This linking is a common promotional strategy. The back cover of my copy of Mark Haddon's *The Curious Incident of the Dog in the Night-time* includes this notice: "A superb achievement. He is a wise and bleakly funny writer with rare gifts of empathy—Ian McEwan, author of *Atonement*." On the cover of John Irving's *A Widow for One Year*, Carol Shields is quoted as saying, "Irving offers ... a faith in patient storytelling and the conviction that narrative hunger is part of our essence."

Readers say they pay attention to such recommendations, but they have to trust the recommender. Jaci said that she chooses books based on the usual earmarks: "author's name, title, cover, what's on the back, whether it's got any nice blurbs from people" (see BEFORE READING). But she warns, it depends on who the recommender is: "If it's Stephen King—Stephen King will give a nice blurb to anybody, so don't trust a Stephen King blurb." Fiona (information specialist, age 31) says, "I will see all kinds of blurbs from authors I hate, and go, 'Okay, well, Piers Anthony loved this book, I won't pick it up.' " Readers looking for a "good book to read," says Joyce Saricks (see X-TRAORDINARY READ-ERS), are often trying to find a book with a certain "feel." Experienced readers familiar with Pynchon, McEwan, Shields, Phillips, or Anthony can gather useful clues about the likely feel of a book these writers are willing to recommend. Ditto the reader who said he decided to buy Phillip Kerr's crime novel *A Philosophical Investigation* because "the blurb included the word Wittgenstein." Unfortunately, Clive (airline pilot, age 60) realized too late that the type of book admired by the blurb sources had a completely different feel from the "slam-bam-gun-'em-down storyline" he wanted:

> Here's a science fiction book I had never heard of before. And I read the front: Orson Scott Card says it's wonderful. Ursula Le Guin says it's wonderful. *Booklist* says it's wonderful. Jean Wolf says it's wonderful. . . . *It's awful!* It really is bad. It's a discussion of philosophy . . . . The author has forgotten that he's writing a novel. I mean, it's the absolute opposite to the slam-bam-gun-'em-down storyline [I wanted]. . . . But I should have guessed it from what I know about [these recommenders]. Card—weird. Le Guin—an Amnesty Greenpeace kind of person. And Wolf—basically an Oxford don and philosophy type of writer.

There is not really a term for this practice of following the breadcrumbs from one book or author to the next, but one of the readers on the discussion group rec.arts.books called it *literary logrolling*:

> I also use literary log-rolling—if I catch authors saying they like each other's books in cover blurbs, I'll try the one I haven't read. I read dedication and acknowledgments pages in search of same.

Along the same lines, another post on rec.arts.books asked about the practice of reading books recommended within other books: "I read Nesbit from Edward Eager's references to her in his books. Actually, I've found quite a few books that way. I read the *Swallows and Amazons* books from a reference in *The Boyhood of Grace Jones* and *Green Mansions* from a reference in *The Saturdays*. . . . Anyone else read books recommended by other books? I think I am beginning to make a habit of it, it's fun, I feel like I'm getting a personal recommendation from the author!" Another reader said, "My mom and I have done this [read books recommended in other books] so often, we started calling it 'the Old Books Network.' "

Social media sites such as LibraryThing and Goodreads have automated the logrolling from one book to a similar one. Look up a book at Library-Thing and you find "LibraryThing recommendations" that rank other books you might like, with the linkages based on users' ratings and similarity of tags assigned by users. In April 2013, I got an e-mail message from Good-reads informing me of new releases that I might like, based on my ratings of other books: Kate Atkinson's *Life after Life*, Julian Barnes's *Levels of Life*, Jane Gardam's *Last Friends*, and, surprisingly, Nancy Atherton's *Aunt Dimity and the Lost Prince*. Goodreads got three right out of four—good odds for a reader.

Marginalia

Librarians frown on it, purists condemn it, but readers persist in doing it: writing in the margins of the books they are reading—their own and sometimes library books. In fact, readers say that one of the things they most like about the physical book is the ease with which they can annotate, make comments, and underline significant passages. Yes, you can do some of these same things with eBooks, they admit, but it's not the same. Noah (student, age 28) says, "I don't want an eBook. . . . I like the pages. I like writing my funny comments on the side. I do that with library books too all the time. That's what the margins are there for. I get in trouble all the time for writing in something." Noah's comment about getting "in trouble all the time" reminds us that these days writing in books is considered transgressive. It is a challenge to authorship. It distracts the eye from the original text to the side notations. It provokes the regulatory zeal of librarians who post signs forbidding the marking of books. But at the same time we are intrigued by traces of earlier readers, especially if the reader has some personal significance for us. When Noah found in the basement an old copy of *Catcher in the Rye* that his dad had read and annotated many decades ago, he considered it a time traveler between a younger version of his dad and himself in the present:

> So it's interesting—this book that can be in two places in the temporal sphere. I like this idea of used books that people have read—people who were someone else and thinking different things. That's why I throw my comments in, just because it's fun to read what people thought were important. It's a connection.

The undisputed expert on marginalia is English Professor Heather Jackson (2001, 2005). Her impressive book *Marginalia* (2001) contains chapters with such titles as "Physical Features," "Motives for Marginalia," "Object Lessons," and "Book Use or Book

Abuse." Jackson has been a seeker out of marginalia of all kinds—both those produced by exceptional, celebrated readers and those produced by common, anonymous readers. An editor of the Coleridge project, she confesses, "Coleridge's marginalia converted me to writing in books" (Jackson 2001, 234). In *Marginalia*, she examined some 3,000 books annotated in English by various readers from 1700 to 2000. Jackson (51) notes continuities over time in the way that readers mark books:

> Readers continue to this day to do what readers did in the Middle Ages, besides doing much more in the way of recording individual impressions. They mark up their books as a way of learning and remembering what they contain, and improve them by correcting errors and adding useful relevant information.

In the book market, the status of marginalia depends on who is doing the writing in the margins and which margins are being written on. In her "Introduction," Jackson provides the example of a copy of Galileo's work on sunspots, acquired with fanfare by the British Library in 1998. A publicity flyer provides this description: "The special interest of this copy lies in the copious annotations in Italian which have been written in the margins throughout the book. While it is not known who wrote the annotations, there appear to be three different hands, all dating from the early seventeenth century" (Jackson 2001, 1). Jackson points out that while the inscriptions by these unidentified, contemporary readers increase the market value of the copy, the same cannot be said for a recent paperback with passages marked in yellow highlighting and inscribed with marginal comments such as "good," "NB," or "don't agree."

However, for students of the history of reading, marginalia of all kinds are of interest. Marginalia are traces that help us recover the experiences of individual readers, but they also reveal codes of reading in use during a particular time period. Marginalia provide clues to "the reading mind."

How and Why to Mark a Book

Jackson points out that there are standardized ways to perform marginalia that have been remarkably consistent over the centuries. Ownership marks and presentation inscriptions (e.g., "To Felix, Christmas 2014 from Aunt Isobel") are written on the inside front cover or on the title page; expressions of opinion are written in the opening pages; side margins are used for a running commentary on the text; and the last page is used for a summary note and possibly an index of subjects and page numbers that the reader may wish to refer to again. Ownership marks are the most common inscription. Writing in books is part of the process of taking possession of a book and making it the reader's own. I recall that in elementary school my friends and I wrote on the inside front covers of our school texts something that Jackson (2001, 24) calls a "reinforcement of the ownership claim": "If this book should chance to roam/ Box its ears and send it home." A more emphatic couplet reported by Jackson (24) was inscribed by one Robert Odell of Petrolia, Ontario, in 1897 in his *Third Reader*: "Steal not this book for fear of life for the owner has a big jackknife." When the presentation inscription has been written, not by your grandmother but by the author (or someone connected with the author, someone of interest in her own right, or even someone connected with the contents), then the copy is considered an "association copy" and becomes more sought-after (Tanselle et al. 2011).

In the library copy of *Marginalia* that I am consulting, an earlier reader has marked selected passages with a faint pencil line tilting upward to the right at a 45-degree angle. Unlike the vandal who underlines library books in yellow highlighter, this person was only slightly transgressive, making unobtrusive marks, presumably as a finding device for personal use. Even so, the marks have subtly altered the text—once I clued in to these penciled lines, I started reading the marked passages with extra attention. One such passage is the following: "The essential and defining character of the marginal note throughout history is that it is a responsive kind of writing permanently anchored to preexisting written words" (81). I began to trust this other reader to mark significant passages, in this case a definition of marginalia that emphasizes the transactional nature of the reading enterprise.

Like reading itself, marginalia writing is a meaning-making activity in which both the original author and the reader have a role. We can see this happening when marginalia writers talk back to authors ("innumerable blunders . . . unparalleled insolence"), correcting errors, agreeing with statements made, debating contentious points, and sometimes, as William Blake so often does (Adams 2009), expressing outrage. In a copy of Francis Bacon's *Essays*, Blake calls Bacon one of "Satan's hirelings" and writes, "Villain! did Christ seek the Praise of the Rulers?" On the title page of a copy of Joshua Reynolds's *Discourses*, Blake observes, "This Man was Hired to Depress Art." For many readers, writing in margins may be the only platform available. Hester Piozzi, a good friend of Dr. Johnson and a compulsive reader, was also a secret writer of marginalia. In 1790, she wrote in her diary, "I have a Trick of writing in the Margins of my books, it is not a good Trick, but one longs to say something" (Jack 2012, 212).

What is the purpose of annotations? Writing in books can be a way of communicating with an imagined author, even dead ones, or with future readers of the text. We may think of marking books as a private act, but producing marginalia can be a public performance done with future readers in mind. Famously, Coleridge published his marginalia, as more recently did Sam Anderson (2012), using technology unavailable to Coleridge to reproduce images of book pages and handwritten annotations for public display. In one image of an annotated page of *Anna Karenina*, we can see that Anderson has drawn a box around Anna's question to Dolly "what's to be done, what's to be done?" The marginal note asks, "key phrase of all C19 Russian lit?" Annotations written with future readers in mind may seem self-consciously crafted as a reading performance. But for most readers, marginalia is less self-display and more a matter of usefulness. Readers who create marginal annotations, summaries, indexes, or even just marginal tick marks beside key passages often see these markings as an information-retrieval aid for future use. In a ground-breaking book on managing scholarly information, Ann Blair (2010) discusses four crucial operations—what she calls "the 4 S's of text management": storing, sorting, selecting, and summarizing. Annotating books is a way of doing all these things. As Jackson (2001, 88) observes, "Annotated books constitute a ready-made filing and retrieval system."

This is why students used to be taught to do annotations as a method for understanding, remembering, and taking mental possession of a text. Writing in books was a privilege of ownership. Seth Lerer (2012, 150) quotes advice that hymn writer Isaac Watts gave to readers in his *Improvement of the Mind* (first published in 1741 and often reprinted): "Mark what is new or unknown to you before. . . . [If the author] does not explain his ideas or prove the positions well, mark the faults or defects, and endeavour to do better, either in the margin of your book, or rather in some papers of your own. . . . If the method of a book be irregular, reduce it into form by a little analysis of your own, or by hints in the margin." The redoubtable Mortimer Adler, author of *How to Read a Book* (1940) and cofounder of the Great Books Foundation, advises serious readers to read with a pencil in hand.

> Why is marking up a book indispensable to reading? First, it keeps you awake. (And I don't mean merely conscious; I mean awake.) In the second place, reading, if it is active, is thinking, and thinking tends to express itself in words, spoken or written. The marked book is usually the thought-through book. Finally, writing helps you remember the thoughts you had, or the thoughts the author expressed. . . . The most famous "active" reader of great books I know is President Hutchins, of the University of Chicago.
>
> But, you may ask, why is writing necessary? Well, the physical act of writing, with your own hand, brings words and sentences more sharply before your mind and preserves them better in your memory. . . .
>
> But don't let anybody tell you that a reader is supposed to be solely on the receiving end. Understanding is a two-way operation; learning doesn't consist in being an empty receptacle. The learner has to question himself and question the teacher. He even has to argue with the teacher, once he understands what the teacher is saying. And marking a book is literally an expression of differences, or agreements of opinion, with the author. (Adler 1941)

Subverting the Text: Some Famous and Not So Famous Child Readers

Young readers are specialists in playful marginalia that subvert the text. Kenneth Grahame (1894) recalls his own early career as a schoolboy writing in the margins of his Latin texts: "For myself, my own early margins chiefly served to note, cite, and illustrate the habits of crocodiles." He reported how his penstroke turned "battle" into "bottle" in this sentence in his Roman history text: "By this single battle of Magnesia, Antiochus the Great lost all his conquests in Asia Minor." The marginalia of ordinary readers also tell revealing stories of readers talking back to texts. Take, for example, a secondhand copy of a Stratemeyer series book that I bought when I was working on a project on series books. It was the Grosset & Dunlap revised 1959 edition of the first book in the Nancy Drew series, *The Secret of the Old Clock*. In an ownership claim, the former owner has printed "Beverley" in ballpoint pen in a child's hand on the book's second page—a blank *recto* page that faces a listing of other books by "Carolyn Keene." Beverley had put checkmarks beside 24 of the 43 titles listed as Nancy Drew Mystery Stories and beside 3 of the Dana Girls Mystery titles. The back cover displayed the same list of Nancy Drew titles, along with instructions: "Check and see how many you have read. You won't want to miss a single one of these exciting mystery cases." Here the annotator Beverley has checked off in red ink the same titles as before, augmented with additional titles checked in pencil for a grand total of 31 Nancy Drew books read. So we are clearly dealing with a reader who is thoroughly familiar with the series and its conventions and who has enjoyed the books sufficiently to read a lot of them.

On the title page, Beverley provided a legend for some idiosyncratic shorthand symbols, which she used to annotate the opening pages of the first chapter, "The Rescue." Here are the symbols and their meaning:

?   do not know

[]   out of sentence

!   or

Two question marks, beside "attractive" and "new," have been added to qualify the book's first sentence: "Nancy Drew, an attractive girl of eighteen, was driving home along a country road in her new dark-blue convertible." On the second page of the text, a little girl about five years old darts into the road right in front of a moving van, miraculously escapes being run over, but then topples over the side of a bridge and out of sight, to Nancy's horror—here the annotator revised "horror" to "delight." The text reads, " 'I hope—' Nancy dared not complete the harrowing thought." Beverley completed the thought by adding, "she is dead!" Nancy finds the little girl at the foot of an embankment, half in the water, but is relieved to find "no water" in her nose and mouth and "no broken bones." Beverley used the "out of sentence" mark [] to delete the "no" in each case so that in the revised version Nancy is relieved to discover water in her nose and broken bones. "Gently Nancy lifted the little girl . . . holding her firmly in both arms" was revised to "Roughly Nancy threw the little girl . . . holding her by the ears." This veteran reader of 31 Nancy Drew books has become an author, rewriting the story as a parody that changes perfect Nancy into a monster.

To turn to fictional writers of marginalia, there is the case of J. K. Rowling, who gave Harry Potter and Ron Weasley some margins to write in when she responded to a request from the charity, Comic Relief, to do something for a fund-raiser to help children living in poverty. She wrote two books, *Fantastic Beasts and Where to Find Them* and *Quidditch through the Ages*, sales of which have raised more than $30 million for the charity. In an interview, Rowling (2001) was asked, "[*Fantastic Beasts*] has extra stuff written in it by Harry. What's all that about?" Rowling explained, "That's Harry and Ron graffitiing the book, as you do to your schoolbooks. You do doodle on them, I always wrote all over mine. Teachers reading this will not be happy that I'm saying it but you do, don't you? So they've just scribbled things on them and said rude things in them, the name of their favourite Quidditch team and stuff in the book."

As it turns out, the markings made by Harry and Ron with a little help from Hermione illustrate many of the elements of marginalia writing as described by Heather Jackson, and they also add a few extra embellishments of their own. The ownership claim on the title page ("This book belongs to Harry Potter") is elaborated in an exchange between Ron ("shared by Ron Weasley because his fell apart") and Hermione ("Why don't you buy a new one then?"). Blank space on the page facing the Contents page is used for a game of hangman, a game of ticktacktoe, and Ron's message "Harry loves Moaning Myrtle" with the last two words crossed out. In the heading, "A Brief History," someone—Harry?—has circled the word "Brief" and added "You liar." The alphabetical entries on the fantastic beasts themselves have been improved with corrections, additions, jokes, and a cartoon illustration of a troll.

References

Adams, Hazard. 2009. *Blake's Margins: An Interpretive Study of the Annotations.* Jefferson, NC: McFarland.

Adler, Mortimer. 1941. "How to Mark a Book." *The Saturday Review of Literature*, July 6. http://chuma.cas.usf.edu/~pinsky/mark_a_book.htm.

Anderson, Sam. 2012. "Marginal Thinking." *New York Times Magazine*, December 21. http://www.nytimes.com/interactive/2012/12/21/magazine/mag-23Riff-970 interactive.html?_r=0.

Blair, Ann M. 2010. *Too Much to Know: Managing Scholarly Information before the Modern Age.* New Haven, CT: Yale University Press.

Grahame, Kenneth. 1894. "Marginalia." In *Pagan Papers*. London: Elkin Mathews and John Lane.

Jack, Brenda. 2012. *The Woman Reader*. New Haven, CT, and London: Yale University Press.

Jackson, Heather J. 2001. *Marginalia: Readers Writing in Books*. New Haven, CT: Yale University Press.

Jackson, Heather J. 2005. *Romantic Readers: The Evidence of Marginalia*. New Haven, CT: Yale University Press.

Lerer, Seth. 2012. "Devotion and Defacement: Reading Children's Marginalia." *Representations* 118, no. 1 (Spring): 126–53.

Rowling, J. K. 2001. "Raincoast Books Interview Transcript, Raincoast Books (Canada), March 2001." http://www.accio-quote.org/articles/2001/0301-raincoast-interview.html

Tanselle, G. Thomas, Hal Kugeler, Kim Coventry, and Susan F. Rossen. 2011. *Other People's Books: Association Copies and the Stories They Tell*. Chicago: The Caxton Club.

Further Reading

Check out Herman Melville's marginalia by browsing digital reproductions of books owned and annotated by the author of *Moby-Dick*.

Olsen-Smith, Steven, Peter Norberg, and Dennis C. Marnon, eds. *Melville's Marginalia Online*. http://melvillesmarginalia.org.

Nonfiction

Here are the opening sentences of seven books. Which of these seven books are nonfiction? What makes you think so?

A   I used to have a cat, an old fighting tom, who would jump through the open window by my bed in the middle of the night and land on my chest. I'd half-awaken. He'd stick his skull under my nose and purr, stinking of urine and blood. Some nights he kneaded my bare chest with his front paws, powerfully, arching his back, as if sharpening his claws, or pummeling a mother for milk. And some mornings I'd wake in daylight to find my body covered with paw prints in blood; I looked as though I'd been painted with roses.

B   To observe your mind in automatic mode, glance at the image below. [Below is a 2-inch by 1.25-inch black-and-white headshot of a dark-haired, frowning woman with her mouth open, evidently saying something.] Your experience as you look at the woman's face seamlessly combines what we normally call seeing and intuitive thinking. As surely and quickly as you saw that the young woman's hair is dark, you knew she is angry. . . . It just happened to you. It was an instance of fast thinking.

C   Then there was the bad weather. It would come in one day when the fall was over. You would have to shut the windows in the night against the rain and the cold wind would strip the leaves from the trees in the Place Contrescarpe. The leaves lay sodden in the rain and the wind drove the rain against the big green autobus at the terminal and the Café des Amateurs was crowded and the windows misted over from the heat and the smoke inside.

D   One warm, spring day in May of 2007, the Medicine Hat Tigers and the Vancouver Giants met for the Memorial Cup hockey championship in Vancouver, British Columbia. The Tigers and the Giants were the two finest teams in the Canadian Hockey League, which in turn is the finest junior hockey league in the world. These were the future stars of the sport—seventeen, eighteen, and nineteen-year-olds who had been skating and shooting pucks since they were barely more than toddlers.

E   There's a photo on my wall of a woman I've never met, its left corner torn and patched together with tape. She looks straight into the camera and smiles, hands on hips, dress suit neatly pressed, lips painted deep red. It's the late 1940s and she hasn't yet reached the age of thirty. Her light brown skin is smooth, her eyes still young and playful, oblivious to the tumor growing inside her—a tumor that would leave her five children motherless and change the future of medicine. Beneath the photo, a caption says her name is "Henrietta Lacks, Helen Lane or Helen Larson."

F   Jim Gallien had driven four miles out of Fairbanks when he spotted the hitchhiker standing in the snow beside the road, thumb raised high, shivering in the gray Alaska dawn. He didn't appear to be very old: 18, maybe 19 at most. A rifle protruded from the young man's backpack, but he looked friendly enough; a hitchhiker with a Remington semiautomatic isn't the sort of thing that gives motorists pause in the forty-ninth state. Gallien steered his truck onto the shoulder and told the kid to climb in.

G   Eat food. Not too much. Mostly plants.
     That, more or less, is the short answer to the supposedly incredibly complicated and confusing question of what we humans should eat in order to be maximally healthy.

Yes, all of them are nonfiction, taken from books that are award-winning, best-selling, and/or on lists of nonfiction favorites. But often it can be hard to tell. Nonfiction writers have learned the standbys of fiction writing: how to set a scene, tell a good story, establish an engaging voice, handle narrative point of view, develop vivid characters, and create suspense. In excerpt C, the opening sentence, "Then there was the bad weather," the "then" puts us right in the midst of things, inviting us to wonder what came before the "then." All the passages but B and G could have been the opening setup for a short story or a novel. Here are the books from which the excerpts were taken:

A   Annie Dillard. 1974. *Pilgrim at Tinker Creek*. Dillard won the Pulitzer Prize for this evocative piece of nature writing—part sharply focused observation and part reflection—about the natural world seen through the turning year in the vicinity of her home near a creek, Tinker Creek, in the Blue Ridge mountains of Virginia.

B   Daniel Kahneman. 2011. *Thinking Fast and Slow.* Written by the recipient of a Nobel Prize in Economics, this book distills a lifetime of empiric research in cognitive psychology on how we think and make decisions. In this popularization of research findings, Kahneman makes complex ideas and concepts accessible to nonexperts.

C   Ernest Hemingway. 1964. *A Moveable Feast.* In his posthumously published memoir of expatriate life in Paris in the 1920s, Hemingway provides an insider's recollection of times with F. Scott Fitzgerald and Zelda, Morley Callaghan, and Gertrude Stein and other writers and artists—writing, talking, and drinking.

D   Malcolm Gladwell. 2007. *Outliers: The Story of Success.* This collection of essays uses case studies of human outliers—for example, NHL hockey players who are almost all born in January or February, Korean airplanes that topped the list for crashes due to pilot error—to reach unexpected conclusions about the nature of success.

E   Rebecca Skoot. 2010. *The Immortal Life of Henrietta Lacks.* This hybrid work of medical science writing draws on medical records, legal documents, and interviews with family members to tell the story of Henrietta Lacks and her immortal cells, called HeLa, that were taken without her knowledge and used in many medical advances, including the development of polio vaccine, chemotherapy, and gene mapping.

F   Jon Krakauer. 1996. *Into the Wild.* Krakauer reconstructs the deadly adventure story of Christopher McCandless, an idealistic, urban kid who ignored local advice and walked alone into the snow-packed bush north of Mt. McKinley, Alaska, in April "to live off the land," with only 10 pounds of rice to eat, inadequate boots and clothing, no snowshoes, no *SAS Survival Handbook*, and no compass or topographical map.

G   Michael Pollan. 2008. *In Defense of Food: An Eater's Manifesto.* New York: Penguin. Science and environmental journalist Pollan argues that the food industry and nutrition science has brought us the toxic Western diet of food-like, processed substitutes.

These seven books are just a few examples of the many different types of nonfiction writing that people read for pleasure: A—nature writing in the form of a memoir, B—popularization of social science research, C—memoir,

D—essays, E—science writing combined with biography, F—true adventure, and G—food and environmental writing.

Why read nonfiction for pleasure? When readers talk about what they enjoy in nonfiction (Ross 2004), this is what they say. They like to read about things that are "real." They like to learn things about topics of long-standing interest. They enjoy expanding their knowledge about the world and acquiring new ideas when they read about, say, the medical importance of the HeLa cells, the way that people evaluate risk when making decisions, or the factors that have led to the toxic Western diet. With essay collections such as Gladwell's *Outliers*, diaries, collections of letters, and cookbooks, readers appreciate being able to dip into the book anywhere. When they don't have long, uninterrupted time for reading, they like a book they can easily pick up and put down and read in short bursts. Insider memoirs such as *A Moveable Feast* offer gossipy accounts of famous people. Memoirs in general are popular because peering into someone else's life gives readers a chance to reflect on their own lives. With such works as Annie Dillard's *Tinker Creek*, readers are drawn to the lyrical writing, the author's voice, and the carefully observed details of the natural world. In other cases, subject matter, not literary style, trumps everything.

Many readers have a passion for a particular topic—dogs, horses, orchids, planes, ancient Egypt, the American Civil War, naval battles, the Shackleton expedition to the Antarctic, the Camino de Santiago, the Bloomsbury Group, the Santa Fe Trail, hockey, and so on—and will read absolutely everything they can find on this favorite topic, well written or not. Others are just looking for a good story. With true adventures or true crime stories such as Jon Krakauer's *Into the Wild* or Truman Capote's *In Cold Blood*, readers say, "it reads like a novel," with the added pathos of knowing the events really happened and often with the bonus of maps and photographs. Readers say that they enjoy all the extras in works of nonfiction: visual elements such as maps, diagrams, tables, charts, colored photographs; formatting enhancements such as sidebars, fact boxes, and pull quotes; finding aids such as tables of contents and indexes; and extensive bibliographies that they can use to pursue an interest in the topic.

In the interviews with avid readers in my study of pleasure reading, some readers said that they *never* read nonfiction (too boring, too much like school, too similar to their work-related reading). Some said they read *only* nonfiction (fiction wasn't "real" enough or was too contrived). But the large majority read both. They often have several books on the go and choose which one to read at any given time depending on their mood and the time available. Jane (student, age 22), who "just like[s] to know things," said she browses in reference works with no particular topic in mind, just for enjoyment: "I like to go through reference sections and browse the dictionaries and other reference books. I like to find out things." Many nonfiction readers find the same satisfaction of good storytelling in biography, history, and travel books that can be found in novels. Marsha (student, age 26) said she "always thought biographies were going to be factual, boring dull stuff, but I realized you can read them like a book, like a fiction book. They're a story." For Clarence (self-employed, age 60), who is primarily a reader of history and biography, the big appeal is that "people existed that did those things" and that he is learning about "real life history"—"you know that they are real and that they actually happened."

Mapping the Nonfiction Landscape

Nonfiction is a category defined by what it is not. Nonfiction is all those books on the other side of what Neal Wyatt (2007) calls the Dewey divide in public libraries—the books that are left over after you take out the novels and short stories. For our purposes here, we can narrow things down even more, because a large percentage of nonfiction is not typically read for pleasure: the task-oriented reference works, manuals, textbooks, and specialized works written for fellow experts in every discipline from astronomy to zoology (but see the case of Jane mentioned earlier, who reads reference books for pleasure). Under consideration here are works that people typically read by choice for their own enjoyment such as biography, autobiography, memoirs, history, travel books, food writing, true adventure, true crime, SELF-HELP, and nonfiction on topics of interest written for a general audience.

Classification of nonfiction is tricky. We are already running into problems with overlapping categories. "Biography, autobiography, and memoir" is a classification by literary form, but it doesn't tell us anything about the subject—there are biographies of presidents, dogs, famous inventors, and serial killers. Memoirs are written by crack addicts, people with miserable childhoods, survivors of hostage-takings, politicians, musicians, novelists, inventors, sports heroes, and so on. This creates a problem for libraries. Should the record-smashing autobiography of Manchester United's Alex Ferguson go into a biography section, or should it be shelved with books on sports? "History" is another classification that does not depend on subject area. The history category is based on the disciplinary approach to the subject matter—the choice to investigate the development through time of any number of things: countries, wars, industries, ideas, sports, food, medicine, science, and so on.

Most of the categories used for nonfiction writing are based on subject. "Travel books," "food writing," "true adventure," and "true crime" are all classifications based on subject matter rather than on literary form or disciplinary approach. Popular books for the general reader get written on a dizzying range of subjects: health and medicine; entertainment such as sports, music, and the media; aspects of power such as politics, warfare, and money; scientific topics such as black holes, scary new viruses, genetics, and climate change; the natural world such as accounts of animals, the wilderness, and oceans; the built environment such as city planning, architecture, and gardens; and so on. For each of these subjects, books can be written of different types. Food writing, say, can be written as a cookbook full of recipes, as a dietary program, as a biography of a famous chef, as a travel memoir focused on experiencing a national cuisine, as the history of a food breakthrough, as an investigative report on some aspect of the food industry, as a study of a single staple such as salt, cod, rice, olive oil, coffee, and chocolate, or as a study that examines the linkage between food and something else such as human health, the rain forest, or industrialized agriculture. The diversity can be daunting—or exhilarating.

Nonfiction in Public Libraries

Nonfiction in public libraries has ridden a roller-coaster. From 1876, when the American Library Association was founded, and continuing for another 100 years or so, librarians considered nonfiction to be much better for readers than fiction. The duty of librarians was to push readers up the reading ladder from dime novels and series books at the bottom to serious fiction and thence to narrative nonfiction such as biography, history, and travel accounts and finally to nonnarrative nonfiction such as philosophy and science. Efforts of public librarians were aimed at getting people to read fewer fiction books and a lot more nonfiction. The "two-book system" was adopted to increase nonfiction circulation and improve library circulation statistics: readers could borrow two books at a time, but the second book had to be nonfiction (Carrier 1965, 172–73). In the 1920s, when readers' advisory (RA) was given a boost as an advertised new service in public libraries, the focus was on nonfiction, self-education, and "reading with a purpose" (Crowley 2004).

Attitudes toward fiction gradually changed until the hierarchy with fiction at the bottom and nonfiction at the top was turned upside down. Thus it was that when RA service returned to public libraries in the early 1980s, the focus was almost entirely on fiction and on helping readers find novels they would enjoy. Fiction was associated with pleasure reading in contrast with nonfiction, which was associated with information and reference services. The Chicago-based Adult Reading Round Table (AART), which has dedicated a year-long study to different genres of popular reading since 1984, finally turned its attention to nonfiction in 2007. From 2000 to 2007, momentum was building, perhaps best exemplified by the collection of essays *Nonfiction Readers' Advisory* (2004), edited by Robert Burgin, who has been a leader in the push to incorporate nonfiction into RA work. More recently, talk has turned to ways of bridging the Dewey divide by including fiction and nonfiction together in displays and on booklists and through creating "whole library" RA tools such as "reading maps" and "read-arounds" (Alpert 2006; Wyatt 2007, 230–45) (see X-TRAORDINARY READERS).

A flurry of books has appeared to map out the nonfiction terrain for pleasure reading. Neal Wyatt's *Readers' Advisory Guide to Nonfiction* (2007) provides an excellent starting point, with separate chapters on specific types—food and cooking; science, mathematics, and nature; memoirs; sports;

true crime; travel; true adventure; history and historical biography; and general nonfiction. For each subject area, Wyatt discusses the appeal for readers and benchmark books. She lists key authors, titles divided according to subtype, and resources and awards. Another go-to source is *The Real Story* (2006) by Sarah Statz Cords, which describes more than 500 nonfiction titles classified by genre—true crime, travel, life stories, and so on—and including a discussion of appeal. More specialized guides include Robert Burgin (2013) on travel narratives; Sarah Statz Cords (2009) on nonfiction investigative writing and exposés; Bernard Drew (2008) on the 100 most popular nonfiction writers; Maureen O'Connor (2011) on memoirs, autobiographies, and diaries; Rick Roche (2009) on biographies; Elizabeth Fraser (2008) on teen nonfiction interests; Melissa Stoeger (2013) on food and eating; and Jessica Zellers (2009) on nonfiction of special interest to women. In these guides, classifications vary somewhat from one to another, depending on whether the primary way to divide up the nonfiction terrain is by audience type, literary form, or subject interest. But Neal Wyatt (2007, 1–2) suggests that it may not be possible, or even desirable, to try to put nonfiction into watertight categories. After all, she says, "Readers don't follow an orderly system when choosing what to read. They make their choices according to a chaotic, whorl of interests based on an ever-changing set of reasons and moods."

Drawing the Line between Fiction and Nonfiction

What about the boundary between fiction and nonfiction itself? Even here it is difficult to draw the line. Australian author Thomas Keneally's Booker Prize–winning *Schindler's Ark* was published as fiction in Great Britain and as nonfiction in North America under the title *Schindler's List*. At one end of the nonfiction continuum, you find work featuring agreed-upon public facts and statistics, empiric evidence, an attempt at objectivity and accuracy, and a purpose to explain or inform. At the other end, you find nonfiction featuring remembered, lived experience presented as anecdotes or stories and written to entertain or inspire. Memoir writers write the truth from their own perspective, relying on memory, which at the best of times is partial and error-prone. David Shields (2010, 57) has argued against distinctions between fiction and nonfiction, memoir and fabrication, claiming, "Anything processed by memory is fiction." Moreover, to shape memories into an interesting narrative, memoir writers must make choices about which characters and events to develop and which to leave out. Autobiographers and memoir writers themselves sometimes directly address issues of subjectivity and memory. Mary Karr's *Lit: A Memoir* (2009), about her downward spiral into alcoholism and craziness and her recovery, begins, "Any way I tell this story is a lie. . . . " Karr acknowledges that her husband would tell a different version of their marriage: "Were Warren laboring over this story, I'd no doubt appear drunkenly shrieking" (87–88). Then there is the problem of memory's unreliability, exacerbated when a person is often, as she says, "blotto":

> How to write without self-deceit. . . . [T]hose years only filter back through the self I had at the time, when I was most certainly—even by my yardstick then—a certain species of crazy.

Or we could say that anything given a narrative shape is fiction. As Jay Parini (1999) puts it in his introduction to the *Norton Book of American Biography*: "Fiction, as it were, means 'shaping' from the Latin *fictio*. The facts of any life are too overwhelming, too detailed, too confusing to constitute a narrative; all narrative works by exclusion. The autobiographer cancels in order to clarify, shaping experience to make it readable, using techniques normally found in fiction such as foreshadowing or scene setting." While narrative nonfiction uses the resources of fiction, conversely many fiction writers use autobiographical material.

So how much shaping, rearranging, and tinkering are allowable in a life story if it's to be labeled nonfiction and not a novel? In his author's note to the *Midnight in the Garden of Good and Evil* (1994), John Berendt says, "Though this is a work of nonfiction, I have taken certain storytelling liberties, particularly having to do with the time of events. Where the narrative strays from strict nonfiction, my intention has been to remain faithful to the characters and to the essential drift of events as they really happened." Annie Dillard has explained that, with permission, she borrowed the story about the "old fighting tom" and being "painted with roses" from a student (Connery 2011, xii). Readers accept such reshapings in the interest of a good story but feel betrayed if they feel the contract with the reader has been broken.

Betrayal is the term often used in the context of the James Frey affair. Praised as a forthright account of addiction and recovery, Frey's *A Million Little Pieces* (2003) was chosen by Oprah Winfrey for her September 2005 Book Club pick, after which it went on to sell millions of copies, becoming the top nonfiction best-seller of 2005 on the *New York Times Best Seller* list. Then on January 6, the investigative Web site The Smoking Gun (2006) published a whistle-blowing article, "A Million Little Lies," forcing Frey to admit that certain key incidents were invented or embellished: he wasn't really an outlaw "wanted in three states"; he had been in jail for just three hours and given two traffic tickets, not incarcerated for 87 days for a multiple-felony bust. The Smoking Gun exposé was quickly picked up and reported around the world in articles with titles that parodied Frey's own title, such as Michiko Kakutani's piece (2006) in the *New York Times*, "Bending the Truth in a Million Little Ways." The ensuing firestorm of controversy swept up Oprah Winfrey (2006), who initially defended Frey but then invited him as a guest for a second appearance to rake him over the coals. On her January 26, 2006, show, she told him that she felt "really duped" and "more importantly, I feel that you betrayed millions of readers." Future printings included Frey's note to readers (2006) admitting that he had "embellished" and "altered" events in the interests of "the greater purpose of the book," seeking the "ebb and flow," the "dramatic arcs," and the tension that "all great stories require." He said that his mistake was "writing about the person I created in my mind to help me cope, and not the person who went through the experience."

Then there are the out-and-out hoaxes, which are not a matter of omission and reshaping but of complete inventions. Margaret B. Jones's memoir, *Love and Consequences: A Memoir of Hope and Survival* (2007), was sold as a story of growing up, half-white, half-Native, as a foster child in an African American family and running drugs for the Bloods in a gang-infested neighborhood in inner-city Los Angeles. The trouble is that the author, Margaret Seltzer, grew up in a well-to-do L.A. neighborhood as the white daughter in a white family, went to an Episcopal day school, and had no gang experience whatsoever. Micha Defonseca's *Misha: A Mémoire of the Holocaust Years* (1997) tells a story of a Jewish child from Brussels who walked alone across war-torn Europe, survived for months in the forest by being adopted by wolves, and spent time in the Warsaw ghetto. However, there were no wolves; her name was Monique, not Micha; she wasn't Jewish; and she stayed in Belgium the whole time, where she was raised by her grandfather after the Nazis arrested her parents for Belgian resistance activities (Van Gelder 2008). The author explained the discrepancy by saying that she had always "felt Jewish." The story, she acknowledged, "is not actually reality, but my reality, my way of surviving."

In such cases, where discrepancies are found, authors may talk of "larger truths," "subjective reality," "strategies for coping," or "feeling like" the outsiders they invented, but readers still feel conned. That's because readers read nonfiction differently. With nonfiction, a major appeal is that these events really happened and that you are learning something real about the world. Nonfiction readers say it's a bonus if, along with the spell-binding narrative, they are also getting insider knowledge or behind-the-scenes information that will give them an edge in their own lives by becoming smarter investors, more in control of their lives, better able to understand other people or other cultures, cannier about avoiding risky or dangerous situations, and so on. People read stories of survival under duress because the intensity of the experience counts more if it's real. We think we are getting hard-won insights into particular human conditions when we read personal accounts such as William Styron's *Darkness Visible* on depression, Susanna Kaysen's *Girl Interrupted* about life in a mental institution, Kay Redford Jamison's *Unquiet Mind* on manic depression, Mary Karr's *Lit: A Memoir* on crazy families and alcoholism, or Naoki Higashida's *The Reason I Jump* on being a 13-year-old boy with autism (Answer: "When I'm jumping, it's as if my feelings are going upward to the sky"). The authors' credentials and authority depend on their actually having lived the experience. In memoirs, as in the anthropological writing discussed by Clifford Gertz, "being there" is critical.

Who Reads Nonfiction and What Do They Read?

When the Harris Poll (2010) conducted an online survey of 2,775 U.S. adults aged 18 and over, 78 percent of readers (defined as those who said they had read at least one book in the previous year) said that they had read a nonfiction book, almost exactly the same percentage as had read a fiction book (79%). Men and women were equally likely to read nonfiction, but they preferred different types. Men were more likely than women to read history (40 versus 23%), political books (25% versus 10%), current affairs (20% versus 9%), and business (16% versus 4%). Women were more likely than men to read self-help (19% versus 12%) and true crime (14% versus 9%).

To dig a bit deeper than the who-reads-what question, Beth Luey (1998) recruited respondents from bookstore customers, reading group members, and library users who self-identified as readers of "serious nonfiction" and who were willing to answer a 20-item questionnaire. Luey was interested not in nonfiction in general but in nonfiction books read for pleasure that are "serious attempts to convey to the lay reader knowledge that has been hard won and is difficult to master" (22). These books are a subset of the nonfiction genre: their authors translate specialized research-based knowledge generated in universities into books that explain complex fields to the nonexpert, but smart, reader. A good example of this kind of book is Daniel Kahneman's *Thinking Fast and Slow* mentioned earlier, but other authors of the sort to interest Luey include Diane Ackerman, Daniel Boorstein, Jared Diamond, John Kenneth Galbraith, Henry Louis Gates, Stephen Jay Gould, John Allen Paulos, Stephen Pinker, David Riesman, and Carl Sagan.

The questionnaire respondents who answered Luey's survey on serious nonfiction were at the very high end of readerliness. They had demographic characteristics in line with what previous readership surveys would lead us to expect of heavily committed readers: 60 percent female, all college educated, belonging to a high-income group, and working at white-collar jobs or retired from such jobs. More than half read 30 or more books a year. They were book buyers who had collections of books at home: "These readers have books all over their houses. More than half reported keeping books in three or more rooms" (27). To qualify to be included in the study, all had to read serious nonfiction; in addition, 75 percent of these nonfiction readers also read fiction. When asked, "What [nonfiction] subjects do you like to read about? Check all that apply," 70 percent indicated that they read books in four to eight subject areas. With 20 subjects to choose from, respondents most often picked history and biography (64%); art, architecture, or philosophy (almost 50%); literary criticism (40%); psychology (38%), and self-help (30%).

When asked to check off all that apply from six possible reasons for reading nonfiction, about 70 percent each said that they read for specific information and to bring themselves up to date on subjects they knew; about 60 percent each reported reading for entertainment and to learn about current events and issues.

About 45 percent said they read to be able to discuss books with others. From Luey's account (1998, 30), a portrait emerges of lifelong learners whose reading of serious nonfiction is part of their engagement with the world. Many discuss their reading with friends, coworkers, family members, and fellow book club members. They display their books in their living rooms and public spaces, and they read at work and on public transportation. Luey contrasts these serious nonfiction readers with ROMANCE readers and SELF-HELP readers, who are reluctant to read in public. Unlike these clandestine readers of down-market, denigrated genres, readers of serious nonfiction are proud of their reading and consider it a badge of being a knowledgeable person. Luey addresses the role of serious nonfiction in self-education in her study of popularization, *Expanding the American Mind: Books and the Popularization of Knowledge* (2010).

The Experience of Nonfiction Reading

In my interviews with avid readers, some additional themes emerged about the special experience of reading nonfiction. Here are some of them.

- *Reading nonfiction for use versus reading for pleasure*

  Readers read nonfiction differently, depending on their purpose. On the one hand, there is reading to find a nugget of information to take away and use—to build a boat, to plant a garden, to choose a dog breed, and so on. On the other hand, there is "recreational reading," which is an end in itself. Virginia (library volunteer, age 65) said, "I will read a gardening book, not so much for the information, but for the ambience of the garden." Rita (homemaker, age 55) said that a train buff had introduced her to Paul Theroux's *The Old Patagonia Express*, which "was really like being on a train journey." Actually, she doesn't like taking trains but loved reading about the journey because "because I didn't have to do any of this dreadful stuff like sitting in this train for ninety-nine hours."

  In *The Reader, the Text, the Poem* (1978), Louise Rosenblatt distinguishes between these two kinds of reading, calling reading for use "efferent reading" and reading as an end in itself "aesthetic reading." She argues that readers bring to their reading not only prior knowledge but also particular dispositions about how they read texts. Readers can choose to see the text as primarily "referential," in which case they take an efferent stance (from the Latin *effere*, to carry away). Efferent readers read to find some particular fact or nugget of information that they can transfer from the reading situation and use in their everyday lives. Or readers can choose to take an aesthetic stance, where the important thing is not the extracted fact but the reader's immediate, lived-through experience of reading. The reader is the one who decides what stance to take, and the same text may be read efferently by one reader and aesthetically by another. A good example is the way some people read encyclopedias, which readers often say they read purely for pleasure, especially in childhood. Maurice (professional engineer, age 57) recalled that at age eight or nine he used to read a 20-volume home encyclopedia for children called *The New Book of Knowledge* "like a novel, from cover to cover." He said, "I would start at Pig and read everything in the P's. . . . Everything I read was brand new information."

- *Interrupted reading*

Readers say they prefer "a long block of time" for reading novels so that they can enter the world of the book and live there for a time. When they lack uninterrupted time, they prefer nonfiction such as letters, memoirs, diaries, travel books, cookbooks, and encyclopedias that can be dipped into and read a bit at a time, just as magazines are read. Rene (physician, age 32) said that now that she is looking after small children, her reading is "so interrupted—I mean you can't concentrate on anything because you're having to stop every page or two. Now I find that I'm more likely to read a nonfiction thing that I'm reading bits of." Derek (student, age 27), who has read books on Eastern religions, Paul Theroux's travel books, books on animals, and "tons of stuff on Malaysia," said, "Fiction really depends on my mood, but nonfiction doesn't as much." Marsha (student, age 26) said, "I'm reading *The Selected Journals of Lucy Maud Montgomery*. These are the kinds of books that I'll read a little bit at a time over a year or something. I don't try and finish them right away." Trevor (student, age 23) said that he often rereads William Shirer's *The Rise and Fall of the Third Reich* because it is "the sort of book that you could dip into at any place and just start reading, which is something I really like about books. Just pick it up, open to a random page, and start reading."

- *Not any old history, biography, or memoir*

When readers say they enjoy history, biography, letters, or memoirs, they don't mean that just any examples of the type will do. They enjoy biographies, autobiographies, or memoirs, they say, but only about particular people in certain categories that interest them. A few may read across the spectrum, but it is more common to find readers who read deeply in one or two given areas—sports heroes, members of the royal family, scientists, writers, film stars, political leaders, or whatever. If they have admired particular novels, buildings, or musical pieces, they may want to find out more about the lives of the creators. Joan (elementary school teacher, age 31) said, "I start with authors and then read their biographies. When Barbara Pym died, I waited for books to come out about her," Dorothy (freelance writer, age 30) said, "I read biographies; I read letters. I like to read about artists and writers. May Sarton's journals, I really love. I like memoirs. I don't read science as a rule. I'll pick a book if it's about or by someone whose work I'm interested in." Aline (student, age 22), said, "I also read biographies. I like to see what happened behind the public persona—Katharine Hepburn for example. Trudeau's memoirs. But I wouldn't sit down and read Neil Armstrong, first astronaut on the moon, because his life doesn't appeal to me."

- *Hedgehogs and the one big thing*

The terms *hedgehogs* and *foxes* refer to two contrasting approaches to life and were popularized in a book by Isaiah Berlin called *The Hedgehog and the Fox*. Berlin got his title from a fragment from an early Greek poet, Archilochus, who said, "The fox knows many little things. The hedgehog knows one big thing." Some readers are hedgehogs, who have one big interest and read on that topic intensively. Roger reads everything he can find about airplanes. Other readers with a passion for, say, horses, ancient Egypt, the American Civil War, or the Shackleton expedition to the Antarctic will read everything on this topic they can get their hands on. Larry (cell biologist, age 24) reads eighteenth-century American history: "That includes all aspects of eighteenth-century American history—sociology, architecture, gardening, landscaping, art, politics, just about every aspect of eighteenth-century history—biographies and diaries." In pursuing an intense interest, these hedgehogs are willing to read any type and format, including histories, biographies, letters, encyclopedias, screenplays, and fictional treatments, so long as the beloved subject matter is the focus.

- *Foxes and serendipitous discovery*

Then there are the foxes, who know many things and have the potential to become interested in many more. Consider the nonfiction book *Rats: Observation on the History and Habitat of the City's Most Unwanted Inhabitants* (2005) by Robert Sullivan, a work that Neal Wyatt (2007, 29) recommends as a book whose appeal to readers is not at all captured by its subject headings ("Rats—New York; Urban pests"). Some potential readers may be drawn to this book by an already existing interest. But for many who end up enjoying this book, it is the book that creates the interest. Similarly, readers may never have heard of William Smith, who first mapped the stratification of rocks in England, until they came upon Simon Winchester's *The Map That Changed the World: William Smith and the Birth of Modern Geology* (2001). Before encountering Stephen Greenblatt's *The Swerve: How the World Became Modern* (2011), who knew that they would want to read about the long-term impact of a rescue by a fifteenth-century bibliophile of the last surviving manuscript copy of Lucretius's *On the Nature of Things*? Recently, there has been a miniboom of micro histories about things that changed the world, for example Steven Johnson's *The Ghost Map: The Story of London's Most Terrifying Epidemic—and How It Changed the World* (2006), Dan Koeppel's *Banana: The Fate of the Fruit That Changed the World* (2008), and Mark Kurlansky's *Cod: A Biography of the Fish That Changed the World* (1997). An important appeal of such books is that they put an incident, a discovery, or a staple product into a larger context, showing its world-changing impact. While nonfiction is a good source to find answers to questions we already have, some readers value even more its capacity to surprise us by stimulating interests we don't realize we have. Mark (music educator and composer, age 42) describes the serendipitous discovery of an amazing book as a kind of fishing:

> When I go to a library . . . a lot of times it's like wading into that river and going fishing. You don't know what's going to happen when you get there. Libraries are still a magical place for me. If I'd gone hunting, I don't know that I would have found that book, but by going fishing and just casting out in different places I could inadvertently come across it. So that's the entertainment side of the library for me, the fun part of reading for pleasure— just seeing what you can come up with. And there's a lot of things that you throw back.

References

Adult Reading Round Table (ARRT). "Nonfiction Genre Study." http://www.arrtreads.org/images/ARRT_genre_NONFICTION.pdf.

Alpert, Abby. 2006. "Incorporating Nonfiction into Readers' Advisory Services." *Reference & User Services Quarterly* 46, no. 1 (Fall): 25–32.

Burgin, Robert, ed. 2004. *Nonfiction Readers' Advisory.* Westport, CT: Libraries Unlimited.

Burgin, Robert. 2013. *Going Places: A Reader's Guide to Travel Narratives.* Santa Barbara, CA: Libraries Unlimited.

Carrier, Esther Jane. 1965. *Fiction in Public Libraries 1876–1900.* New York and London: The Scarecrow Press.

Connery, Thomas B. 2011. *Journalism and Realism: Rendering American Life.* Evanston, IL: Northwestern University Press.

Cords, Sarah Statz. 2006. *The Real Story: A Guide to Nonfiction Reading Interests.* Westport, CT: Libraries Unlimited.

Cords, Sarah Statz. 2009. *The Inside Scoop: A Guide to Nonfiction Investigative Writing and Exposés.* Santa Barbara, CA: Libraries Unlimited.

Crowley, Bill. 2004. "A History of Readers' Advisory Service in the Public Library." In *Nonfiction Readers' Advisory*, 3–29. Edited by Robert Burgin. Westport, CT: Libraries Unlimited.

Drew, Bernard A. 2008. *100 Most Popular Nonfiction Authors: Biographical Sketches and Bibliographies.* Westport, CT: Libraries Unlimited.

Fraser, Elizabeth. 2008. *Reality Rules! A Guide to Teen Nonfiction Reading Interests.* Westport, CT: Libraries Unlimited.

Frey, James. 2006. "A Note to the Reader." http://www.randomhouse.biz/media/pdfs/AMLP020106.pdf.

The Harris Poll. 2010. "Stephen King Is America's Favorite Author: Mystery, Crime and Thriller Novels Are the Genre Most Read." October 7. http://multivu.prnewswire.com/mnr/harrisinteractive/44732/.

Kakutani, Michiko. 2006. "Bending the Truth in a Million Little Ways." *New York Times*, January 17. http://www.nytimes.com/2006/01/17/books/17kaku.html?_r=1&.

Karr, Mary. 2009. *Lit: A Memoir.* New York: HarperCollins.

Luey, Beth. 1998. "Who Reads Nonfiction?" *Publishing Research Quarterly* 14, no. 1 (Spring): 21–35.

Luey, Beth. 2010. *Expanding the American Mind: Books and the Popularization of Knowledge.* Amherst: University of Massachusetts Press.

O'Connor, Maureen. 2011. *Life Stories: A Guide to Reading Interests in Memoirs, Autobiographies, and Diaries.* Santa Barbara, CA: Libraries Unlimited.

Parini, Jay, ed. 1999. *The Norton Book of American Autobiography.* New York: W.W. Norton & Company.

Roche, Rick. 2009. *Real Lives Revealed: A Guide to Reading Interests in Biography.* Santa Barbara, CA: Libraries Unlimited.

Rosenblatt, Louise. 1978. *The Reader, the Text, the Poem: The Transactional Theory of the Literary Work.* Carbondale: Southern Illinois Press.

Ross, Catherine Sheldrick. 2004. "Reading Nonfiction for Pleasure: What Motivates Readers?" In *Nonfiction Readers' Advisory*, 105–20. Edited by Robert Burgin. Westport, CT: Libraries Unlimited.

Shields, David. 2010. *Reality Hunger: A Manifesto.* New York: Alfred A. Knopf.

The Smoking Gun. 2006. "A Million Little Lies: Exposing James Frey's Fiction Addiction." January 4. http://www.thesmokinggun.com/documents/celebrity/million-little-lies?cid=free_tout.

Stoeger, Melissa. 2013. *Food Lit: A Reader's Guide to Epicurean Nonfiction*. Santa Barbara, CA: Libraries Unlimited.

Van Gelder, Lawrence. 2008. "Holocaust Memoir Turns Out to Be Fiction." *New York Times*, March 3. http://www.nytimes.com/2008/03/03/books/03arts-HOLOCAUSTMEM_BRF.html.

Winfrey, Oprah. 2006. "Oprah's Questions for James." Oprah.com, January 26. http://www.oprah.com/oprahshow/Oprahs-Questions-for-James.

Wyatt, Neal. 2007. *The Readers' Advisory Guide to Nonfiction*. Chicago: ALA.

Zellers, Jessica. 2009. *Women's Nonfiction: A Guide to Reading Interests*. Santa Barbara, CA: Libraries Unlimited.

Only the Best

Outsiders might wonder what the fuss was about. So what if kids read Nancy Drew? Why have so many librarians fought to the death against series books and their hated predecessor, dime novels? Growing up, I was a big fan of the Nancy Drew, Hardy Boys, and Trixie Belden series books and could not understand at the time why librarians and teachers hated them so much. The children's library in my city refused to stock them. But my friends and I got these books as presents, traded them, and read them assiduously. Without being exactly sure what Nancy's "traveling suit" or her "blue roadster" might look like, I nevertheless felt these appurtenances were marks of her specialness. Nancy, Frank, and Joe were always on the go—they had roadsters and iceboats and could pilot planes and sail Chinese junks. Evocative words appeared in almost every TITLE, such as *clue, sinister, secret, haunted, sign*, and *mystery.* Nancy Drew and the Hardy Boys provided my first encounter with motifs and plot devices that seemed resonant and compelling: coded messages, letters left in a hollow oak tree, a moss-covered mansion, moldy attics and secret caves, an unclaimed inheritance, a hidden box of treasure, a stolen legacy, and a mistaken identity. This repertory of storytelling devices (see PLOTS) may seem formulaic to jaded adults, but not to the apprentice reader who is reading for the first time about lost gold mines and fresh footprints under the window. The children I knew who were the most committed readers were also the ones who were the biggest readers of series books.

Since this puzzling, early introduction to the politics of reading, I have heard from many avid readers who claim that series books got them started on their lifetime love of reading. Describing reading Enid Blyton, one reader said, "It was my first experience (of many!) of not being able to put a book down! After that I read just about everything by her that I could get my hands on." When my students and I interviewed avid readers (see QUESTIONS ABOUT READING), it turned out that 60 percent of these avid readers had read series books as children. And not just any book written in a series such as Harry Potter, but the bad kind of series specifically denounced by librarians such as Enid Blyton books; Stratemeyer series books including The Bobbsey Twins, Happy Hollisters, Tom Swift, and Nancy Drew; and the more recent series of Sweet Valley High and the horror books of Christopher Pike and R. L. Stine (Ross 1995). Rachel (lawn specialist, age 27) talked about the series book reading experience as shared and repetitive: "My sister Claire and I . . . went through the whole Nancy Drew series, the whole Hardy boys series, over and over again. There's a whole group of books that we kept going through." For Zelda (student, age 25), the idea of series books involved a constellation of bookish activities that included gift-giving, trading, and collecting books as well as reading: "My neighbour and I used to trade Nancy Drew back and forth, try and collect new titles. . . . I read *The Famous Five* and *The Secret Seven*. We all read them. And we all got them at birthday parties." For Daphne (student, age 29), series books were associated with being able to make her own choices: "By the time I was old enough to kind of pick my own books, I really liked those *Baby-sitter* series ones and the horror-y ones by Christopher Pike."

Many avid readers used the language of developmental stages, saying that after reading their first book in a particular series, they would "keep on going" through the others until they outgrew the series. For a while, they would be in a Baby-sitters Club "stage" or an Animorphs "phase" and then they "graduated" or "moved on" to series for older readers. Gitta (student, age 41) said, "I was really into *Animorphs* by K.A. Applegate. And then I got up to some number in the 30s or 40s and lost interest in the series. I think I outgrew it." After reading sometimes dozens in the same series, readers suddenly would find them predictable, even boring, and turn to something less formulaic. But note that until the reader "moves on," this formulaic quality is what makes the series pleasurable for novice readers. S. J. Appleyard in *Becoming a Reader* (1990, 62) speculates that the popularity of series books "seems to have something to do with the combination of sameness and diversity that is common to these books." Each book has novelty—a new puzzle for Nancy Drew, a new technological gadget for Tom Swift, a new horror on Fear Street—but is not *so* different that the reader can't figure out what's going on.

The obvious point about series books is that they provide a predictably pleasurable experience to beginning readers, there are so many of them, and they are cheap enough that kids could buy them on their own and get them as gifts. Young readers like the continuity of reading about characters that they know and consider to be old friends. The key element here is pleasure. Once readers have experienced the entrancement of Nancy Drew, Captain Underpants, Junie B. Jones, or Lemony Snicket's Baudelaire children in *A Series of Unfortunate Events*, they can repeat the pleasurable experience as often as they wish. And they do. Grown-up readers recall with nostalgic fondness the series book reading of their childhoods, and many are now turning to online communities and booksellers to share memories and reacquire long-lost favorites.

So why did children's librarians denounce series books as "pernicious" and as the enemies of genuine reading? It seems to have been a case of a smashup of two forces that were simultaneously gathering momentum during the early decades of the twentieth century: the Stratemeyer Syndicate and the professionalization of children's librarians.

Edward Stratemeyer and the Syndicate

Series book momentum was building as the twentieth century began, with 160 new series launched between 1900 and 1909 and almost 500 additional series started in the following two decades (Johnson 2002, 158). What turned the series book phenomenon into "The Series Book Problem" was the stunning popularity of Edward Stratemeyer, which as early as 1901 had prompted a backlash—the Newark Public Library removed Stratemeyer books from its shelves, along with those of Horatio Alger and Oliver Optic (Rehak 2005, 97). Stratemeyer's background as a dime novelist was probably a red flag for librarians, who had spent the 1880s and 1890s in a failed campaign against dime novels (Hewins 1883). In *Traps for the Young* (1883), Anthony Comstock, a tireless worker in the "suppression of vice," inveighed against "evil reading" (ix) and detected "sure-ruin traps" in "a large variety of half-dime novels, five and ten cent story papers, and low-priced pamphlets for boys and girls" (21). Therefore, librarians were unlikely to be reassured by Stratemeyer's apprenticeship during the 1890s, writing and editing dime novels for the New York publisher Street & Smith.

At Street & Smith, Stratemeyer met such dime novel greats as William T. Adams (Oliver Optic), Horatio Alger Jr., Frederic Van Rensselaer Dey, Edward S. Ellis, and William Gilbert Patten. According to the Hardy Boys ghostwriter Leslie McFarlane (1976, 48), "He learned from the inside. He rid himself of any fancy notions about literature as an art." What he did learn a lot about was how to tell the kinds of exciting stories that turned kids into repeat readers. Stratemeyer made his biggest impact as a book packager and founder of the Stratemeyer Syndicate. According to Deidre Johnson (1993, ix), who has written the definitive book on Stratemeyer and his Syndicate, Stratemeyer series books have sold over 200 million copies. Stratemeyer generated new series for different market segments—boys, girls, young children, and adolescents—and in many different genres—the school story, the family story, travel adventure, the sports story, science fiction, the western, the outdoor and campfire story, and the detective story—and waited for the market to decide. How many titles, series, house names, and writers were there? A staggering number.

Stratemeyer's practice was to devise series concepts, market them to publishers, and recruit ghostwriters to write the books. He was clear about what style he wanted. In a 1904 interview, he declared, "I have no toleration for that which is namby-pamby or wishy-washy in juvenile literature. This is a strenuous age. . . . [The boys and girls] of today are clever and up-to-date" (Johnson 1993, 5). Writers who could produce vigorous, "up-to-date" copy were paid from $75 to $150 for a manuscript (Rehak 2005, 25) or about what a journalist would be paid for two or three weeks of work. Stratemeyer generated a title and brief plot outline, the ghostwriter expanded the outline into a book of some 200 pages, and Stratemeyer edited the manuscript, always having the final say. The book was published under a Syndicate house name such as Arthur M. Winfield (Rover Boys), Laura Lee Hope (Bobbsey Twins), Victor Appleton (Tom Swift), Alice B. Emerson (Ruth Fielding), Roy Rockwood (Bomba the Jungle Boy), Franklin W. Dixon (Hardy Boys), and Carolyn Keene (Nancy Drew). Individual writers could come and go, but the author names beloved by readers stayed with the Syndicate.

At a time when hardcover fiction for children was selling for $1.00 or $1.25 a book, Stratemeyer invented an economic model for children's publishing that did an end-run around cultural gatekeepers. Soderbergh (1974, 866) reports that Stratemeyer was fond of saying, "Any writer who has the young for an audience can snap his fingers at all the other critics." In 1906, he approached publisher Cupples & Leon with a proposal: a set of breeders for a new series, "The Motor Boys," and a plan for selling cloth-covered, hard-bound books directly to kids by lowering the unit price. The profit margin for an individual book would be low, but publishers would make up for it in volume. By the 1930s, series books were selling for 50 cents and were referred to as fifty-cent juveniles or fifty-centers. According to an anonymous *Fortune* magazine reviewer identified by Rehak as Ayers Brinser (1934), Grosset & Dunlap was printing 3 million fifty-centers a year and its major competitors Cupples & Leon and A.L. Burt were printing 1 million apiece. Stratemeyer became known as the Henry Ford of children's publishing: he speeded up production by the use of ghost writers; he achieved uniformity by controlling the story outlines and retaining editorial control; and he kept unit costs low through large production runs and economies of scale.

The thought of this rising tide of cheap books triggered the usual anxieties associated with mass media. First, was the charge that the counterpart to the assembly-line form of production is mass consumption by a mass audience turned into passive dupes and made supine by meretricious pleasure. The designation *fifty-center*, like *dime novel* and *penny dreadful*, became a term of opprobrium used by critics who associated cheap purchase price with cheap content and called it "cheap reading." Indignation over the fifty-center was heightened by the respectable, hardcover binding of the books. Some felt that at least the dime novel was honest: a shoddy product in a shoddy and lurid package. The fifty-center was a wolf in sheep's clothing, an imposter in the fold of children's books, deceiving unwary children and their parents into mistaking series books for genuine literature.

The Professionalization of Children's Librarianship

The Stratemeyer series books were strikingly popular in the early twentieth century, just at the time when children's librarians were establishing themselves as professionals. Children's librarians staked their claim to professional knowledge on the battleground of childhood and children's reading. The child reader was thought to need firm guidance and a strong push toward quality books. Left to their own devices, it was thought, children followed the path of least resistance and embraced the "mediocre." The overwhelming popularity among children of series books was the unwelcome finding of the Winnetka Survey of 1925, directed by Carleton Washburne, superintendent of the Winnetka, Illinois, public schools and sponsored by the American Library Association. The kicker was the big gap between children's own preferences and what reading authorities thought children *should* like. Washburne asked 36,750 students in 34 representative cities, among other things, to fill out "ballots" on all the books they had read during the school year. Almost 100,000 ballots were submitted. It turned out that 98 percent of the pupils reported reading the inexpensive series books known as "fifty-centers," the most often mentioned being Tom Swift. The reading choices of fifth-, sixth-, and seventh-grade readers were dominated by Edward Stratemeyer series books such as the Bobbsey Twins, Tom Swift, and others " 'unanimously rated trashy' *a priori* by a select panel of librarians" (Soderbergh 1974).

Children's librarians embarked on a campaign against the "mediocre," advocating nothing but "the best" for children. The first task was to win recognition for the critical importance of childhood as a formative time. Esther Jane Carrier in *Fiction in Public Libraries, 1876–1900* (1965) quotes generously from the library literature to illustrate debates on the rights of children to public library service and controversies about what kinds of materials children should read. In 1894, the American Library Association declared that children, formerly unwelcome in some public libraries, should be given free access to books in children's rooms staffed by qualified people. Six years later in 1900, the American Library Association founded the group that later became the Library Service to Children Division. A new breed of children's librarian was trained to take up leadership roles in children's rooms that were being established in public libraries across North America. According to Alison Parker (1997, 94), a key move in establishing their authority was to claim that they, not parents, knew best what children should read. In their backlash against series books, children's librarians were galvanized into positive initiatives that made a permanent contribution to children's literacy and reading, among which were Children's Book Week and the Newberry Medal (Jenkins 2000, 112).

Anne Carroll Moore (1920, 23), the first superintendant of the Department of Work with Children at the New York Public Library, did a lot through her regular column of reviews of children's books in *The Bookman* to argue for a rigorous, sustained criticism of children's books that would draw a clear line between "mediocrity, condescension," and "cheap optimism" on the one hand and "the best" on the other hand. In these reviews, many of which were collected in *Roads to Childhood* (1920), *New Roads to Childhood* (1923), and *Cross Roads to Childhood* (1926), Moore (1920, 23) proved herself a tireless enemy of low standards and "the commonplace in theme, treatment and language." Critical of what she calls "the series idea," Moore said, "It is inevitable that it should result in just such a state of arrested development as we find today" (92). In her influential reviews, she demonstrated the distinguishing mark of the new professionalized children's librarian: the ability to discern the best in children's books and identify and promote those few that deserve to be called literature. Moore's vision was carried on by her apprentice, the Canadian librarian, Lillian H. Smith. In the often-reprinted *The Unreluctant Years* (1953), Smith argues that the same high standards of good writing and literary excellence used to judge adult literature should be used in the evaluation and selection of children's literature. For librarians, the key in doing collection development is to recognize the very best. Smith warns against "time-fillers," "written-to-formula books," and "encroaching mediocrity," all of which need to be distinguished from "books of genuine quality" (189–90).

From the 1910s onward, librarians led the charge against series books, which were seen as the enemy of the best. Kathleen Chamberlain (2002) has provided a balanced summary of the scorn directed toward series books. Series books were denounced for their lack of realism, their tendency to instill false views of life, and their assembly-line methods of production (see ROMANCE FICTION for similar complaints). The newly emerging profession of children's librarianship defined itself by what it was not. It was *not* a friend of series books, trash, or mediocrity. This point is made repeatedly in the titles of articles in the library literature: Franklin K. Mathiews's "Blowing Out the Boy's Brains" (1914), Irene Bowman's "Why the American Library Association Does Not Endorse Serials for Boys and Girls" (1921), Mary E. S. Root's "Not to Be Circulated" (1929), Lucy Kinlock's "The Menace of the Series Books" (1935), Margaret Beckman's "Why Not the Bobbsey Twins" (1964), Lou Willett Stanek's "Stunting Readers' Growth" (1986), and Judith Saltman's "Groaning under the Weight of Series Books" (1997). Given the impulsiveness of the child reader and the "deluge" of series books, Saltman (1997, 25) concludes that "now, more than ever," knowledgeable and informed experts are needed to help children grow from "mediocre reading . . . to more challenging and exhilarating literary experiences."

Smith's *The Unreluctant Years* and other similar guides consolidated two opposed repertoires of vocabulary and concepts for use in discussing children's books. On the one hand, there is the repertoire of "the best"—here one speaks of "books of honesty, integrity and vision" (Smith 1953, 13) that provide genuine pleasure, insight, and growth because they embody permanent and universal values. On the other hand, there is the repertoire of "mediocrity"—here one speaks of inauthentically written, ephemeral, commodified books that lack all the positive qualities of the best and provide only meretricious pleasure, distraction, and stultification. A good example of the deployment of this repertoire can be found in an article by Margaret Beckman (1964), "Why Not the Bobbsey Twins?" reprinted in 1970: "[W]e should select the *best* when we can't buy all"; it's a crime for a child to waste the "few precious years" of childhood in reading inferior work when "there are so many wonderful books to be read he will never have time to read them all"; reading the Bobbsey Twins has a baleful effect "on youthful minds," which if limited to "mind-stultifying series books" will "follow the path of least resistance" and without mental stimulation will fail to develop sufficiently ever to be able to read anything else. "If we feel that public funds can be spent on the mediocre rather than on books of lasting value ... then the Bobbsey Twins and Nancy Drew *don't* matter." But if we believe "that reading is vital, we will remember that a child wants only the best until we, as adults, teach him to accept mediocrity."

Librarians' century-long campaign against series books failed because it overlooked the experience of the child reader. The rhetoric of "the best" is a text-centered approach to reading that assumes that books in themselves can be ordered on a single, universal scale of literary value. "The best" leaves no room for the contingencies of what may be best for an apprentice reader. Series books provide the security of a contract with readers. They make a promise about what kind of reading experience to expect: exciting, pleasurable, and easy enough to be successful. Predictability bores practiced readers, but it provides a scaffold for novices that helps them get into the story. And in the course of reading dozens, sometimes hundreds, of series books, readers are given lessons in reading. They are taught by the books themselves how to distinguish good guys from bad guys, how to size up the significance of events, and how to know that apparently unrelated plot lines will eventually come together if you just keep reading (Ross 1995). In an excellent discussion of the Baby-sitters Club and its role in supporting literacy, Margaret Mackey (1990) argues that children make "valuable reading discoveries, almost without noticing"—reading for the story but learning about "the value of practice in prediction, extrapolation, and pattern-making."

Case studies confirm the role of series books in helping struggling readers: for example, Wickstrom and colleagues (2005) describe how Ashley, a special needs child, made her first genuine connection with books through listening to Barbara Park's *Junie B. Jones and Her Big Fat Mouth* (1993) followed by others in the series about the rambunctious kindergartner. Ashley memorized recurrent lines or patterns from the books, she connected with the character of Junie B., and eventually she was able to read on her own the books that had been read to her. Librarians and literacy specialists are now paying more attention to the reader and to the context of reading and are more likely to consider "the best for whom" and "the best for when." Here's Robert (English Professor, age 57) on the rhetoric of "the best":

> They don't know what is best from the perspective of the child. They remember what they think they thought was the best. We all see our past reading through one change after another. And how clearly we see it, who knows? Every time we reread a book, we're creating another work, so that the *Gulliver Travels* you read in second year university is not the same *Gulliver* you would read now. What the child may really need may be literature that is a waste of time from an adult point of view. It may give the child relief from adults for one thing.

References

Appleyard, J. A. 1990. *Becoming a Reader: The Experience of Fiction from Childhood to Adulthood*. Cambridge and New York: Cambridge University Press.

Beckman, Margaret. 1964. "Why Not the Bobbsey Twins?" *Library Journal* 89, no. 20: 4612–13, 4627.

Bowman, Irene K. 1921. "Why the American Library Association Does Not Endorse Serials for Boys and Girls." *Iowa Library Quarterly* 9: 212.

Brinser, Ayers. 1934. "For It Was Indeed He." *Fortune* (April): 86–90.

Carrier, Esther Jane. 1965. *Fiction in Public Libraries, 1876–1900*. New York and London: The Scarecrow Press.

Chamberlain, Kathleen. 2002. " 'Wise Censorship': Cultural Authority and the Scorning of Juvenile Series Books, 1890–1940." In *Scorned Literature: Essays on the History and Criticism of Popular Mass-Produced Fiction in America*, 187–211. Edited by Lydia Cushman Schurman and Deidre Johnson. Westport, CT: Greenwood Press.

Comstock, Anthony. 1883. *Traps for the Young*, 3rd ed. New York: Funk & Wagnalls Company.

Hewins, Carolyn M. 1883. "Dime Novel Work." *Library Journal* 8: 57.

Jenkins, Christine A. 2000. "The History of Youth Services Librarianship: A Review of the Research Literature." *Libraries & Culture* 35, no. 1 (Winter): 103–40. http://people.lis.illinois.edu/~cajenkin/papers/researchreview.pdf.

Johnson, Deidre. 1993. *Edward Stratemeyer and the Stratemeyer Syndicate*. New York: Twayne.

Johnson, Deidre. 2002. "From Abbott to Animorphs, from Godly Books to Goosebumps: The Nineteenth-Century Origins of Modern Stories." In *Scorned Literature: Essays on the History and Criticism of Popular Mass-Produced Fiction in America*, 147–65. Edited by Lydia Cushman Schurman and Deidre Johnson. Westport, CT: Greenwood Press.

Kinlock, Lucy M. 1935. "The Menace of the Series Books." *Elementary English Review* 12 (January): 9–11.

Mackey, Margaret. 1990. "Filling the Gaps: 'The Baby-sitters Club,' the Series Book, and the Learning Reader." *Language Arts* 67, no. 5 (September): 484–89.

Mathiews, Franklin K. 1914. "Blowing Out the Boy's Brains." *Outlook*, November 18: 653.

McFarlane, Leslie. 1976. *Ghost of the Hardy Boys: An Autobiography by Leslie McFarlane*. Toronto & New York: Methuen/Two Continents.

Moore, Anne Carroll. 1920. *My Roads to Childhood: Views and Reviews of Children's Books*. Boston: The Horn Book.

Parker, Alison Marie. 1997. *Purifying America: Women, Cultural Reform, and Pro-Censorship Activism, 1873–1933*. Urbana: University of Illinois.

Rehak, Melanie. 2005. *Nancy Drew and the Women Who Created Her*. New York: Harcourt, Inc.

Root, Mary E. S. 1929. "Not to Be Circulated." *Wilson Bulletin* 3, no. 17: 446.

Ross, Catherine Sheldrick. 1995. "If They Read Nancy Drew, So What? Series Book Readers Talk Back." *Library and Information Science Research* 17, no. 3: 201–36.

Saltman, Judith. 1997. "Groaning under the Weight of Series Books." *Emergency Librarian* 24, no. 5 (May–June): 23–25.

Smith, Lillian H. 1953. *The Unreluctant Years: A Critical Approach to Children's Literature*. New York: Penguin.

Soderbergh, Peter A. 1974. "The Stratemeyer Strain: Educators and the Juvenile Series Book, 1900–1973." *Journal of Popular Culture* 7, no. 4: 864–72.

Stanek, Lou Willett. 1986. "Stunting Readers' Growth." *School Library Journal* 33, no. 3: 46–47.

Wickstrom, Carol D., et al. 2005. "Ashley and Junie B. Jones: A Struggling Reader Makes a Connection to Literacy." *Language Arts* 83, 1 (September): 16–21.

Plots

Many readers chose books on the basis of the plot—they are looking, they say, for a good story. Or they are looking for one particular story, the retelling of which never grows stale because it speaks to a particular desire in the reader to hear that special story again and again. Storyline is one of the four "appeal elements" that Joyce Saricks (2005, 40–41) has identified in her discussion of factors that contribute to the particular "feel" or experience of a book (see X-EXTRAORDINARY READERS). For Nancy Pearl (2012), plot or story is one of the four "gateways" or "doorways" to reading, the others being character, setting, and language. When Saricks and Pearl talk about plot, they consider it in relation to readers: what elements make the most difference to particular readers when they are look for "a good book to read"? In contrast, a lot of scholarly work has studied plot as a formal element in composition rather than the relation of plot to readers' experience. From Stith Thomson's *Motif Index of Folk Literature* (1955–1958) to Christopher Booker's *The Basic Seven Plots* (2004), the thrust has been to identify and classify the various kinds of plots and plot elements or motifs. This approach is not reader-centered, but it can be helpful to readers. When readers reflect on the typical ways in which stories get told, they tend to gain an understanding of the kinds of stories that they themselves enjoy and why they like them.

How Many Plots Are There?

How many can you think of? OK, there's the heroine who marries a tramp on a dare, but it turns out he is really a duke in disguise (ROMANCE). There's the frontiersman who becomes a relentless Indian killer after his cabin is burned and his family massacred (WESTERNS). There is the story of threatened psychological or physical absorption in which one person is consumed by another (VAMPIRES). There is the young hero and his band of loyal comrades who go on a quest to find a precious object or defeat a fearsome enemy (fantasy). There is the secret organization that is hatching a conspiracy to gain world domination (thrillers). There is the kidnapped woman/child/king who must be rescued against the odds from pirates/Indians/usurpers. There is the ragged orphan who escapes poverty and hardship through luck and a deserving nature (RAGS TO RICHES). And so on.

But how many different plots are there? Some say 36, some say 1,462, and some, like Booker (2004), say 7. It all depends on what you count and on what principle you use to find common patterns. In 1894, the French critic Georges Polti claimed that all possible stories are just variations on 36 basic plots. In the eighteenth century, the Venetian playwright Carlo Gozzi, author of *Turandot*, had claimed that there were only 36 "dramatic situations." Gozzi remained vexingly silent on what these plots might be, but Polti took up the challenge. In *The Thirty-six Dramatic Situations*, he ransacked literature from classical Greek theatre onward to find the 1,200 examples that he used to illustrate his 36 categories. Fortunately, this book has been translated, reprinted (Polti 1921), and made available free online. Here are some of the categories Polti used:

2   Deliverance. Elements: an Unfortunate, a Threatener, a Rescuer.

3   Crime Pursued by Vengeance. Elements: An Avenger and a Criminal. (This category includes Professional Pursuit of Criminals.)

6   Disaster. Elements: A Vanquished Power; a Victorious Enemy or a Messenger. (This category also includes natural disasters.)

9   Daring Enterprise. Elements: A Bold Leader; an Object; an Adversary. (This category includes Adventurous Expeditions.)

10   Abduction (Elements: The Abductor; the Abducted; the Guardian)

11   The Enigma. Elements: Interrogator, Seeker and Problem. (In this category, Polti includes "*Turandot* of the incomparable Gozzi.")

22   All Sacrificed for a Passion. Elements: The Lover; the Object of the Fatal Passion; the Person or Thing Sacrificed.

25   Adultery. Elements: A Deceived Husband or Wife; Two Adulterers.

26   Obstacles to Love. Elements: Two Lovers; an Obstacle.

35   Recovery of a Lost One. Elements: The Seeker; the One Found.

Each situation allows for multiple variations. For example, in category 3, "Crime Pursued by Vengeance," the avenger could be a child, parent, husband, wife, friend, sibling, or detective. The crime could be a seduction, rape, death, attempted slaying, intentional injury, robbery, false accusation, or deception. Hence, category 3 is expansive enough to include *The Tempest, The Count of*

Monte Cristo, and the Sherlock Holmes stories, not to mention all those Indian-hater westerns that Polti didn't know about (see Jones 1978, 27–34).

The Fiction Factory

With the insatiable demand for new stories by the dime novel and series book industries (see ONLY THE BEST), authors needed to write quickly and come up with new plots. Pulp writer William Wallace Cook came to the rescue with *Plotto*, which was described by the *Singapore Free Press and Mercantile Advertiser* (October 19, 1928) under the dramatic, if inaccurate, headline, "Last Word in Robots. Makes Novels to Measure. Plots While You Wait." By the time Cook produced *Plotto*, he had worked in the trenches some 40 years, turning out as many as 50 stories a year for the 5- and 10-cent libraries. He wrote fast. In his autobiographical *The Fiction Factory* (1912, 54), he reports that he has "begun a Five Cent Library story at 7 o'clock in the morning and worked the clock around, completing the manuscript at 7 the next morning." Cook quotes with approval Jack London, who advises authors "not to wait for inspiration but to 'go after it with a club' " (52).

What Cook learned about plots by writing westerns, detective stories, love stories, and sea stories he systematized in his 1928 manual *Plotto: The Master Book of All Plots*. Paul Collins, who wrote the introduction to the Tin House 2011 reissue of *Plotto*, describes how the manual was unveiled "at the Plotto Studio of Authorship at 1658 Broadway in New York" and announced as "an invention which reduces literature to an exact science." Unlike those writers who depend entirely on the "divine afflatus," Cook ([1928] 2011, 5) recommends combining inspiration with a "hard, consistent, carefully calculated effort." The result of the systematic approach, he says, is a "carefully developed plot as framework" for the story. Getting the armature right is only the first step: writers still need to enliven the plot with specific details and incidents drawn from personal experience and newspaper headlines.

Using a fiendishly complicated classification scheme and system of symbols involving letters, numbers, dashes, and asterisks, Cook provided a coded system that he claimed could generate millions of different stories. (So complicated is his system, in fact, that Cook (1934) was obliged to write a supplementary 32-page instruction book, now available online.) Fortunately, Cook's core concept is clear enough. *Plotto* is a plot generator that works by ringing the changes on three different elements called *clauses*: (A) the protagonist, (B) the conflict situation, and (C) the resolution. A simple master plot consists of one A, one B, and one C clause. Here's an example offered by Cook ([1928] 2011, 6):

A11   A Person Swayed by Pretense.

B11   Assuming a fictitious character when embarking upon a certain enterprise.

C2   Emerges happily from a serious entanglement.

Compound plots should be attempted, we are warned, only by the most "advanced plottist." Beginners should content themselves with picking one of the 15 protagonist types, one of the 62 conflict situations, and one of the 15 resolutions. For the protagonist, you can chose among such types as Person in Love, Married Person, Lawless Person, Erring Person, Benevolent Person, Protecting Person, Person of Ideals, Person Swayed by Pretense, Resentful Person, and even Person Influenced by the Occult and the Mysterious. The B clauses, which initiate the action, each specify a conflict situation that involves a purpose and an obstacle. Here are some examples of B clauses:

1   Engaging in a difficult enterprise when promised a reward for high achievement.

8   Confronting a situation in which wealth is conditional upon a certain course of action in a love affair.

12   Falling into misfortune through disloyalty in love.

13   Seeking by craftiness to escape misfortune.

15   Finding a sustaining power in misfortune.

19   Meeting with misfortune and being cast away in a primitive, isolated and savage environment.

26   Seeking secretly to preserve another from danger.

29   Aiding another to hide from the world a fateful secret.

56   Seeking to test the value of a mysterious communication and becoming. involved in weird complexities.

58   Engaging in an enterprise and then mysteriously disappearing.

Finally, for the ending or resolution that terminates the action, here are some options to choose from:

1   Pays a grim penalty in an unfortunate undertaking.

2   Emerges happily from a serious entanglement.

3   Foils a guilty plotter and defeats a subtle plot.

4   Undertakes a role that leads straight to catastrophe.

5   Emerges from a trying ordeal with sorely garnered wisdom.

6   Makes the supreme sacrifice in carrying out an undertaking.

7   Reverses certain opinions when their fallacy is revealed.

8   Achieves a spiritual victory.

13   Comes finally to the blank wall of enigma.

14   Achieves a complete and permanent character transformation.

With these three sets of "interchangeable clauses" as starting points, Cook provided 1,462 plots. And each plot is cross-referenced with other plots that combine well with it to dramatically increase into the millions the number of combinations possible. Yikes! Michelle Legro (2012) observes, "Crack open the book at any page and you'll find conflicts you never knew existed, between character A and character B, whose individual quirks manage to shine through." Here are examples, some of which sound familiar (e.g., 9—any number of western romances; 101—any number of Regency romances; 639—O Henry's "The Ransom of Red Chief"):

9. B's [female protagonist's] cattle ranch was left to her by her father, and every man B hires as foreman makes love to her sooner or later, and is discharged. B hires A as a foreman on her ranch, and he promises to keep his place and not to make love to her, but B falls in love with him, and is presently glad to learn that A's sole purpose in taking the job of foreman was to win her love.

101. A [male protagonist] is so besieged by match-making mammas that their meddling seriously interferes with the practice of his profession. He resolves to escape the annoyance by a stratagem.

227. B is unable to marry A because her father, F-B, in using B for his subject in a scientific experiment, has instilled a poison into her blood.

639. A, abducted by A-5 [male criminal] and held for ransom, is a meddlesome, disagreeable person and his family and friends are glad to be rid of him and will not pay the ransom. ** A, abducted by A-5 and held for ransom, makes A-5's life so miserable that he pays a round sum to have A taken off his hands.

1210. A, wealthy miser, told by his doctor that he has only three months to live, decides to spend all his money before he dies so none will be left for his heirs.

1426. A, engaged in a hazardous search for A-4 [male stranger], finds himself in a strange lost community that has no direct communication with the outside world.

Reviewing *Plotto* on Goodreads (July 31, 2012), Sarah says, "*I love this book!* It breaks down writing stories into a formula. A little from here, a little from there, and voila! I can't wait to get writing! Also fascinating to read because I recognize many books and film plot lines."

Boiling It All Down to Seven Stories—or One

If identifying 1,462 plots seems to be bordering on the obsessive, check out Christopher Booker who boils it all back down again into seven basic plots. Booker is an avid and wide-ranging reader, not a fiction writer. He reports that, after immersing himself in stories of all kinds, he made a "startling discovery ... that there were a number of basic themes or plots which continually recurred in the storytelling of mankind, shaping tales of very different types and from almost every age and culture" (2004, 5). Moreover, the details that make up any given plot remain the same, whether an ancient Greek epic, a Middle Eastern folk tale, a nineteenth-century novel, or a modern children's story. There are certain typical ways that stories get told, according to Booker, and here they are:

> *Overcoming the Monster.* A deadly embodiment of evil power threatens destruction to a court, society, or the entire world. A hero, armed with special weapons, tracks the monster to its cave or mere and, after a tremendous struggle, slays the monster and gets the monster's gold hoard. This is the story of Beowulf defeating Grendel's mother, St. George killing the dragon, Jonathan Harker killing Dracula, and the Magnificent Seven defeating the thugs who are terrorizing a Mexican farming village. In displaced versions that are more realistic, the "monster" may be a human being, but remnants of the folk-tale dragon remain in the description of the evil force as "reptilian."

> *Rags to Riches.* An orphan, who has been abused and treated as of no account, emerges from obscurity, at which point everyone recognizes how truly exceptional he or she really is. This is the plain secretary who, taking off her glasses and unpinning her bun, is recognized as the radiant beauty she has been all along (see RAGS TO RICHES).

> *The Quest.* Far away, there is "some priceless goal, worth any effort to achieve: a treasure; a promised land; something of infinite value" (Booker 2004, 69). We can see this pattern in the story of the hero and his companions who set off on a perilous journey through a waste land in, for example, *The Odyssey, Watership Down,* or *The Lord of the Rings* in which the priceless goal is to return home, to find a new home, or to defeat dark forces and redeem society.

> *Voyage and Return.* A hero, heroine, or a group of characters leave behind the familiar, everyday world for a strange world completely cut off from the first. The second world may at first seem marvelous and exciting, but eventually it becomes menacing and frightening. Then, by a lucky turn, the central characters escape and

arrive safely home. In this group of stories, we can include *Goldilocks and the Three Bears*, *Alice in Wonderland*, C. S. Lewis's *The Lion the Witch and the Wardrobe*, Jules Verne's *Journey to the Centre of the Earth*, and Maurice Sendak's *Where the Wild Things Are*.

Comedy. All starts in confusion and conflict, with everything in a tangle, with the real identities of some characters disguised, and with lovers separated by blocking figures. Then, in a turn called the *recognition*, disguises are thrown off, identities are revealed, and bad hats either "come to themselves" by being redeemed or are universally recognized as bad hats. A newly regenerated society is ushered in by declarations of love and wedding bells. Notable examples include the Shakespearean comedies, *The Marriage of Figaro*, Fielding's *Tom Jones*, the novels of Jane Austen and their imitators, *Crocodile Dundee*, and, in parody form, Oscar Wilde's *The Importance of Being Ernest*.

Tragedy. All starts out fine, with the central character successful and prosperous but dissatisfied. Tempted by ambition or some other flaw, the hero allows his nature to be taken over by the dark side of himself. He prospers initially but becomes increasingly isolated until the story ends in destruction and death. Notable examples include the Shakespearean tragedies, Marlowe's *Dr. Faustus*, *Don Giovanni*, and Tolstoy's *Anna Karenina*.

Rebirth. A hero or heroine "fall under a dark spell which eventually traps them in some wintry state, akin to living death: physical or spiritual imprisonment, sleep, sickness or some other form of enchantment" (Booker 2004, 194). After a long period of dark, icy imprisonment, a sunny hero wakes up the imprisoned one and brings new life to the whole castle, community, or kingdom. In Sleeping Beauty, the princess awakened by the kiss of the solar prince, but there are also male versions such as the Frog Prince, Dickens's *A Christmas Carol*, and George Eliot's *Silas Marner* in which an imprisoned male figure is reborn to new life through the power of love.

Booker's seventh plot type, Rebirth, hews very closely to a solar myth in which the world is imprisoned in the icy grip of winter until a solar prince breaks through the imprisoning thorns, melts the ice, and wakes up both the heroine and her society to the rebirth of spring. It's not much of a step to claim that all these stories are episodes in one great unifying story of the battle of darkness and light, having connections to the yearly cycle of the sun. Booker in fact does exactly that. In seeing these seven plots as different periods in one great cyclic story, Booker is following the English poet and novelist, Robert Graves, who claimed that there is one story only and wrote a book about it, *The White Goddess* (1947). In a poem written for his son Juan on the shortest day of the year when the sun is in retreat, Graves begins:

> There is one story and one story only
> That will prove worth your telling,
> Whether as learned bard or gifted child;
> To it all lines or lesser gauds belong
> That startle with their shining
> Such common stories as they stray into.
>
> ("To Juan at the Winter Solstice")

All true poetry, Graves says, is inspired by the "white goddess," the triple-faced moon goddess who governs birth, love, and death. The only story worth telling is about the relation of the male hero to a female figure associated with the moon. Sometimes she appears as a maiden, sometimes as a wife, sometimes as an old hag, and sometimes as a siren or witch who lures men to their doom. As Northrop Frye (1963, 20) explains in *The Educated Imagination*:

> By saying it's the only story worth telling in literature, Graves means that the great types of stories, such as comedies and tragedies, start out as episodes from it. Comedies derive from the phase in which god and goddess are happy wedded lovers; tragedies from the phase in which the lover is cast off and killed while the white goddess renews her youth and waits for another round of victims.

References

Anon. 1928. "Last Word in Robots." *Singapore Free Press and Mercantile Advertiser*, October 19. http://newspapers.nl.sg/Digitised/Article/singfreepressb19281019-1.2.87.aspx.

Booker, Christopher. 2004. *The Seven Basic Plots: Why We Tell Stories*. London and New York: Continuum.

Cook, William Wallace. 1912. *The Fiction Factory*. Ridgewood, NJ: The Editor Company. https://archive.org/details/fictionfactoryb00compgoog.

Cook, William Wallace. (1928) 2011. *Plotto: The Master Book of All Plots*. Reprint, Portland, OR: Tin House Books.

Cook, William Wallace. 1934. *Instruction Book*. New York: Writer's Digest. http://www.plamondon.com/plotto_instruction_book.pdf.

Frye, Northrop. 1963. *The Educated Imagination*. Toronto: CBC Enterprises.

Graves, Robert. 1947. *The White Goddess: A Historical Grammar of Poetic Myth.* London: Faber and Faber.

Jones, Daryl. 1978. *The Dime Novel Western.* Bowling Green, OH: Popular Press, Bowling Green State University.

Legro, Michelle. 2012. "Plotto: The Master Book of All Plots." *Brainpickings* (blog), January 6, 2012. http://www.brainpickings.org/index.php/2012/01/06/plotto/.

Pearl, Nancy. 2012. "Check It Out with Nancy Pearl: Finding That Next Good Book." *Publishers Weekly*, March 16. http://publishersweekly.com/pw/by-topic/columns-and-blogs/nancy-pearl/article/51109-check-it-out-with-nancy-pearl-finding-that-next-good-book.html.

Polti, Georges. 1921. *The Thirty-Six Dramatic Situations.* Translated by Lucille Ray. Boston: The Writer, Inc. http://archive.org/details/thirtysixdramati00polt.

Saricks, Joyce G. 2005. *Readers' Advisory Service in the Public Library*, 3rd ed., 40–41. Chicago and London: American Library Association.

Thomson, Stith. 1955–1958. *Motif Index of Folk Literature: A Classification of Narrative Elements in Folktales, Ballads, Myths, Fables, Medieval Romances, Exempla, Fabliaux, Jest-Books, and Local Legends*, 6 vols. Bloomington: Indiana University Press.

Questions about Reading

To start first with some answers, here are statements that avid readers have made about their pleasure-reading experience in the course of open-ended, conversational interviews on the reading experience. To qualify to be interviewed, these readers had to identify themselves as keen pleasure readers, people who read a lot and read by choice. I now have 302 interviews with avid readers that explore such themes as these: What fostered (or hindered) reading in childhood? How do avid readers choose a book to read? What particular elements in a book make the reading experience rewarding for a particular reader? How important is the book as a physical object to be handled, shelved, and passed on to others? I interviewed 26 of the readers, and the rest were interviewed by Masters of Library and Information Science students in successive offerings of my course on genres of fiction and reading at the University of Western Ontario. Here are some of the ways in which avid readers have described their experience of reading.

- *Nathan on a wonderful children's librarian and the empire of texts*

  My first experience with books was in the library, when I was three or four years old. There was a librarian there called Miss Lovehart, who *read* every Saturday at this library. She read in the part of the library, which was basically a turret. A whole group of children would sit around her and she would read these marvelous books. And the first experience of books was oral, but it was more than that—it was *textual*. I remember her turning the pages, I remember the delicious feeling, the sound of the book, the smell of the book. It was a wholly tactile experience. Miss Lovehart created this whole empire, this atmosphere of books. (English professor, age 50) (see E-READING)

- *Jean on the centrality of reading in her life*

  I hate to say that reading is everything, but I think sometimes it's more important than people, and that scares me. It is—it's everything. If I don't have a book, I'm bare. If I have three or four at one time, that's all the better. I remember when I was in school in a guidance class and one of the girls said to the guidance teacher, "I want to become an artist, and my parents won't let me draw. What do I do?" And the teacher said, "If you are going to be an artist, you *will* draw. Nobody can stop you from drawing." And that's what it's like being a reader. If you're going to be a reader, nobody can stop you. You are going to be that. That's what reading is to me. I just am. It's part of me. (teacher–librarian, age 44)

- *Sally on reading as a way of demonstrating competence and mastery*

  I had a really desperately unhappy childhood and adolescence and, when I got to be in my teens, books became a place for me to go. They also became a way of establishing a certain self-esteem that I wouldn't have had otherwise. I could read, so I couldn't really be all that stupid. I read big thick books so I must be really, essentially, a smart person. (library assistant, age 40)

- *Elizabeth on choosing a book to read*

  Normally I browse through library shelves, usually looking for books by authors I already knew and expanding from that. My eye might fall on a book that had an interesting title or cover. I would read the brief account on the cover, and then I would leaf through it and read the ending. That, by the way, is why thrillers had to be well written, because I wasn't reading them for the surprise. If the ending looked safe enough, then I would probably read the book. [Ross: What do you mean by "safe"?] Well, after I had read *The Mill on the Floss* at the age of ten, I automatically rejected any book in which anybody died on the last two pages. It traumatized me. And I don't like suspense books much. I don't like what they do to me. And when I had to read *The Turn of the Screw* for a university course, I read it from the back page to the front page, page by page, and it was hard enough reading it that way. (PhD candidate in English, age 35) (see BEFORE READING)

- *Angus on living in a chosen world*

  Reading is an experience of travel. I can go to the world of a book and I can live in that world. I can come to know the people who lived in that world and I can insert myself into the life of that world and think of how I would react to it. And so, yes, I do travel when

I read. And quite often coming to the end of a book is very jarring, sometimes a heart-rending experience, because I have to come back again. And it's not because I don't like this world particularly. It's not pure escapism. It's like going someplace you really enjoy, and eventually you have to leave, and being quite upset because you've found so many things to enjoy or to move you in that world. Quite regularly when I read, I am very sad when I come to the end. Not because people die, although that saddens me, but because I have to go leave that world behind. But I find another one. (graduate student, age 26)

- *Regna on formats*

  I like them all because they all have different purposes. I like hard cover. I like it for collecting's sake—all my *Harry Potters* are hard covers, and I like to hear the crack of the spine when you open it. And they just last longer, which is nice. Paperbacks are definitely my favorites, just because they fit in my bag. Audiobooks I can see for long drives, or if your eyes are too tired to read, or if you want to listen to *Harry Potter* and get all those little things you never noticed before. eBooks I like, but it's not for me. I like having a collection. I like having a different book in my bag every week. I like appreciating the physical design and typesetting of the book. But I do like them for the people who read tons and tons of mass market paperbacks, and they just can't have that many physical books. Or for travelling. And then there is the anonymity and storage that are advantages of eBooks. (proof-reader, age 29) (see E-READING)

- *Hunter on the bookshelf as home*

  When I see people's bookshelves I don't assume they're reading them. That's why we separate reading out from a constellation of actions and attitudes around books. Reading books is just one thing to do with them. I love the sight of a bookshelf and just the flights of fancy that the sight of a book can raise. I've got 13 boxes of books. It's the only thing of any substance that I own. Every time I move, I spend hundreds of dollars shipping them. My bookshelf is definitely home. Books do a lot of things and there are a lot of acts and concepts and values associated with them. I think that they're a particularly convenient intersection of material possession and of flights of fancy, of comfort, and of intellectual stimulation, and of self-indulgent "me" time. Maybe you can find other things in life that make a home a home. But I just find something about books that is a particularly convenient and pleasurable way to meet all those needs. (student, age 27)

So who are these avid readers? The interviewers were instructed to pick the most readerly person they knew. These were individuals who, when asked, "What would it be like for you if you *couldn't* read?" did *not* say, "Oh well, I guess I would have to take up knitting or play more card games or more golf." They said things like "Oh, my God. That would be terrible. It would be like not being able to see color; I wouldn't be the person I am if I didn't read." Or, "I can't imagine a life without reading. I guess I would learn Braille." Laurie (student, age 34) was aghast at the thought of not reading: "Oh God! That would be awful. That would be really, really bad. That would be worse then not being able to have sex! I can't imagine what I'd do. I'd go crazy."

The demographic profile of these 302 interviewees matches the profile of so-called heavy readers that survey research has repeatedly uncovered: more likely to be female than male and more likely to have attained higher levels of education. Of the 302 interviewees, two-thirds (199) were female and one-third (103) were male. The age range was 16 to 84 with the following distribution: 47 percent (141) were between the ages of 16 and 29, 31 percent were between 30 and 50, and 22 percent were between 51 and 84. Clearly, these interviewees differ significantly from what we would get from a random sample of the population at large. And the main way they differ is in their passion for books. These are the kinds of people who disproportionately buy books, borrow books, give books as gifts, read books, collect books, talk about books, join bookclubs, listen to audiobooks, and write about books in blogs, journals, and diaries.

A large majority said that their love of books and reading began in childhood. They talked about bedtime stories, favorite childhood books, personal collections preserved into adulthood, trips to the bookstore or library, and parents who modeled the love of reading. But not everybody. When asked if his parents encouraged him in reading, Clarence (self-employed, age 60) said: "Actually not. My parents were not big readers at all. I'm not even sure my dad has ever read a book. . . . I really don't recall my mother reading a book. She didn't have time anyway with six kids." Shirley Brice Heath, a notable ethnographer of childhood reading, acknowledges the common story of a middle-class childhood rich in books but tells her own counter story out of "a sense of difference." Recalling her own fragmented childhood, raised in rural Virginia by a grandmother who could not really read and whose only book was the Bible, Heath (2011, 33) argues that the trajectories that can bring someone to reading are "divergent and multiple." It is important to hear these multiple and divergent stories from the readers themselves.

Questions for Avid Readers

The interviewees were instructed to use a schedule of questions, but use it flexibly, pursuing themes that were important and salient to the reader. The interviews all began with a question about the reader's earliest memory, either of reading or of being read to. Differences among the interviewees emerged right at the first question. Some said that they couldn't remember much at all about childhood reading and had not really read for pleasure until high school or university or later. The majority, however, launched into stories of family reading, bedtime stories, favorite childhood books, books as gifts, trips to the library, and sometimes having independently learned to read before going to school. After that first question established a starting point, interviewers asked nondirective questions such as "What did you read next?" or "Was there any change in your reading?" Interviewers were all aware of the desirability of asking questions that invite an open-ended response ("Do you have favorite genres?") rather than closed questions ("Did you read series books as a child?" "Do you like cyberpunk?"). They progressed through the interviewee's reading history using open questions ("What can you remember after that?"), probes ("What do you mean when you say 'a safe book'?"), encouragers ("Yes, that's interesting"), and paraphrasings ("So you found *The Mill on the Floss* traumatic").

In preparation for conducting the interviews, we had classroom discussions about the various skills involved in conducting an interview when the goal is to understand the reading experience from the reader's perspective. I had learned the hard way what happens if you start with your own categories and try to get interviewees to fit their experience into your categories. In the very first reading interview I conducted (the one that got me started on this long project), I asked Elizabeth, "What about thrillers? Do you enjoy those?" She said, "I'm not quite sure what a thriller is, as compared with a murder mystery." Oh well, I said and launched into my definition: "In a murder mystery, you have the appeal of clues and solving a puzzle, whereas in a thriller you have a high-octane story in which every twist and turn puts the main character in high danger." The rest of the interview showed that I had taught her to use my vocabulary successfully, when I should have been finding out what terms she normally would use. With this horrible example before them, interviewers were encouraged to let the readers supply the terms for the book and categories of books they read. Interviewers then asked the readers to define what they meant by the particular terms they had used—*fluff books, wifty elves, important books, new weird.*

As you look at the questions that the interviewers asked, you might want to think about your own reading experience. What kind of a reader are you? Have you thought of yourself as a reader from earliest childhood, or did you get turned on later to the pleasures of reading? Do you read voraciously and indiscriminately, or are you very selective (see IMPORTANT BOOKS VERSUS INDISCRIMINATE READING)? Do you often reread books, or do you think that there are so many wonderful books out that you can't afford to read any book more than once? Are you a reader who enjoys a fast-paced page-turner with plot twists, or are you more attracted to books with strongly developed characters? Do you read eBooks or listen to audio books, and, if so, how does that experience compare for you with reading a physical book? Here are the questions that avid readers were asked. How would you answer them?

- What is the first book that you can remember either having read to you as a child or reading yourself?

  Secondary questions for each question are probes, as appropriate, such as:

  - What can you remember about it?
  - Can you think of an example?
  - Was there anything special about it?
  - Can you explain what you mean by X?

- What do you remember reading next? Next? After that?

- Was there anything in your childhood experience that you would say fostered reading? Discouraged reading?

- When you were a child, did you think of yourself as a reader? [probe: if not, then when did you start to think of yourself as reader? what made the difference?]

- How, if at all, did your reading interests change as you reached adolescence?

- What are you currently reading?

- What would the pattern of your reading be like in a typical week? [probe: how much?]

- How do you choose a book to read?

- Where do you get the books that you read?

- Do you have different categories for books? What are they? Can you give examples?

- Do you have favorite genres? favorite authors?

- Are there genres that you do *not* enjoy and would not choose?

- Has there ever been a book that has made a big difference to your life in one way or another? [probe: what kind of a difference? how did it help you?]

- What would it be like for you if for one reason or other you *couldn't* read?

- How do you feel about rereading books?

- If you could get an author to write for the "Perfect Book," what would it be like? What elements would it include?

- How do you feel about different formats for reading—for example, audio books or eBooks? [This question was asked for the first time in 2011.]

- What would you say is the role of reading in your life?

- Is there something important to you about your reading experience that I have omitted to ask you?

Reflecting on Reading

For class members who conducted and transcribed these interviews, the next step was to read through and reflect on what the readers interviewed by fellow class members had said about their reading experience. (I gave each interview a code name to protect the reader's anonymity and put hard copies of the interviews into a binder for the class to read.) Class members said that one result of reading these transcripts was that it prompted them to reflect on their own reading, which previously they had taken for granted. They began to recover their own reading autobiographies. One student recalled being pulled in a red wagon by her grandmother to the library, something she hadn't thought about for years. The major eye-opener was how very different other people's experiences could be from one's own—and from each other.

The interviewees also reported making discoveries about themselves as readers. During the interview itself, they sometimes interrupted their accounts of reading to interject a comment on the interview process. Angus said, "God, the interview process is wonderful, because I'm getting insights into myself. I put two and two together." Shelley (student, age 26), who had been describing a run on reading nonfiction about mental illness as well as her repeated rereadings of Sylvia Plath's *The Bell Jar* right after a devastating breakup with her boyfriend, then remarked in some surprise, "I just made that connection right now. Wow. So that's pretty neat." Diane (social worker, age 37) said that only now, "all grown up and in retrospect," did she understand her father's reasons for the weekly Sunday comic book gift:

> We used to get comic books every Sunday. My Dad always felt bad about us going to church. He thought that church was hard on children. Dad has this theory about children's brains being fresh and young. They shouldn't be subjected to sermons. He thinks that sermons are infinitely boring and a fresh young brain finds this particularly long. [Ross: He doesn't have views about fresh young brains being subjected to comic books?] No. In fact, after church every Sunday, he'd take my brothers and me and get us each a comic book. My father was forbidden from reading comic books as a child, and I think that had something to do with how come we weren't forbidden from reading them. He thought that as long

> as we were reading, that was good. It's only now, that I'm all grown up and in retrospect, that I make a connection between the fresh young mind and the long sermon and the comic book that came afterward.

Other readers made discoveries about why they valued reading and what kinds of books resonated with them. The interview allowed Linda (student, age 25) to discover that she derived from reading a value that she can't get any other way: "You really prompted me to think about my reading. You don't always think about it, but I think the main thing I have gotten out of this interview is that you just have to appreciate reading so much because it's not the same as really anything else. It's something I just don't want to lose in my life." Rihanna (student, age 26) ended the interview by saying that in talking about the books that she enjoys she understands far more clearly the kind of reader she is:

> Your questions really got me thinking about reading. I guess I didn't really realize before how important character is for me. I just feel like I've really discussed the importance of character a lot during this interview. It's something I keep going back to. So it's nice that you did this interview with me, because it made me realize that about what I'm reading.

References

Heath, Shirley Brice. 2011. "The Book as Home: It All Depends." In *Handbook of Research on Children's and Young Adult Literature*, 32–47. Edited by Shelby A. Wolf, Karen Coats, Patricia Enciso, and Christine A. Jenkins. New York and London: Routledge.

Rags to Riches

The rags to riches plot is a special case of the wish-fulfillment story in which the hero starts off in a desperate situation—orphaned, hungry, in rags, unloved, without either family or home or friends—and ends up gaining the heart's desire. The story of the redheaded orphan in L. M. Montgomery's *Anne of Green Gables* is an example, and so are all Cinderella stories. Cockney Eliza Doolittle was dressed in rags when Professor Henry Higgins spotted her on the street corner and turned her into someone who could pass for a duchess. In a male version of the story, the poor orphan Dick Whittington goes to London and, after setbacks and hardships, ends up as the rich Lord Mayor of London with a little help from his cat. In his monumental study, *The Seven Basic Plots* (2004), Christopher Booker identifies the Rags to Riches story as one of the seven basic shapes that underlie all stories. (The other six are Overcoming the Monster, The Quest, Voyage and Return, Tragedy, Comedy, and Rebirth—see Plots). Booker (2004, 65–66) argues that all rags to riches stories involve common elements. The hero begins in the depths, poor, unrecognized, and marginalized. He or she is called to a new life, but, after an initial success, everything falls apart. Just when the situation looks most bleak, however, the hero rallies and in a final test draws on inner resources of virtue and good character. Success, when it comes, is universally recognized as well deserved: the hero is self-evidently the sort of person who deserves good luck and a happy ending.

For many North American readers, the term *rags to riches* brings to mind the Horatio Alger stories, of which *Ragged Dick* is only the most celebrated example. The "riches" in question don't have to be gold coins or large amounts of money—in the Alger stories, the heroes never become really rich, but they gain respectability. Ragged Dick began as an orphaned, illiterate bootblack living in a straw-filled box on a New York City sidewalk and became " 'spectable"—an apprentice with a new set of clothes, who has learned to read, has opened a bank account, and is making $10 a week in a counting house. Riches in these stories turn out to be the particular form of wealth most desired by the hero or heroine. In Ragged Dick's case, it is respectability. In the ugly duckling story by Hans Christian Andersen, it is beauty and acceptance. In the case of Anne, it is a home—during the novel she is transformed from being Anne of nowhere to Anne of Green Gables. Real-life examples can be found in biographies of people as different as Benjamin Franklin and Oprah Winfrey. In the introduction to the Yale edition, *The Autobiography of Benjamin Franklin* was described as "the most widely read autobiography ever written by an American." It tells the story of the youngest son of 17 children of a Boston tallow chandler, who left school at 10, ran away from his apprenticeship, and after many adventures became a successful publisher, inventor, diplomat, and American founding father. What makes these stories so enduringly popular is that they are all about successful transformation.

Horatio Alger and the American Dream

By the 1920s, the Horatio Alger hero was taken to epitomize the American dream of material success, of starting off poor and becoming fabulously wealthy. Horatio Alger, Jr. (1832–99) published some 125 novels for boys about heroes who succeed by pluck, luck, virtue, and hard work (Bennett 1999). The titles of Alger's novels indicate the shape of a much-repeated plot in which a ragged street boy starts off in a lower world and rises—though not quite to actual riches: *Ragged Dick: or, Street Life in New York with the Bootblacks* (1868); *Struggling Upward: or, Luke Lankin's Luck* (1868); *Luck and Pluck: or, John Oakley's Inheritance* (1869); *Tattered Tom: or, The Story of a Street Arab* (1871); *Bound to Rise: or, Up the Ladder* (1873); *Risen from the Ranks: or, Harry Walton's Success* (1874); *Ned Newton: or, The Fortunes of a New York Bootblack* (1890); and *Cast Upon the Breakers* (1893). The prototypical Horatio Alger plot tells the story of a poor boy whose luck turns when he rescues a child from a runaway horse or returns a lost, valuable object to its owner, thereby attracting the favorable attention and gratitude of a philanthropic older man. These stories had once sold in their millions, initially in books priced at $1.25 and later in dime novel formats, but were out of print and little read after 1920 (Scharnhorst 1985, 152). Alger's most reliable biographer, Gary Scharnhorst (149–50), quotes Malcolm Cowley's complaint made in 1945, "I cannot understand how [Alger] should come to be regarded as the prophet of business enterprise; nor why the family melodrama that he wrote and rewrote for boys should be confused with the American dream of success." Nevertheless a Horatio Alger Association was founded in 1947 to "dispel the mounting belief among the nation's youth that the American Dream was no longer attainable" and "to remind Americans of the limitless possibilities that exist through the free-enterprise system."

Like almost everything that was thought to be known about Alger, the idea of the Alger hero as the epitome of the American dream is inexact. As Hugh Kenner (1975, 21) put it, "Alger did not typically see his boy through to riches, he merely saw him out of rags, driving a pen in a countinghouse, reading industriously, attending Sunday School, and plainly destined Upward." *Ragged Dick*, which was Alger's first big success and the prototype for his later stories, was based on Alger's first-hand knowledge of street Arabs, bootblacks, and newsboys gained after he arrived in New York City in 1868, having quit his calling as a Unitarian minister. The 14-year-old hero is first presented as ragged and dirty, wearing pants torn in several places, a vest with all but two buttons gone, a grimy shirt, and a too-long coat apparently dating back "to a remote antiquity." What money Dick earns at 10 cents a shine he spends on cigars, going to the Old Bowery Theatre, treating his friends to oyster-stew, and sometimes losing at cards. The call to a new life comes when he encounters a gentleman, Mr. Whitney, and his country-boy nephew Frank and when Dick volunteers to give Frank a tour of New York City. "He has an open face, and I think can be depended upon," opines Frank's uncle.

But first Dick needs to be washed and dressed in a new suit of clothes. Catching sight of himself in a mirror, Dick says, "It reminds me of Cinderella . . . when she was changed into a fairy princess" (Chapter 4). Dick "aint much on reading" but he knows a lot about the way stories work from going to plays at the Old Bowery. He tells Frank about the current play, *Demon of the Danube*: "The Demon falls in love with a young woman, and drags her by the hair up to the top of a steep rock where his castle stands." To rescue her, the hero has to sneak into the castle "by some underground passage" and fight the Demon. Dick reports, "Oh, it was bully seein' 'em roll round on the stage, cuttin' and slashin' at each other." They fight fiercely until finally the young Baron strikes a dagger into the Demon's heart, saying, " 'Die, false and perjured villain! The dogs shall feast upon thy carcass!' and then the Demon give an awful howl and died."

The guided tour through the city, which occupies eight chapters, is a double education. Dick, who has lived by his wits on the street since he was seven, wises Frank up to the "swindlin' shops," "regular cheats," drop-games, and cons that are to be met with at every corner in New York City. And Frank teaches Dick to aspire higher than boot blacking: "I'd like to be a office boy, and learn business, and grow up 'spectable." "Did you ever hear of Dick Whittington?" asks Frank, and then tells the story of another "very poor" boy named Dick who was taken into the house of a rich merchant and who parlayed his only possession—a kitten—into great fortune. "You may not become rich,—it isn't everybody that becomes rich, you know—but you can obtain a good position, and be respected."

The secret is not only to work hard "but work in the right way" (Chapter 8). And what is the right way? The first thing needful is an honest character, which Dick already has. The next thing, advises Frank, is "to get as good an education as you can. Until you do, you cannot get a position in an office or countingroom, even to run errands." Frank's uncle's parting gift to Dick is a $5 bill and some similar advice: "Save your money, my lad, buy books, and determine to be somebody." In short order, Dick starts on the path to respectability. He rents a room, opens a bank account for his five dollars, exchanges the name

Ragged Dick for Dick Hunter, and "now, for the first time, he felt himself a capitalist." The transformation has begun.

When Dick befriends Fosdick, a 12-year-old orphan, and invites him to share the rented room, he acquires a private tutor. The well-educated son of a printer, Fosdick initiates Dick's education in reading, writing, arithmetic, grammar, and geography. But honest industry is necessary but not sufficient. As Kenner (1975, 21) points out:

> If you scrutinized [Alger's] plots closely, there was always a key no amount of honest industry could simulate: as when you turned out to be the long-lost grandchild of someone important, or as when, less implausibly, the child you pluckily saved from drowning was claimed by a man of affluence who called you "my brave boy," acknowledged that "but for your timely service I should now be plunged into an anguish which I cannot now think of without a shudder," and gave you a job in his countinghouse at ten dollars a week. Insofar as there was a practical formula it was this: that you should strive to be the kind of person who should deserve this sort of luck.

At $10 a week, Dick Hunter is clearly no Jay Gatsby—he of the great mansion, the garden parties like an amusement park, the full orchestra, the five crates of oranges ordered in every week to be squeezed for guests' drinks, the hydroplane, and the legendary car "terraced with a labyrinth of wind-shields that mirrored a dozen suns." However, there are certain resemblances in their stories: the unpromising origins, being taken up and befriended by an older man following the rendering of a significant service, the taking on a new name as a baptism into a new life (in Fitzgerald's novel Jay Gatsby begins life as Jimmy Gatz), and the deliberate program of education of the self-invented man, which recalls Benjamin Franklin's self-improvement program outlined in his *Autobiography*. When he was 16, Gatz wrote out a self-improvement schedule on the flyleaf of a copy of *Hopalong Cassidy* (Chapter 9):

Rise from bed	6:00 A.M.
Dumbbell exercises and wall-scaling	6:15–6:30
Study electricity, etc.	7:15–8:15
Work	8:30–4:30 P.M.
Baseball and sports	4:30–5:00
Practice elocution, poise and how to attain it	5:00–6:00
Study needed inventions	7:00–9:00

Something about Horatio Alger, Jr.

For a long time, most of what was known about Alger's life was wrong. The misleading source was *Alger: A Biography without a Hero* published in 1928 by Willard Mayes. Commissioned to write the first full-length biography some 30 years after Alger's death, Mayes immediately ran into a snag. The sources that biographers normally depend upon—diaries, correspondence with family, friends and publishers, working notes, writer's journals, draft manuscripts, and so on—were all missing. A setback certainly, but Mayes, who later became editor of *Good Housekeeping* and president of McCall Corporation, was resourceful. Lacking any reliable sources, he made everything up—the letters, the diaries, the life events, everything (see NONFICTION for other examples of invented lives).

Meyes supplied Alger with a repressed childhood and a stern Unitarian preacher father, who trained his son for the ministry from the cradle onward. He concocted diary entries, purportedly written when Alger was a teenager, in which he muses, "Have I the ability to write? Why not—if I am conscientious and observe closely all that goes on around me?" In Meyes's account, after graduating from divinity school, Alger fled to Paris, where all good American novelists wanted to go at the time when Meyes was writing. There Alger got entangled with a café singer named Elise. Symmetrically, Mayes provided Alger, near the end of his life, with another romantic entanglement, this time with an entrepreneur's wife, who got him mixed up in a murder charge. The irony of Alger's life, claimed Meyes, was that the creator of the rags to riches formula failed at the very thing he most desired: to write a great novel.

Meyes's biography was accepted for many years as authoritative—it was the major source of the *Dictionary of American Biography* entry on Horatio Alger. Then in 1972, Mayes 'fessed up: he said that his book had been "a complete fabrication, with virtually no scintilla of basis in fact. Any word of truth in it got in unwittingly." His original intention had been, he said, to write a "delightful spoof," but when reviewers took the hoax seriously it seemed too late to set the record straight (Scharnhorst 1985, x–xiii). Scharnhorst quotes Mayes as saying:

> I provided [Alger] with mistresses. I had him adopt and become attached to a little Chinese boy, and then had the boy killed by a runaway horse. I credited to him as a child essays and verses— never existent—that a child of ten might have written. I had Alger dreaming of a great novel that someday he would write. (xi)

If Meyes had taken the time to consider *why* all the evidence of Alger's life was missing, he might have discovered that it was no accident that documentary sources for Alger's life were unfindable. Alger had taken pains to cover his tracks. According to Scharnhorst (1985, 159), Alger charged his sister Augusta with destroying all his private papers after his death. Horatio Alger, Jr., and his family were protecting a secret: Alger had been driven out of his post as Unitarian minister in Brewster, Massachusetts, charged with molesting young boys.

References

Bennett, Bob. 1999. *A Collector's Guide to the Published Works of Horatio Alger, Jr.* Newark, DE: MAD Book Company.

Booker, Christopher. 2004. *The Seven Basic Plots: Why We Tell Stories.* London and New York: Continuum.

Horatio Alger Association. http://www.horatioalger.org/aboutus.cfm.

Kenner, Hugh. 1975. "The Promised Land." In *A Homemade World: The American Modernist Writers,* 20–49. New York: Alfred A. Knopf.

Mayes, Herbert R. 1928. *Alger: A Biography without a Hero.* New York: Macy-Masius.

Scharnhorst, Gary, with Jack Bales. 1985. *The Lost Life of Horatio Alger, Jr.* Bloomington: Indiana University Press.

Romance Fiction

In my Genres of Fiction and Reading course that I have taught for many years in a graduate program in Library and Information Science, students are required to read an example of each genre that we study. The class on the romance almost always evokes the most controversy and raw emotion. One female student who checked out a Harlequin from a public library for this assignment reported with some indignation that the circulation assistant had said, "Why are you reading *that*? Couldn't you find something better?" Male students said that, in order to read their chosen romance in a public place such as a bus or laundromat, they had to conceal its cover in a brown paper bag. How embarrassing to be seen with a book with a mauve die-cut cover and swash lettering. For various reasons, both the men and the women in the class, even those who enjoyed the novel they chose, admitted that they felt like saying to anyone seeing them with a romance novel, "I'm just reading this for an assignment; I'm not really *reading* it." Romance is the genre, along with SELF-HELP, whose readers are most apt to be judged and found wanting. Bestselling romance writer Jayne Ann Krentz (1992, 1) begins her edited collection of essays by established romance writers, *Dangerous Men and Adventurous Women*, with this observation: "Few people realize how much courage it takes for a woman to open a romance novel in an airplane. . . . When it comes to romance novels, society has always felt free to sit in judgment not only on the literature but on the reader herself."

One thing that everyone agrees upon—both detractors and fans—is the enormous commercial success of romance fiction. The Romance Writers of America (RWA) Web site takes pains to present annually updated statistics on the production and consumption of romance fiction. Here are some figures for North American readership presented by RWA, based on the source *Business of Consumer Book Publishing* 2013 and other sources:

- Romance fiction generated $1.438 billion in sales in 2012.

- 8,240 new romance titles were released in 2010.

- 74.8 million people read at least one romance novel in 2008 (RWA Reader Survey).

Readership surveys have consistently found that romance readers resemble a normal cross-section of the female population, apart from their reading more books than average and apart from their having attained a higher level of education. This picture of the romance reader has not changed over 40 years (Mann 1974, 1981; Mussell 1984, 11–15; Thurston 1987, 115–21; Linz 1992, 12; Owen 1997). Readership surveys repeatedly find that romance is a top-ranking genre with female readers. *Reading and Buying Books for Pleasure* (Createc 2005, 69), based on a national telephone survey of 1963 Canadians aged 16 or older, reported that romance fiction was read by 51 percent of the women in the study who had read a book in the past 12 months and by 10 percent of the men. Romance readers read and buy more books a year than do readers of other genres. They have been early adopters of E-READING and are among the readers most likely to buy and borrow eBooks. According to information posted on the "Reader Statistics" page of the RWA Web site, as of the first quarter of 2012, 44 percent of romance titles were bought in digital eBook format.

All this leads to two important questions about the romance. Why has this genre, more than any other popular genre, attracted denigration so intense that its readers feel stigmatized (Brackett 2000) and try to conceal their reading preferences? And why, despite efforts to marginalize the romance, has it survived and thrived? Narratives that continue to be told over and over must tell a story that readers want to read. So what is it about the romance that its audience— mostly women—wants to hear? In a nutshell, why is the romance both the least respected and the most popular of all the genres?

Something about the Romance Genre

The love story has a long history, including plots both with happy outcomes such Chaucer's "The Wife of Bath's Tale" and with tragic outcomes such as *Orpheus and Euridice*, *Romeo and Juliet*, and *Tristan and Isolde*. But the romantic novel, as understood by contemporary publishers and readers, is narrower in scope and more restricted in definition. The consensus seems to be that the definition of the romance novel must be broad enough to include *Jane Eyre*, *Pride and Prejudice*, *Gone with the Wind*, and lesbian romances but narrow enough to exclude *Middlemarch*, *The Bridges of Madison County*, and the novels of Danielle Steel. As the Romance Writers of America put it, "Two basic elements comprise every romance novel: a central love story and an emotionally-satisfying and optimistic ending." In a romance novel, there can be various elements that might be at home in other genres—characters can be threatened by enemy agents, kidnapped, get involved in espionage plots, uncover a deep secret, have an encounter with a VAMPIRE, or go on a journey quest. But the central concern must always be the developing love relationship between the hero and heroine (or in lesbian or gay romances between the two protagonists) as they move from misunderstanding, and often actually disliking, each other at the outset to declared love at the end. Everything else is secondary to the development of a committed relationship and to the powerful emotions evoked as the characters struggle in dynamic tension until the final recognition of their mutually shared love. Successful romance writers do not aim for detachment and irony but for reader engagement. Readers want to be drawn into the story and feel an emotional involvement with the characters.

In addition to the steady focus on the developing love relationship, the other non-negotiable element in a romance is the happily-ever-after ending. Abbreviated in discussions by romance fans to HEA, the happy ending is expected as part of the contract made with the reader. It is a premise of the genre itself. As Andrea posts on a *Likesbooks.com* discussion of the HEA requirement: "The HEA is an absolute must for me. This is what makes romance as a genre so appealing—the ending can be depended upon to be happy. And even though I know this is a given, I still take a quick peek at the last page 'just to make sure.' " This means that if the lovers are killed off at the end as in Dryden's *All for Love: or The World Well Lost* or if the heroine hurls herself under a train as in *Anna Karenina* or if the lovers opt for renunciation as in *The Bridges of Madison County* or even if one lover sets off on a journey part way through the book and never comes back, the resulting novel may be about love but it won't be a well-formed or satisfying example of the romance genre.

The romance genre is a comedy in the formal sense of its being a story that starts off with obstacles, difficulties, and misunderstandings and ends with a happy resolution and what Northrop Frye (1957, 44) has called "a society ushered in with a happy rustle of bridal gowns and banknotes." The well-known first sentence of Jane Austen's *Pride and Prejudice* (1813) makes clear the connection between marriage and money that has dominated the romance: "It is a truth universally acknowledged, that a single man in possession of a good fortune, must be in want of a wife." So begins the novel of courtship that Pamela Regis (2003), in *A Natural History of the Romance Novel*, calls "the best romance novel ever written." But despite happy outcomes in which the heroine gets to be mistress of Pemberley or becomes a duchess or, in contemporary romances, marries a billionaire, the reader has to feel that the relationship is based not on a prudential concern for economic security but on a deeply shared love. The heroine is loved not for anything she does but simply because of who she is. Like the hero of the RAGS TO RICHES story, she is someone who self-evidently deserves good luck and a happy ending.

Regis (2003, 30–38) says that there are eight obligatory narrative events in a romance novel, all of which can be found in *Pride and Prejudice*. These are:

1. the defining of the special society in which the courtship takes place

2. the meeting of the heroine and hero for the first time

3. the barriers, internal and external, that separate the heroine and hero and defer their union

4. the attraction, developed in a series of scenes, that shows the characters' increasing regard for each other

5. the declaration in which the characters declare their love for each other, something which may be split into two parts and made at different times

6. the "point of ritual death" at which the hoped-for coming together of heroine and hero seems impossible and the whole story seems to be veering off into a tragic crisis

7. the "recognition" in which new information is presented that will overcome the barrier

8. the betrothal or the equivalent in which it is made clear that the heroine and hero will end up together for life

Taken together, these eight narrative events carry the heroine on the satisfying trajectory from a state characterized by illusion, disguise, constraints, and barriers to a state of freedom and the discovery of true identity. In freeing herself, the heroine likewise frees the hero.

Critics have noted the structure of the fairy tale—especially the Cinderella story—lying not far below the surface of romance and worry that readers will derive "false views of life"—the Mme Bovary problem. Romance writers, on the other hand, are very aware that what readers expect is a fantasy, not a gritty representation of what life is really like for a young woman who is orphaned or left penniless by the bad behavior of gambling fathers or feckless brothers. In *Reading the Romance*, a pioneering study based on interviews with avid romance readers, Janice A. Radway (1984, 91) reported that a dominating theme in her interviews was the idea of "romance reading as a special gift a woman gives herself."

The fantasy is achieved through the choice of coded language and descriptive details. As Krentz (2000) puts it, "The language of the romance is rich in its ability to describe intense emotion, strong sensual attraction, and acute physical awareness." The key is to achieve the right balance of fantasy and realism, with a fairy tale narrative trajectory displaced into a recognizable, everyday world. As is the case with genre fiction in general, readers demand certain fixed elements—in romance, it's the presence of the hero and heroine in almost every scene, the emotional tension of the developing relationship, evocative language that reflects the intensity of the desire felt by the two protagonists, and the happy ending. Above all the mark of a successful romance is its ability to draw readers into the emotional world of the characters. But beyond these requirements, innovation is expected. Romance writers are free to explore different settings in the past, present, or future; can examine changing social roles for women; can include social criticism; and in some subgenres can include paranormal elements such as time travel, ghosts, witches, or vampires.

Studying Romance Fiction and Its Readers

One explanation for the romance's massive popularity is that its readers, being women, are easily duped. A more plausible explanation is that writers and publishers have been exceptionally adept at finding out what pleases readers and then providing it. The feedback loop between readers and producers is rapid and direct. Industry gatekeepers have created lots of ways for readers to connect with publishers and writers and tell them what they like. Publishers, authors, fans, romance-based associations, and booksellers have set up websites, blogs, and discussion forums where readers can find out about new work and can talk about what they like and don't like in a romance. Of all the popular genres, romance fiction is the one whose publishers have been keenest on surveying readers and finding out about readers' changing tastes and attitudes, starting with sociologist Peter Mann's survey (1974) of Mills & Boon readers in the United Kingdom.

Moreover most successful romance writers start off as avid readers of romance. They are fans who have thoroughly learned the romance conventions and then make the transition from reader to writer by writing the book that they themselves would like to read. Conferences such as those organized by Harlequin or by the Romance Writers of America are important ways of connecting the nodes on the circuit from writer to publisher to reader to writer and back around the circle again. The Romance Writers of America, with its 10,000 members of published writers and not-yet-published hopeful, holds an annual July conference, which is usually advertised as follows: "Conference attendees will enhance their writing and knowledge of the ins and outs of publishing at workshops; get the inside track at panels and round-tables featuring publishing professionals; schedule a one-on-one pitch meeting with an acquiring editor or literary agent; attend parties and network with the stars of romance fiction."

The relative neglect of the romance genre as an object of academic study is striking but not surprising. Academics prefer to study up. Romance fiction, as a genre written and read primarily by women, is considered decidedly downmarket. For that reason, academic studies of the romance have tended, with a few notable exceptions, to concentrate not on readers but on the texts themselves or on the political economy of mass taste. One line of scholarly work has examined the most successful publisher of romance fiction, Harlequin Enterprises, in terms of its business model that has standardized a product and used branding and marketing strategies to sell books in a global marketplace (Jensen 1984; Grescoe 1996; McAleer 1999). The political economic approach used in such studies looks at large-scale processes of ownership, production, consumption, and globalization.

A second line of scholarly work has examined texts, often focusing narrowly on a particular subgenre or a limited time period (e.g., Jones 1986; Dixon 1999; Betz 2009; Vivanco 2011; Teo 2012). Theorists of the mass-market romance often "conflate all romance genres and call them 'Harlequins,' " says

Deborah Lutz (2006, 2–3). In contrast, Regis's study of romantic fiction (2003) or Lutz's study of the dangerous lover (2006) each provide a dazzlingly grand sweep through centuries of romance writing, considering literary texts and popular romances side by side. Third, with the turn toward cultural studies, critics following John Cawelti (1976) have largely jettisoned the high culture/low culture hierarchy and examined romance texts as a window into popular culture (Mussell 1997; Frantz and Selinger 2012). Fourth, a handful of researchers have studied real readers. Janice A. Radway's *Reading the Romance* (1984), an ethnographic study of committed romance readers, was a ground-breaking work that put the spotlight on empirical readers, not implied readers as they might be deduced from the texts. In another landmark study, Carol Thurston (1987) used surveys of readers, interviews with authors and editors, and content analysis of texts to examine romance production and consumption during a period from 1972 to the mid-1980s when both were undergoing rapid changes. Fifth, romance writers and fans have written about romance fiction, publishing how-to-write manuals as well as spirited defenses of the genre (e.g., Krentz 1992; Wendell and Tan 2009). And sixth, forward-looking librarians and library educators involved in readers' advisory work have taken a lead in mapping the field and explaining the appeal to readers of romance and its many subgenres (Chelton 1991; Bouricius 2000; Wyatt et al. 2007; Saricks 2009; Ramsdell 1982/2012).

Like the romance readers who have adopted e-reading so enthusiastically and like the romance authors who are in touch with their readers through Web sites and social media, a new breed of romance scholar has established online spaces for publishing and distributing research. Declaring popular romance studies to be an "emerging field," the newly established International Association for the Study of Popular Romance (IASPR) started publishing in 2010 an online, open-access *Journal of Popular Romance Studies*. The bibliographic control of romance scholarship has also gone online. Check out the Romance-Wiki, which provides a comprehensive bibliography of scholarly articles and books on romance.

Hating Romance

Pressed to account for the enormous popularity of books that are said to be "badly written" and "all the same," critics have settled on three explanations: "romance as porn" (Snitow 1979); the "duped" reader, in which women are seduced by mass marketing to read against their own best interests; and the "empty life" syndrome, in which romance reading is compensatory for something lacking in the reader. Germaine Greer (1970, 180) argued that the traits given by romance novels to alpha heroes "have been invented by women cherishing the chains of their bondage." Jeanne Dubino (1993, 107–8) explained that "the hero is usually dominant and forceful, the heroine yielding and submissive," but the readers like them anyway because of their empty lives:

"Not finding what they want in 'real' life, millions of women turn to romances in a vicarious attempt to compensate for the lack of attention and validation they get in their own lives."

Romance reading seems to activate a deeply held anxiety over the connection between pleasure and consumption. The metaphor "reading is eating" is commonly used for all types of reading (see INDISCRIMINATE READING), but romance reading is apt to be likened to eating sugary treats or, even worse, to taking opiates. Reading romance fiction might provide momentary pleasure, but the worry is that in the long run it creates a debilitating dependency. In *Loving with a Vengeance,* Tania Modleski (1982, 57), claims that repetitive romance reading is driven by the reader/addict's compulsion to resolve a disturbing psychic conflict through fantasy when the conflict can't be resolved in real life. And worse: "The user must constantly increase the dosage of the drug in order to alleviate problems aggravated by the drug itself."

The term *Harlequin* has often been used as a shorthand for everything that is wrong with *all* romance novels, not just with category romances or with works actually published by Harlequin. The industry itself divides romances into single title romances published by a large number of publishers and category romances, in which Harlequin is the dominant publisher. Category romances are shorter books released as part of a numbered series or line, each line having its own predictable elements of appeal to readers. Harlequin is a Canadian company that started off republishing British Mills & Boon romances for North American audiences and subsequently expanded its markets to international lines in 110 countries and 34 languages. Harlequin releases some 110 titles a month under a number of different imprints and lines, including some exclusively in eBooks. Harlequin standardizes the reading experience within the line through writing guidelines that specify recommended elements of plot and character and suggested word lengths (e.g., 50,000 words for Harlequin Presents and 85,000 words for Harlequin Superromance).

Harlequin Enterprises has excelled in regulating supply and demand through interventions at different nodes in the circuit from author to reader. Aware from surveys that romance fans read voraciously, often as many as five or six romance novels a week, Harlequin has kept the price low and made titles easy to get, initially through mail order and now through eBooks. Harlequin has recruited new readers through advertising and book giveaways, while at the same time it has recruited new writers and has been willing to take a chance on new storylines. In contrast to works of literary fiction, which must be marketed one book at a time, Harlequin sells a brand, every book in the line guaranteed to deliver the same satisfaction. Harlequin books are marketed as a luxurious pleasure that a woman can give herself. Writing guidelines declare, "A Harlequin Presents is more than just a book; it's an experience, an everyday luxury."

Complaints that used to be made about series books and the Stratemeyer Syndicate (see ONLY THE BEST) predictably have been redirected at Harlequin Enterprises, namely that Harlequin is a gigantic fiction factory in which books are produced and marketed like soap for commercial gain; that the books are mass-produced according to a repetitive formula by a stable of authors (some 1,300 authors currently write for Harlequin); that they purvey false values and inculcate false views of life; and that they have a mind-weakening effect on their duped, impressionable readers. The scandal of Harlequin is two-fold. Its romance novels are produced as profitable commodities cannily designed to please readers. And readers—almost all women—like them a lot and read them repetitively. Popularity with readers, in this context thought of as "the masses," confirm the status of romances as "lowbrow," "fluff," and "trashy"—terms that are used alike by romance readers and non-readers.

Defending Romance

In response, romance readers, writers, and advocates have marshaled their defenses. One strategy has been to demonstrate that romance is not a recent Mills & Boon/Harlequin upstart but a genre with a long and respectable history and with an especially adept practitioner in Jane Austen. Regis devotes almost a third of her *Natural History of the Romance Novel* to chapters on Samuel Richardson's *Pamela* (the first bestseller—1740), *Pride and Prejudice* (the best romance novel ever written—1813), Charlotte Bronte's *Jane Eyre* (freedom and Mr. Rochester—1847), Anthony Trollope's *Framley Parsonage* (romance form in the Victorian multiplot novel—1861), and E. M. Forster's *A Room with a View* (the ideal romance novel—1908).

Countering the theme of the duped or enslaved reader, romance advocates make the case for the romance reader as empowered. Suzanne Juhasz (1988, 239) explains, "The love story tells a tale of female aspiration to self-realization, for in women's fantasy, love and identity are concurrent." Librarian and romance-writer Ann Bouricius (2000, 5) claims, "Romances are about women winning," and she quotes Deborah Smith as saying, "In romances, the woman always ends up on top." Krentz agrees. In her introduction to *Dangerous Men and Adventurous Women*, Krentz (1992, 5) describes romance as a fantasy of female empowerment in which the woman always wins: "In romance the success of an individual author is . . . [based] on how compellingly she can create her fantasy and on how many readers discover they can step into it with her for a couple of hours." Krentz argues that readers have no difficulty distinguishing the inevitably happy endings of the fantasy from the reality of their everyday experience. They *choose* to enter the romance world for a couple of hours to experience a reaffirmation of hope and the importance of love. Many readers support this claim. For example, Petra (student, age 24) says, "What actually happens in the romance novels is that the female actually wills the man to change his ways to suit her needs. I think that is something really nice for women to read. They won't necessarily get that in their life." Women read romances because romances tell a story that they want to hear about the transformative power of love.

In response to the criticism that romances are all the same with a preordained ending, romance fans argue that *all* popular genres involve a contract with the reader about what ending to expect. DETECTIVE fiction ends with the murderer unmasked; WESTERNS end with the lone hero winning the shoot-out and riding off into the sunset; spy stories and thrillers end with the free world saved from evil agents and killer viruses. We know the ending. The interest of the genre is in the *way* the book achieves that anticipated ending—the novel combination of situations, complications, and solutions that lead to the hoped-for conclusion. The reader is kept guessing about how the author will pull the fat from the fire this time. In an address given to the National Book Festival, Eloisa James (2012) said that the key thing in romance, as in all genre fiction, is "that you surprise the reader within the bounds of what they already know." Eloisa James is the pen name used for her more than 20 bestselling romances by Dr. Mary Bly, who is also an English professor and Shakespeare scholar at Fordham University. James/Bly describes the process of creating surprise within the boundaries of the known and "already promised." Readers have to be made to think in the middle of the book, whether it's romance or detective fiction, "This book isn't going to work." She says, "There's a dream at the heart of every genre fiction that has to be dispelled in the middle."

Defenders of romance also deny the charge that romance lacks complexity and diversification. Readership studies (Radway 1984; Owen 1990) have demonstrated that there is considerable complexity in the cultural use that romance readers made of the books in the context of their own lives. Then there is the growing diversification of the texts themselves—the multiplying subgenres of romance, each with its own set of writers and its characteristic conventions. These subgenres are rapidly evolving, with some fading and others such as military romance and urban fantasy romance coming on strong. Subgenres include historical romance, regencies (which are historical romances set in England under the Prince Regent—1811–20), frontier romance, romantic suspense, inspirational (in which religious or spiritual values are a cornerstone of the love relationship), contemporary romance, gay/lesbian, science fiction romance, time-travel romance, military romance, dark fantasy, and paranormal.

Demonstrably, subgenres vary in many ways: in the place or geographical setting of the book; in the time period represented, whether past, present, or future; in the degree to which the characters and the society represented resemble what might be expected to happen in the known world; and in the depictions of the sexual encounter. Is this a Georgette Heyer–type novel in which the courtship is framed within Regency high society in London with its season of balls and its strict rules of decorum? Does the story center on characters with paranormal powers such as the shape-shifting Carpathians in Christine Feehan's Dark series? Is the hero a tech entrepreneur in contemporary Seattle, a veterinarian in a small town in Maine, an eighteenth-century Highlander, a Cherokee warrior on the frontier, or possibly a Navy SEAL lieutenant countering international terrorists? Is the romance "sweet" or "spicy"? Kristin Ramsdell's *Romance*

Fiction: A Guide to the Genre (2012) provides an excellent map of all these various differences among the subgenres of romance and provides examples of recommended authors and titles.

In summary, even when critics and fans are reading the same text, they are *not* reading the same text. These two adversarial groups bring differing understandings, prior commitments, and expectations to their reading of romance. One group reads a text of female bondage; the other of female empowerment and liberation. One group sees readers being duped into false expectations; the other sees readers choosing to enjoy a fantasy for a while as a break from the demands of everyday life. One group says, "nothing happens" in a story that is "badly written," which is to say overly evocative and emotional. In contrast, fans insist that something important *is* happening when a plot incident advances the developing love relationship. For fans, the criterion of good writing is whether or not the book draws them in and involves them in the emotional life of the characters. And even among romance fans themselves, readers take different things from the same novel. This is not surprising when we consider the creative role of readers in making sense of any text. When Mairead Owen (1990, 123) surveyed 137 romance readers and interviewed 40 more for her doctoral research, she found that, "More than with most books, the reader writes the text."

What Do Romance Readers Know?

Fans who enjoy romance give themselves lifelong lessons in reading the genre. They may start with teen romances, move on to category romances, and then settle in to read longer, single title romances (which, however, are often written in a series of books linked by a common setting and related characters). A key thing about fans is that they have read lots—probably hundreds—of romance novels. When they read a particular novel, instead of its being a one-off experience, they are always comparing *this* novel's treatment of a particular trope—the mail order bride, the cross-dressing heroine, the second chance romance, friends-into-lovers, the captivity—with the handling of that same trope in other books. They are comparing *this* heroine and *this* hero with countless others. Being able to discriminate the excellent treatments from the not-so-good ones is part of their repertoire as a knowledgeable connoisseur.

The blog *Dear Author* (2010a, 2010b) sponsored two polls that asked readers if there were storylines that they absolutely *wouldn't* read (80% said yes) and conversely if there were storylines that they almost always *would* read. Some stories were decisively in the not-read category. Readers said no adultery, no abusive relationships, no forced seduction, and no rapist-and-victim hookups. Some readers also said no secret babies, no revenge stories, no time travel, no shape-shifters, no Navy SEALs or paramilitary, no Christian storylines, no billionaire/doormat secretary relationships, and no stories featuring much older heroes "teaching lessons" to younger women. But, apart from the secret baby, which was mostly rejected, and the marriage of convenience, which was mostly a favorite, the same tropes showed up on both the "wouldn't read" and "always would read" lists. Some readers said that they avoid vampires or time travel, while others said that those books are their very favorites. Most readers, it turns out, are selective. They avoid certain story types, and they read other types intensively. One reader said, "My favorite storyline is anything where the couple already knows each other, regardless of how. Friends to lovers; antagonists to lovers; marriage of convenience; former lovers." Another said she would almost always read anything with a "strong channeling of Beauty and the Beast (or any fairytale really)." This method of intensive reading means that fans become highly knowledgeable in their preferred storylines and tropes.

Isobel, posting on the *Dear Author* blog (2010c), said, "A lot of what I look for is variations on a theme. I really like identifying storylines or tropes and then seeing how different authors treat them (or even the same author with different novels), whether that's using them straight, inverting them, pointing them out, exploring their deeper meanings and possible complications, or whatever. I love re-told fairy tales and archetypical characters." Each work that features, say, the triumph of the undervalued heroine—the Cinderella story—is in conversation with every other such story that the reader has read. But also part of this conversation are works, such as Jane Austen's *Emma*, which invert the Cinderella story by starting off with a heroine who is "handsome, clever, and rich."

When experienced readers pick up a new romance to read, they can therefore recognize the hooks that are provided on the book JACKET—references, for example, to friends-to-lovers, enforced proximity, a sham marriage, a hidden identity, or a dissolute rake in need of redemption. Each of these situations comes with its own set of conflicts and related themes. The reader who has read many novels featuring, say, the marriage of convenience wants the latest book to provide a new twist. How does the book in hand set up the situation (e.g., the heroine suddenly discovers she will be disinherited unless she is married by her 25th birthday, which is in three weeks), and how does the book develop the emergent conflicts? Romance reading is thus an activity that does not drill deep into a single text but involves comparing the text in hand with similar, but different, versions. A real source of pleasure is to see how an old familiar plot element becomes new again.

The tropes that work best set up the conflict between hero and heroine and supply the push–pull energy that generates longing and sexual tension. Often two very different people from very different worlds are brought together in forced proximity: for example, a snowstorm or shipwreck traps characters together; a bodyguard and the guarded person announce a sham engagement as a cover story; a character is kidnapped and held in captivity; a woman is persuaded to marry a stranger who has two weeks to live, but then he miraculously recovers; a single woman seduces a strange man as an unwitting sperm donor, but then he finds out about the baby. Each of these situations is a productive source of conflict that produces misunderstandings and drives the couple apart.

The conflict may include such themes as deception, betrayal, remorse, abandonment, revenge, and denial which must be resolved before the happy ending. The key to a successful romance is to maintain almost to the end the tension between the forces that bring the characters together and the forces that drive them apart.

Heroines and Heroes

Romance readers distinguish between what they call "keepers" and "wall-bangers" (so terrible that they deserve to be hurled across the room) in large part on the basis of their satisfaction with the book's hero and the heroine. Moderator Sarah Wendell (2008) posted a question on the Web site, "Smart Bitches, Trashy Books": "Who are your favorite heroines from Days of Yore?" In response, Shannon said, "I am one of those readers who has to like the heroine in order to like the romance. I can lust after a hero, but if he's paired with a limp rag for a heroine, I don't feel that the hero has found a satisfying love match and I don't get invested in the book."

Respondents to the "Days of Yore" question supplied many examples of favorite heroines, including Austen's Elizabeth Bennet, Sophy from Georgette Heyer's *The Grand Sophy*, Penelope from Julia Quinn's *Romancing Mr. Bridgerton*, and Pru from Mary Balogh's *A Precious Jewel* ("It's tough to write a heroine who decides to make the best of being a whore"). Reasons for favoring particular heroines included: she is "a brainy bluestocking done well"; she has "real problems but responds by pulling up her socks and getting on with it"; and "she's smart, sexy and small but she can seriously kick your ass to the moon." Some heroines were considered total failures ("an utterly flat, two-dimensional character"), while those who were most appreciated were seen to have changed and developed ("I loved her wit and spunk and adored the fact that . . . I had watched this character grow up"). Merry Patricia Wilding from Tom and Sharon Curtis's *The Windflower* is "my favorite heroine of all time," said one reader, because she "starts as this incredibly sheltered heroine who is kidnapped by pirates (of course!), shoots at someone with a crossbow, nearly drowns, catches malaria, and becomes this resilient, strong, feisty heroine by the end of the story." Another said that she had read Jude Deveraux's *The Duchess* "a million times": "I think Claire was the archetypal heroine who is not particularly physically attractive, but makes up for it in wit and intellectual curiosity."

Readers prefer rich heroes—Regency dukes or modern millionaires (or in these inflationary times, billionaires), but they don't all have to be alpha heroes. In Georgette Heyer's *Cotillion* (1953), for example, rich Freddy Standish is a thoroughly nice, easygoing guy who wins over the heroine Kitty Charing by his unerring fashion sense, his steady reliability, and his ability to negotiate the social pitfalls of Regency London. The heroine and hero must be equal in some important way, even when at first there seems to be an inequality of power or wealth or social status or beauty between them. One reader said, "I love stories that start off with an obvious imbalance of power—like when characters come from different social classes, or one is beholden to the other—because I like seeing how the author will flip this balance on its head and keep the tension going between the characters." Mary K said, "The reason I love all these military romances is that the honorable and tender but badass heroes resist falling in love, despite being great lovers, but when they do, it's like watching a redwood fall over!" The energy of the romance comes from the dynamic of attraction and repulsion between the two central characters. It works best when the two are well-matched sparring partners, one character's power advantage offset by some rare personal quality in the other character.

Dangerous Lovers

Why do some genres such as the WESTERN become exhausted, while others have the capacity for continued renewal, appealing to new generations of readers? In the case of the romance, the trick has involved adjusting the treatment of the hero and heroine to respond to changing social attitudes and reader preferences. Consider the book that Pamela Regis (2003, 115) has called the "ur-romance of the twentieth century." *The Sheik* (1919) by British author E. M. Hull was a huge bestseller that was made into a film starring Rudolph Valentino and gave its name to a brand of condoms. It inspired a whole flock of imitators in which a virginal heroine with golden hair is abducted by a fierce, hard, dark lover—a sheik, a pirate, an outlaw—and raped. Reprinted 32 times in the first nine months after publication, *The Sheik* tells the story of Diana Mayo, a bored, willful, and wealthy English aristocrat who sets off unprotected on horseback on a trek into the Algerian desert, where she rides into a trap and is kidnapped by Sheik Ahmed Ben Hassan. By removing Diana from her social world and making her a captive in the empty desert, Hull was able to focus almost exclusively on intense emotions—initially terror, horror, anger, and hatred but later ardor, longing, and love.

Soon after her abduction, Diana discovers that she, who has been accustomed to dominating others, is now powerless: "For the first time she had met a man who had failed to bow to her wishes, whom a look had been powerless to transform into a willing slave. . . . His dark, passionate eyes burnt into her like a hot flame." The sheik is a prototype of what Deborah Lutz (2006, ix) has called the "dangerous lover"—"the one whose eroticism lies in his dark past, his restless inquietude, his remorseful and rebellious exile from comfortable everyday living." In Hull's novel, this dangerous lover is vengeful, moody, and subject to "taciturn fits." He has "dark fierce eyes," "steely strength," and animal savagery: "The cruel lines about his mouth were accentuated and the tiger-look in his face was more marked than ever." In this Beauty and the Beast variant, the dangerous lover is tamed, as Diana and the sheik (providentially revealed to be the son of the Earl of Glencaryle) declare their mutual love.

Sheik Ahmed Ben Hassan stands in a long line of charismatic hero/villains who have descended from Milton's Satan in *Paradise Lost* and the dark villains of the GOTHIC and who have morphed into the cruel sheiks, plundering pirates, and predatory vampires of twentieth- and twenty-first-century popular romances. Byron's tormented, exiled heroes belong in this genealogy, as do Emily Bronte's Heathcliffe and Charlotte Bronte's Rochester. In gothic novels, male characters were split into virtuous but boring heroes and sexy, but irredeemably bad, villains. Byron's self-punishing heroes couldn't be redeemed either. Byron gave enormous currency to the brooding, scornful, despairing, self-loathing, misanthropic hero with a guilty secret who wanders in exile, forever cut off from everyday happiness. In *The Vampyre*, Byron's personal surgeon, Polidori, invents a Byron-inspired VAMPIRE, Lord Ruthven, who uses his irresistible magnetism to lure women to their death. No happy endings with any of these villain/heroes. But in *Jane Eyre*, Charlotte Bronte transformed the gothic/Byronic villain into a character who can be saved through the redemptive power of love. The dangerous lover was now available to be adopted by a genre of fiction that insists on the happy ending.

Deborah Lutz (2006, 1) claims that the "dangerous lover lurks in almost all the categories of romance"—all but the contemporary romance with the beta hero, who is sensitive, supportive, easygoing, and laid-back. In an attenuated form, the enemy lover provided the sexual energy of the "sweet" Harlequins with contemporary settings written in the 1960s and 1970s. In these, a young virginal heroine, either orphaned or rendered penniless by an unreliable father or brother, works as a nurse, secretary, assistant librarian, or child-care worker for an older, richer, arrogant hero whose history has left him moody, cynical, and embittered about women. In the historical romances, including the gothic, the Regency, and especially the erotic historical, the dangerous lover is given much more scope. After the runaway success of Kathleen Woodiwiss's erotic historical, *The Flame and the Flower* (1972), single title romances got a lot sexier and started to feature sea travel, plundering pirates, dark brooding heroes, captivity, rape, and a strong female lead. Lutz (2006, 6) asks:

> What was it about the "bodice-ripper" that caused such a historical break, a radical shift in romance formulas thereafter? Their essential charm stems from their erotic dangerousness, their near-pornographic sexual violence, and their eroticization of travel, of the world and all its exhilarating experiences. . . . The formula hinges on the elusive and cryptic hero who gestures toward the endless possibility of erotic darkness.

Significantly, these stories of forced seduction start with a large power differential between hero and heroine and trace the gradual transfer of power to the heroine.

By the mid-1980s and following, readers were telling researchers (Thurston 1987, 129) and each other that they were fed up with arrogant, moody, violent heroes and were definitely turned off by rape scenes. Captivity-and-forced-seduction stories, however popular they were formerly, began to evoke strong antipathy and are no longer published. In a discussion in the Amazon Romance Forum (March 21, 2008) that asked, "What are the worst romance books you've read and why?" the majority of respondents singled out books with abusive, violent heroes (one respondent thought a particular author must actually be a man "because I honestly can't believe that women find anything about her creepy heroes remotely appealing"). One reader said, "I like a sometimes harsh, alpha hero, but deliberately and calculatingly cruel and abusive is a total turn off and makes my stomach turn."

Which is not to say that readers don't still find the dangerous, demon lover attractive—just not in the guise of violent abuser or rapist. Romance fiction has renewed its appeal for readers in large part through updating elements of the formula in response to changing social standards and the demands of its readers. The dangerous lover, without the forced seduction element, has recently returned in paranormal romances. A new line, Harlequin Nocturne, wants "stories of vampires, shape-shifters, werewolves, psychic powers, etc. set in contemporary times." The guidelines for writers specify that these stories must "deliver a dark, very sexy read. . . . The hero is a key figure—powerful, mysterious and totally attractive to the heroine." Deborah Lutz (2006, 89) gets the last word: "But finally the dangerous lover's meaning comes from those who desire him: those who themselves long as deeply as he does. One must wonder whether or not the dangerous lover can even be seen except through the lens of women's desire." The heroine's desire, perhaps, but more importantly the reader's.

References

Amazon Romance Forum. 2008. "What Is the Worst Romance You've Read?" March 21. http://www.amazon.com/forum/romance/Tx3V88YODYKUDL4/tag =peekycom03-20/10.

Betz, Phyllis M. 2009. *Lesbian Romance Novels: A History and Critical Analysis.* Jefferson, NC: McFarland & Company, Inc.

Brackett, Kim Pettigrew. 2000. "Facework Strategies among Romance Fiction Readers." *Social Science Journal* 37, 3.

Bouricius, Ann. 2000. *The Romance Readers' Advisory: The Librarian's Guide to Love in the Stacks.* Chicago and London: American Library Association.

Cawelti, John G. 1976. *Adventure, Mystery, and Romance: Formula Stories as Art and Popular Culture.* Chicago: University of Chicago Press.

Chelton, Mary K. 1991. "Unrestricted Body Parts and Predictable Bliss: The Audience Appeal of Formula Romances." *Library Journal* 116, no. 12: 44–49.

Createc. 2005. *Reading and Buying Books for Pleasure: 2005 National Survey, Final Report.* Department of Canadian Heritage. http://data.library.utoronto.ca/datapub/ codebooks/utm/srbb05/srbb05_report.pdf.

Dear Author. 2010a. "Poll Time Are There Storylines You Just Won't Read." *Dear Author: A Romance Review Blog for Readers by Readers.* September 7. http://

dearauthor.com/features/poll-misc/poll-time-are-there-storylines-you-just-wont
-read/.

Dear Author. 2010b. "Are There Storylines You'll Always Read (or Almost Always?)."
Dear Author: A Romance Review Blog for Readers by Readers. September 14.
http://dearauthor.com/features/letters-of-opinion/are-there-storylines-youll-always
-read-or-almost-always/

Dear Author. 2010c. "Originality in Genre Fiction—an Oxymoron?" *Dear Author: A
Romance Review Blog for Readers by Readers.* October 19. http://dearauthor
.com/features/letters-of-opinion/originality-in-genre-fiction-an-oxymoron/

Dixon, Jay. 1999. *The Romance Fiction of Mills & Boon, 1909–1990s.* London: UCL
Press.

Dubino, Jeanne. 1993. "The Cinderella Complex: Romance Fiction, Patriarchy, and
Capitalism." *Journal of Popular Culture* 27, no. 3: 103–18.

Frantz, Sarah S. G., and Eric Murphy Selinger, eds. 2012. *New Approaches to Popular
Romance Fiction: Critical Essays.* Jefferson, NG: McFarland and Company.

Frye, Northrop. 1957. *The Anatomy of Criticism.* Princeton, NJ: Princeton University
Press.

Greer, Germaine. 1970. *The Female Eunuch.* New York: McGraw Hill.

Grescoe, Paul. 1996. *The Merchants of Venus: Inside Harlequin and the Empire of
Romance.* Vancouver: Raincoast.

Harlequin. "Writing Guidelines." http://www.harlequin.com/articlepage.html?
articleId=538&chapter=0.

International Association for the Study of Popular Romance (IASPR). http://iaspr.org/.

James, Eloisa. 2012. "The National Book Festival." *Popular Romance Project.* http://
popularromanceproject.org/behind-scenes/4090/.

Jensen, Margaret Ann. 1984. *Love's $weet Return: The Harlequin Story.* Toronto:
Women's Educational Press.

Jones, Ann Rosalind. 1986. "Mills & Boon Meets Feminism." In *The Progress of
Romance: The Politics of Popular Fiction*, 195–18. Edited by Jean Radford.
London and New York: Routledge and Kegan Paul.

Juhasz, Suzanne. 1988. "Texts to Grow On: Reading Women's Romance Fiction."
Tulsa Studies in Women's Literature 7, no. 2: 239–59.

Krentz, Jayne Ann, ed. 1992. *Dangerous Men and Adventurous Women: Romance Writers on the Appeal of the Romance.* Philadelphia: University of Pennsylvania Press.

Krentz, Jayne Ann. 2000. "Are We There Yet? Mainstreaming the Romance." Keynote
Address, Bowling Green State University Conference on Romance, August. http://
www.krentz-quick.com/bgspeech.html.

Likesbooks.com. n.d. HEA, part 1. http://www.likesbooks.com/hea.html.

Linz, Cathie. 1992. "Setting the Stage." In Jayne Ann Krentz, ed. *Dangerous Men and
Adventurous Women*, 12–13. Philadelphia: University of Pennsylvania Press.

Lutz, Deborah. 2006. *The Dangerous Lover: Gothic Villains, Byronism, and the Nineteenth Century Seduction Narrative*. Columbus: Ohio University Press.

Mann, Peter. 1974. *A New Survey: The Facts about Romantic Fiction*. London: Mills & Boon.

Mann, Peter H. 1981. "The Romantic Novel and Its Readers." *Journal of Popular Culture* 15, no. 1 (summer): 9–18.

McAleer, Joseph. 1999. *Passion's Fortune: The Story of Mills & Boon*. Oxford: Oxford University Press.

Modleski, Tania. 1982. *Loving With a Vengeance: Mass-Produced Fantasies for Women*. Hamden, CT: Archon Books.

Mussell, Kay, ed. 1997. "Where's Love Gone? Transformations in Romance Fiction and Scholarship." *Where's Love Gone?: Transformations in the Romance Genre*, special issue of *Para-Doxa* 3, no. 1–2: 9.

Mussell, Kay. 1984. *Fantasy and Reconciliation: Contemporary Formulas of Women's Romance Fiction*. Westport, CT: Greenwood Press.

Owen, Mairead. 1990. *Women's Reading of Popular Romantic Fiction: A Case Study in the Mass Media, A Key to the Ideology of Women*. PhD Thesis. University of Liverpool.

Owen, Mairead. 1997. "Re-inventing Romance: Reading Popular Romantic Fiction." *Women's Studies International Forum* 20, no. 4: 537–46. http://www.brown.uk.com/brownlibrary/RM.htm.

Radway, Janice A. 1984/ 1991. *Reading the Romance: Women, Patriarchy and Popular Literature*. Chapel Hill: University of North Carolina Press.

Ramsdell, Kristin. 1982/2012. *Romance Fiction: A Guide to the Genre*, 2nd ed. Santa Barbara, CA: Libraries Unlimited.

Regis, Pamela. 2003. *A Natural History of the Romance Novel*. Philadelphia: University of Pennsylvania Press.

Romance Wiki. "Romance Scholarship." http://www.romancewiki.com/Romance_Scholarship.

Romance Writers of America Website. "The Romance Genre." http://www.rwa.org/p/cm/ld/fid=582

Romance Writers of America. "Romance Industry Statistics." http://www.rwa.org/p/cm/ld/fid=580.

Saricks, Joyce G. 2009. "Romance." *The Readers' Advisory Guide to Genre Fiction*, 131–53. Chicago: American Library Association.

Snitow, Ann Barr. 1979. "Mass Market Romance: Pornography for Women Is Different." *Radical History Review* 20: 141–61.

Teo, Hsu-Ming. 2012. *Desert Passions: Orientalism and Romance Novels*. Austin, TX: Texas University Press.

Thurston, Carol. 1987. *The Romance Revolution: Erotic Novels for Women and the Quest for a New Sexual Identity*. Urbana: The University of Illinois Press.

Vivanco, Laura. 2011. *For Love and Money: The Literary Art of the Harlequin Mills & Boon Romance*. Tirril, Penrith: Humanities Ebooks.

Wendell, Sarah. 2008. "My Favorite Heroines." *Smart Bitches, Trashy Books*. (June 1) http://smartbitchestrashybooks.com/m/blog/my-favorite-heroines.

Wendell, Sarah, and Candy Tan. 2009. *Beyond Heaving Bosoms: The Smart Bitches' Guide to Romance Novels*. New York: Simon and Schuster.

Wyatt, Neal, Georgine Olson, Kristin Ramsdell, Joyce Saricks, and Lynne Welch. 2007. "Core Collections in Genre Studies: Romance Fiction 101." *Reference and User Services Quarterly* 47, 2 (Winter): 120–26.

Self-help

The self-help genre shares two characteristics with the ROMANCE genre: it sells in huge numbers, and academic critics hate it. Self-help is scorned for some of the same reasons that people scorn romance: the audience for self-help is assumed to be largely female; its content is repetitive; and it has become an enormous commercial moneymaker. Undeniably, self-help is big business—many billions of dollars a year by some estimates, if you include spin-offs, audio and video products, seminars, workshops, and life-coaching. Critics find this commercial success undeserving and attribute it to the easily duped nature of the mass reader. And, as if all this isn't bad enough, there are additional reasons for uneasiness: self-help books focus on problems—interpersonal relationships, questions of identity and self-discovery, money problems, employment problems, addictions, problems with health and diet, coping with difficult situations, living with stress—and the books often frame these problems as illnesses in need of therapy. The advice provided is considered to be overly simplified: it is broken down into discrete steps or stages or numbered tips (e.g., four agreements; five dysfunctions; seven habits, ten stupid things, twelve steps, one hundred simple things).

And finally, and most damning of all, self-help emphasizes the self. Advice is directed to an individual reader, who works to fix the self rather than taking collective action in the public sphere to address the sociopolitical ills that are root causes of the problems. Self-help readers are encouraged to invest in and rely upon themselves (and sometimes God). According to Micki McGee in *Self-Help, Inc.* (2005), the idea of individual self-help is a trap that results in "endless cycles of self-invention" and the "belabored self." Elayne Rapping (1996, 11) argues that self-help and the associated recovery movement enmeshes women in a master narrative that constructs female unhappiness as an illness in need of recovery, when the real problem is inequality in the home and in the workforce.

Satirical glee is a common response from those who write academically about self-help books. Self-help book titles, especially in the aggregate, lend themselves to ridicule. Critics such as Kelefa Sanneh (2010) in *The New Yorker* have singled out ludicrous passages from self-help texts such as Rhonda Byrne's explanation in *The Secret* (2006) of the "Laws of Attraction": "Thoughts are magnetic, and thoughts have a frequency. As you think, those thoughts are sent out into the Universe and they magnetically attract all *like* things that are on the same frequency. Everything sent out returns to the source. And that source is you." And for a genre in which the bedrock of moral authority is good character, the satiric impulse is awakened when there is a big gap between the public advice and the author's private life. For example, Ellen Fein, co-author of *The Rules for Marriage: Time-Tested Secrets for Making Your Marriage Work* (2001), filed for divorce on the eve of her book's release. Jack Canfield, "Success Coach" and author of the *Chicken Soup for the Soul*, walked out on his pregnant wife and took up with his masseuse—this according to a tell-all memoir *Freefall* (2009) by Canfield's son.

Self-help books are works of NONFICTION that offer advice on how to change your life for the better. The topics of best-selling self-help books have remained stable over the years: personal growth, communication and relationships, love, marriage, parenting, diet and health, money, job success, happiness, and spiritual life. At Amazon, the "self-help" category included some 175,000 paperback book titles in December 2013, with the largest sub-categories in personal transformation, relationships, and motivational. No wonder cultural authorities worry that self-help books are completely swamping nonfiction lists. When in 1983 the *New York Times Book Review* added the category of advice books to its best-seller lists, the explanation given apparently was that this new category was needed to free up the nonfiction list for genuine works of nonfiction such as biographies, histories, travel narratives, scientific accounts, political analysis, and so on.

Readers have for a long time made self-help a hugely popular segment of the nonfiction market. But recently self-help has been given a push by a government program in which self-help books are prescribed as bibliotherapy. In July 2013, the British government announced a new program, "Reading Well Books on Prescription," which has partnered with public libraries to make available across England a core list of 30 recommended books that take a cognitive behavioral approach to overcoming various mental health problems such as anxiety, eating disorders, chronic pain, and mood disorders (Reading Agency 2013). We usually think of self-help books as nonfiction, but *The Novel Cure* (2013) by British bibliotherapists Susan Elderkin and Ella Berthoud prescribe 751 novels for whatever ails you from abandonment to zestlessness. (Suffering from "Common Sense, Lack of"? Try Stella Gibson's *Cold Comfort Farm*.) The burgeoning field of bibliotherapy and self-help books has also called forth efforts at bibliographic control. *Self-Help That Works* by John C. Norcross and colleagues (2013) is designed to help laypersons and mental health professionals sort out the wheat from the chaff. This comprehensive guide evaluates some 2,000 titles in 41 categories from abuse and addictions to violent youth and women's issues.

Something about the Self-help Genre

The self-help genre is a very diverse category of books with a long history. Unlike writers of MYSTERY, WESTERN, or ROMANCE, writers of self-help books have not organized themselves into a self-help writers association for purposes of marketing, professional support, and the awarding of prizes. Nevertheless, despite marked differences in the domains in which advice is offered, from decluttering your closets to facing death, there are key features that most self-help books share. Describing the psychological self-help book, sociologist Arlie Russell Hochschild (1994, 3–4) claims that most have four parts. These are:

1. The "establishment of a tone of voice" that connects the reader to a source of authority such as the Bible, psychoanalysis, new research on how the brain works, or corporate expertise.

2. A "description of a moral or social reality" such as "This is how men are" or "That's what the job market's like."

3. "Concrete practices" such as "With your boyfriend, listen, with your girlfriend, you can talk" or "Wear blue to a 'power breakfast meeting' at work."

4. Illustrative stories that illustrate key points of the advice. Such stories, Hochschild says, "tend to be either exemplary or cautionary. Exemplary stories tell one what to do and cautionary stories tell one what not to do." These stories "contain magnified moments, episodes of heightened importance" that reveal a feeling, either wonderful or terrible. An examination of these magnified moments provides clues to the "cultural premises" undergirding the advice.

To this analysis, Sandra Dolby (2005, 69) adds the idea of the "problem/ solution framework." In *Self-help Books: Why Americans Keep Buying Them* (2005), Dolby uses the tools of folklore studies to analyze motifs found in some 300 self-help books. She explains the genre's popularity in terms of its problem–solution structure and its use of stories and aphorisms as rhetorical resources. She notes that Scott Peck starts off his book *A World Waiting to Be Born* (1993) with a statement about the problem: "There is an illness abroad in the land" and later on the first page, "Something is seriously wrong." Self-help writers, Dolby (2005, 75) argues, present the solution as the result of the reader's engagement, first unlearning the faulty conventional thinking that is causing the problem and then learning and acting on new ways of thinking:

Writers who do this most effectively usually follow a seven-step sequence: (1) They identify a given problem—for example, poor time management, failed intimacy in personal relationships, a tendency to overwork or underachieve, worry about death, general unhappiness. (2) They explain the problem's strength and endurance as a consequence of faulty thinking. (3) They account for both the presence and persistence of the faulty thinking itself by examining the traditional (or sometimes inherent or archetypal) sources that maintain that thinking in the culture. (4) If possible, they offer vehicles for alternative patterns of thinking—often stories, slogans, or sayings. (5) They interpret the information they have presented to the reader as supportive of the new, enlightened thinking they hope to promote. (6) Often, they then suggest changes in behavior and practice that will move the reader away from the old thinking and reinforce the new. (7) Finally, they include an epilogue or conclusion in which they remind the reader that the message of the book can only be realized in the reader's own application. This is the writer's last word—the rhetorical and inspirational send-off.

Dolby's account underlines the rhetorical nature of the genre and provides another reminder that the term *well-written* is genre dependent. Many of the stylistic features of the self-help book are well-suited to goals of persuasion and teaching, including the direct address to the reader as "you," memorable slogans that encapsulate the advice, repetition of key points, bullet points and numbered lists, illustrative stories, and the "inspirational send-off" that reminds readers that it's all down to them.

The book that gave its name to the entire genre is Samuel Smiles's *Self-Help: With Illustrations of Character, Conduct, and Perseverence* (1854). Disillusioned after 20 years of tireless work for parliamentary and social reform, Smiles turned to "individual reform." In his introduction, Smiles, a Scotsman, provides an origin story for what turned into a 300-page book: 15 years earlier he was approached by members of a self-improvement group of working-class men who met in the evenings in a northern town in Scotland and asked to "talk to them a bit." Impressed by the "admirable self helping spirit which they had displayed," he spoke several times to the group, telling them stories "of what other men had done, as illustrations of what each might, in a greater or less degree, do for himself and pointing out that their happiness . . . must necessarily depend mainly upon themselves." Chapter One starts, "The spirit of self-help is the root of all genuine growth in the individual; and, exhibited in the lives of many, it constitutes the true source of national vigor and strength." Smiles followed up the big success of *Self-Help* with *Character* (1871) and *Thrift* (1875). He captured in these inaugural self-help books characteristics that still define the genre: the optimistic tone; the confidence that the individual can change things for the better by adopting certain new habits or practices; and the educational intent.

The self-help book has a long history from the treatises by ancient Greek and Roman philosophers on how to lead the good life to conduct books dating from the Middle Ages to Renaissance courtesy books such as *The Courtier* to advice found in Farmer's Almanacs such as Benjamin Franklin's *Poor Richard's Almanac*. In 1757, Franklin provided a brief summary of 25 years of Poor Richard's pithy advice in *The Way to Wealth*, an eight-page essay. In the opening paragraphs of an account structured as a tale within a tale, Poor Richard relates how he stopped his horse where a lot of people were gathered waiting for a sale of merchant goods to start. People were complaining about the badness of the times, and one asked an old man with white locks, "Won't these high taxes quite ruin the country?" Father Abraham responded with a "harangue" on industry, thrift, the effective use of time, and avoiding debt— all based on Poor Richard's proverbial sayings. Here's a sampling that emphasizes a topic dear to Poor Richard's heart—time management:

> *If time be of all things the most precious, wasting time must be*, as Poor Richard says, *the greatest prodigality*; since, as he elsewhere tells us, *Lost time is never found again; and what we call time enough, always proves little enough*. Let us then up and be doing, and doing to the purpose; so by diligence shall we do more with less perplexity. *Sloth makes all things difficult but industry all easy; and He that riseth late must trot all day, and shall scarce overtake his business at night* while *Laziness travels so slowly, that poverty soon overtakes him. Drive thy business, let not that drive thee; and Early to bed, and early to rise, makes a man healthy, wealthy, and wise*, as Poor Richard says.

Like the modern self-help books described by Wendy Dolby, Father Abraham ends by exhorting the advice-recipient to translate advice into action: "we may give advice, but we cannot give conduct." Poor Richard, who was listening all the while, noted that the crowd approved the advice on frugality and avoiding debt but "immediately practiced the contrary" and "began to buy extravagantly." All the same, Poor Richard says that he felt flattered that the old man had studied and digested his almanacs, even though "I was conscious that not a tenth part of the wisdom was my own which he ascribed to me, but rather the gleanings I had made of the sense of all ages and nations." Called to his senses by this echo of his own advice, Poor Richard decides against his former plan of buying material for a new coat: "I went away resolved to wear my old one a little longer. Reader, if thou wilt do the same, thy profit will be as great as mine." In short, Franklin's *The Way to Wealth* demonstrates many of the features that came to characterize self-help books: the use of the second person "you"; the retelling of conventional wisdom in a novel way; the optimistic sense that the individual can be healthy, wealthy and wise by adopting new habits; the pithy slogans that sum up the desirable new habits; the warning that others—the crowd—may fail; and finally the exhortation to the reader to succeed by turning new knowledge into deeds. All that remained for the development of the self-help genre was to flesh out the pithy essay format into a full-length book with the help of the illustrative cases, examples, and checklists that are now required.

Who Reads Self-help Books?

The imagined reader of self-help books is a self-involved woman with fragile mental health. In an article on whether " 'self-help' is really any help at all" published in *The Observer* (October 26, 2003), Polly Vernon starts off with an anecdote about a friend of hers. The friend met a woman at a party, accepted an invitation to crash at her house, but then noticed with alarm that her bookshelves "were monopolised by upwards of 50 titles from the self-help genre. *I'm OK— You're OK. Feel The Fear and Do It Anyway. Men Are From Mars, Women Are From Venus. The Road Less Travelled. Women Who Love Too Much. Chicken Soup for the Soul. A Course in Miracles.*" The friend realized in a millisecond that he had wandered into the home of "a nutter." "Alarm bells started ringing," and he knew that he "must leave immediately."

If the imagined readers are nutters, who then are the actual readers? National readership surveys indicate that a large percentage of people who claim to be book-readers in general say that they read self-help books. Polls indicate that between one-third and one-half of Americans have bought a self-help book (Whelan 2004, 2). Women read them, but men read them too, though men and women favor different titles. In August 2010, the Harris Poll (2010) conducted an online survey of 2,775 U.S. adults ages 18 and over. Among the readers who said that they had read a book in the past year, 16 percent reported reading self-help books, 26 percent reported reading religious and spirituality books, and 10 percent reported reading business books. In the Canadian study *Reading and Buying Books for Pleasure* (Createc 2005), based on a national telephone survey of 1963 Canadians who were 16 or older, 87 percent of respondents reported that they had read at least one book for pleasure in the past 12 months. Of these readers, at least half reported reading what we might consider a self-help book, although that category was not used explicitly. Presented with a "pre-established list of 24 genres," respondents were asked to identify which genres of books they had read in the past 12 months. On average, respondents reported reading 17 books spread across nine different genres. We can't know how respondents understood these categories or whether there was much consistency from one respondent to the next about how they applied the labels. Nevertheless, it is safe to say that, except for business books, women read more than men do of books that could be considered self-help books: books on health, fitness, childcare (read by 63% of female book readers versus 44% of male book readers), and personal growth and self-awareness (read by 50% of female book readers versus 33% of male book readers).

One of the questions asked in the Createc (2005, 85) survey may provide insight into self-help reading. To tap the factor "Reading as a Way of Life," the 1,963 respondents were asked if they agreed or disagreed with the statement, "When I encounter a problem, I find a book to help me deal with the situation." Presumably the 13 percent who reported not having read a book in the past 12 months were among the 31 percent who disagreed totally or somewhat that they turned to books for help with a problem. Adding together those who agreed somewhat or totally, we find 58 percent who say they turn to books for help with a problem. These readers find a close text-to-life connection and believe that in a wide range of situations books are a reliable source of help—a preferred place to go when help is needed. When these 58 percent encounter a problem in their life, they find a helpful book. I am betting that, for many among this 58 percent, the book they found helpful was a self-help book. Self-help books are directed to readers who think that they can fix problems and change their lives.

When sociologist Christine Whelan (2004, 317) studied the self-help phenomenon in the United States for her D.Phil dissertation, she concluded that the typical "self-help reader is a well-educated, middle-class American in his or her late 30s or early 40s, who is more self-confident, sophisticated and open to innovation than the average American." In her review of the admittedly spotty survey research on who reads self-help books, Whelan (2004, 68) concluded that reading self-help books is strongly correlated with having higher levels of education and income. The gist of her argument is that people in this demographic already have a lot of control in their lives, that they value this self-control, and that they seek out more of it when they read self-help books. It's the "Matthew Effect": to those that hath shall be given even more of what they already have. Because self-help readers, like readers in general, have more money and more education than average, they have resources that can help them to make changes in themselves or in their environments, and they have confidence in their ability to change things for the better.

Reading Self-help as a Critic, or "Something Is Seriously Wrong"

If self-help books, which are sold in huge numbers, really work to help people with their problems, then why aren't people healthier, richer, and happier? Why does one out of every two marriages end in divorce? Why are so many people struggling with drug or alcohol addictions? Why are so many North Americans taking antidepressants? Why are people too fat and getting fatter? It's *because* people are reading self-help books, some say (although others say the main problem is high fructose corn syrup). Titles of some recent books provide a good index to what critics think of self-help: Wendy Kaminer's *I'm Dysfunctional, You're Dysfunctional* (1992); Tom Tiede's *Self-Help Nation: The Long Overdue, Entirely Justified, Delightfully Hostile Guide to the Snake-Oil Peddlers Who Are Sapping Our Nation's Soul* (2001); Micki McGee's *Self-Help, Inc.: Makeover Culture in American Life* (2005); Steve Salerno's *SHAM: How the Self-Help Movement Made America Helpless* (2005); and

Barbara Ehrenreich's *Bright-Sided: How the Relentless Promotion of Positive Thinking Has Undermined America* (2009).

Sapping and undermining America and making it helpless—yikes! Salerno's book, which bills itself on its cover blurb as an "exposé" of the "Self-Help and Actualization Movement (SHAM)," promises to reveal the "real damage" this multibillion-dollar industry "is doing—not just to its paying customers, but to all of American society." As evidence that the industry is a boondoggle, Salerno reveals that the most likely purchaser of a self-help book is someone who has bought a similar book in the past 18 months. Using terms such as *infected* and *infiltrate*, Salerno warns that the self-help phenomenon is an invisible toxin all around us, secretly working harm. "What if it's actually SHAM that's screwing people up?" Salerno (2005, 39) asks. Without offering evidence, Salerno holds self-help books responsible for, among other things, rising divorce rates, threats to the nuclear family, and increasing rates of substance abuse.

Wendy Kaminer (1992), a forerunner in the critique of the self-help industry, also thinks that the recovery movement is making us sick. Her target is what she calls "personal (how to be happy) books" that focus on the inner self. Following the success of Alcoholics Anonymous and the famous Twelve Steps, these self-help books have taken a therapeutic turn, immersing readers in the language of illness and recovery. Furthermore, according to Kaminer (1992, Introduction), the self-help industry gives lip service to individual choice while actually taking choice away. It emphasizes self-efficacy and independence while promoting conformity by delivering readers into the hands of experts who tell them all to follow the very same steps and techniques. In a nutshell, she says that the self-help tradition is "conformist, authoritarian, an exercise in majority rule," and the "popularity of books comprising slogans, sound bites, and recipes for success" is part of a larger trend to be "blamed for political apathy." Critics such as Kaminer (1992), Salerno (2005), and Ehrenreich (2009) hold the self-help phenomenon culpable as a *cause* of societal decline, whereas McGee (2005) sees the huge sales of self-help books as a *response* to a crumbling social structure, where jobs are disappearing and families are breaking apart. McGee (2005, 12) warns that "the promise of self-help can lead workers into a new sort of enslavement: into a cycle where the self is not improved but endlessly belabored."

Framing her critique of self-help in a more personal way, Barbara Ehrenreich (2009) begins her book with an account of how the obligation to engage in "positive thinking" was harmful when she herself was diagnosed with cancer. (For the UK edition, the TITLE was changed from *Bright-sided* to *Smile or Die*.) The term *positive thinking* was of course popularized by Norman Vincent Peale's book, *The Power of Positive Thinking* (1952), but earlier versions of the concept predated Peale. Notably there was the autosuggestion method of the French psychologist Emile Coué, who in the 1920s recommended frequent daily repetitions of "Every day, in every way, I'm getting better and better."

Ehrenreich traces the "dark roots" of positive thinking from Calvinism through nineteenth-century thinkers such as Mary Baker Eddy and William James to such twentieth-century best-selling writers as Napoleon Hill, author of *Think and Grow Rich* (1937). The idea behind positive thinking is that thinking something makes it happen. Visualize the body's illness-fighting forces eating up cancer cells, and the cancer will recede. Imagine yourself rich or popular or successful, and you will become so. Ehrenreich reserves her greatest scorn for what she calls the "inescapable pseudoscientific flapdoodle" (71) that is used to explain this power of mind over matter: invocations to quantum physics, vibrations, magnetism, or the "Laws of Attraction."

Reading as a Reader

Self-help critics deliberately distance themselves from ordinary readers who read self-help books to get help. In her introduction, Wendy Kaminer (1992) says specifically, "I have attended support groups only as an observer, not as a participant. I have read self-help books only as a critic, not as a seeker, and I was rarely engaged by the books that I read (one hundred or so), except as a critic." To understand the reading experience of people who are not reading as distanced observers, we need to turn to the readers themselves and what they say about the role of self-books in their lives. For this, we can use evidence from published accounts of reading, interviews with readers, and statements posted by readers in public forums such as in Amazon reviews and online discussion groups. One of the key things that readers tell us is the importance of their personal situation at the time of reading: readers turn to self-help books that speak directly to their individual and current concerns.

In *Promised Land: Thirteen Books That Changed America* (2008), Jay Parini includes a chapter on Dale Carnegie's *How to Win Friends and Influence People* (1936), a self-help benchmark that has now sold more than 16 million copies worldwide. In it, Parini positions himself, among other things, as a reader. The chapter starts with a general acknowledgement, "People often feel helpless, out of their depth, powerless," followed by an historical stage-setting of 1936 as a time of breadlines, unemployed breadwinners, helpless wives, and hungry children. "In the midst of this dismal scene came Dale Carnegie, with a cheerful book that turned the heads of millions, giving them a specific way to reinvent themselves in a country where self-invention itself defines our culture" (2008, 239). Then comes the more personal statement: "Like many others, I have a personal debt to this book" (241). Parini describes how, growing up in the 1950s and early 1960s as a quiet, shy, unbefriended boy in Scranton, Pennsylvania, he found in the public library a battered copy of *How to Win Friends*. Following Carnegie's advice, he bought a dime-store notebook, wrote out the steps (listen to people; seek out qualities that you can admire and praise in others, etc.), and spent the year systematically working his way through the Carnegie system. Not without some retrospective reservations about the advice, Parini (241) reports, "I still think the Carnegie method had its benefits and that it worked wonders in my own life, making me much less self-conscious, more interested in the lives of others . . . and more likely to see good things in people."

Parini's account of self-help reading shares features with accounts of other readers. Readers are typically selective—they do not read indiscriminately across the whole spectrum of self-help books but pick a book that addresses the situation they are currently facing. If the book isn't helpful, they stop reading it. Unlike readers of DETECTIVE or ROMANCE fiction who read steadily in the preferred genre from one year to the next and often throughout a lifetime, readers read self-help books in bursts, often with long gaps in between. During some troubling personal situation—a child is doing badly at school, a loved one has been diagnosed with a terminal illness, a personal relationship is failing, a retirement is imminent—readers may read a number of books on the particular topic. Remember that these are people who say that when they encounter a problem in their life, they find a book to help them with the situation.

A good example is Sue, age 45, whose story is told in Polly Vernon's *Observer* article (2003). Sue had just been through a very difficult break-up, the second in five years. After the first split, she had gone to therapy, which didn't give her any answers and left her feeling like a patient. After the second breakup, she read self-help books, which made her "feel like I was taking responsibility for myself, but being supported":

> I could go at my own pace. I could take certain elements and dismiss others, while I'd felt that my therapist thought I was failing if I didn't embrace everything she offered. There's a lot of rubbish out there, certainly, but there's a lot of good stuff. I shopped around for the things that resonated with me, and discarded the rest.

Sue's comment introduces some key themes that are repeated by other self-help readers. They say that they feel in control and can go at their own pace. They like the fact that they can return to certain passages and reread them over and over. Aware that there is a "lot of rubbish out there," they nevertheless trust themselves to be able to pick and choose, keeping the nuggets and discarding the dross.

Wendy Simonds's *Women and Self-Help Culture* (1992) is based in part on open-ended, qualitative interviews with 30 women who identified themselves as readers of self-help books. Simonds (1992, 16–19) describes her interviewees as "highly educated," "employed outside the home," and wide readers of "a variety of books for instructive purposes." Simonds (26) reports that her readers "were unanimous in their recognition that self-help books were repetitive, and thus secure. Reading could be a ritual of self-assurance where repetition was *desired*." These women spoke of self-help books "as 'tools' for accomplishing specific goals" and valued them for their immediate helpfulness at the specific time of reading (31). Readers were also well aware that self-help books are a denigrated genre. One interviewee told Simonds (44) that on learning that the interviewee read self-help books, a friend said, "You're so intelligent; I can't believe you read that crap!"

Active Readers as Gleaners and Miners

Sociologist Paul Lichterman (1992) conducted depth interviews on self-help reading with six men and nine women. Lichterman (1992, 423) explains his model of reading upfront: he rejects "the model of a passive audience through which ideological messages diffuse," embracing instead the reader-response model that "self-help readers construct meanings through their reading." From this second model, it follows that we can't deduce what meanings readers make of self-help books by conducting a close textual examination of self-help books themselves. Why not? Well, because ordinary readers don't feel obligated to read every word, but skip over parts that don't speak to their personal situations. They give extra weight to other parts, reading and rereading the passages that resonate. In this way, they take a generic book written to address a problem shared by millions and individualize it to suit their own needs, thereby creating their own version. The book might offer seven tips or twelve steps, but the reader might focus on just one or two. When Lichterman (1992, 430) asked his interviewees to tell him what is good about self-help books, "most of the readers spoke in terms of gleaning a 'nugget' in the books." One interviewee, Sheila, told him:

> You might only get maybe one or two sentences out of one of these books, that really apply to you in a way that you say, 'that's it. Aha!' And if you can apply that to your life, you've learned a tremendous thing.

In an attempt to answer the question of how self-help books may actually help readers, commentators often turn to metaphor. We have already encountered the idea in Poor Richard's account that self-help writers, and indirectly readers, are gleaners, gathering the leftover grain "of all ages and nations." Then there are Lichterman's readers who mine self-help materials to find the occasional gold nugget. Bergsma (2008, 356) speculates that maybe self-help books work more like travel guides: "Most readers will not follow the book page by page, but will study parts of the book and will select some travel options they would have never heard of without the book." All three of these metaphors of gleaning, mining nuggets, and selecting travel options put the reader in charge. Unlike the conformist readers who Wendy Kaminer imagines are mindlessly following prescribed steps, these readers pick and choose according to their own interests and needs. Introducing a therapeutic metaphor, Starker (1988, 171–73) suggests that self-help books are a placebo: it's the readers' belief that they can improve their lives that does the trick. Starker's conclusion: "the powerful inspirational message of the self-help book can, by itself, mobilize the healing forces of faith, hope, and courage."

In my own interviews with avid readers, many readers mentioned self-help books either as a genre they do not enjoy or, in contrast, as a book that has helped or made a difference (see QUESTIONS ABOUT READING). Here's what four readers said in response to the "book that has made a big difference in your life" question.

- *The Road Less Travelled* by M. Scott Peck has influenced a fair bit my thinking and perhaps my approach to life. It's not an entertaining book. It's one that deals with spiritual growth. I think the book has helped me to be a more open person. I've grown up with perhaps some very closed ideas with regard to the way other people should live, the way they should act, and this book has helped me to accept people for their differences and for their different ways of life. (Beverly, dietician, age 22)

- *I'm Okay You're Okay* by Eric Berne was important in my life because it made me realize that you can change yourself, if you put your mind to it. You can eliminate bad habits or change the way you do things. . . . I don't think that I ever really thought that you could do that before I read that book, and it made me decide that you could, so I think that book changed my life in some way. (Simon, lawyer, age 39)

- *Personal Power* by Tony Robbins changed the way I think because he emphasizes that you can learn things or learn how to achieve things by emulating other people, who have succeeded. Since reading that, I've tried to read more biographies or autobiographies. And I've also thought more about what I want to do with my life. (Sebastian, recording engineer, age 22)

- The most useful book that I've read recently has been a book called *Changes*, which is written by two psychologists. The idea is that when things are in flux, most of us are a bit uncomfortable. When people are going through life crises or depressions, quite often the need for change is very great. I found it a fascinating book—and really useful personally. [Ross: It helped you to do something in your own life?] Yes. It helped me understand how sometimes one's frustrations lead to the feeling that you have to change something. You have to change your job or your husband or your way of life or your world-view or whatever. But, in many cases, what you really have to do is to look at what you are doing yourself and not change all the other things around you. (Lisa, family physician, age 38)

Each of these four readers described the helpful book as life-changing: it "helped me to be a more open person" (Beverley); "it made me realize that you can change yourself" (Simon); it "changed the way I think" (Sebastian); "It helped me understand" that when life is frustrating, you should look first to change yourself and not try to change "all the other things around you" (Lisa). Readers who singled out self-help as a genre they *wouldn't* choose disliked the idea that a self-described expert presumes to change your life from the outside, sometimes arguing, "You have to figure it out for yourself." Self-help fans would probably say that their characteristic way of figuring out things for themselves is to read about it. What they get from the self-help books—gleanings or nuggets or travel options—they take selectively and read back again into their own lives.

References

Bergsma, Ad. 2008. "Do Self-help Books Help?" *Journal of Happiness Studies* 9: 341–60.

Createc. 2005. *Reading and Buying Books for Pleasure: 2005 National Survey, Final Report*. Canadian Heritage. http://publications.gc.ca/collections/Collection/CH44-61-2005E.pdf.

Dolby, Sandra K. 2005. *Self-help Books: Why Americans Keep Reading Them*. Urbana: University of Illinois Press.

Ehrenreich, Barbara. 2009. *Bright-sided: How the Relentless Promotion of Positive Thinking Has Undermined America*. New York: Henry Holt.

Elderkin, Susan, and Ella Berthoud. 2013. *The Novel Cure: An A–Z of Literary Remedies*. Edinburgh: Canongate.

Harris Interactive. 2010. "Stephen King Is America's Favorite Author; Mystery, Crime and Thriller Novels Are the Genre Most Read." *The Harris Poll*, October 7. http://multivu.prnewswire.com/mnr/harrisinteractive/44732/.

Hochschild, A. 1994. "The Commercial Spirit of Intimate Life and the Abduction of Feminism: Signs from Women's Advice Books." *Theory, Culture & Society* 11, no. 2: 1–24.

Kaminer, Wendy. 1992. *I'm Dysfunctional, You're Dysfunctional: The Recovery Movement and Other Self-Help Fashions*. Reading, MA: Addison-Wesley.

Lichterman, P. 1992. "Self-help Reading as Thin Culture," *Media, Culture & Society* 14: 421–47.

McGee, M. 2005. *Self-help, Inc.: Makeover Culture in American Life*. New York: Oxford University Press.

Norcross, John C., Linda F. Campbell, John M. Grohol, John W. Santrock, Florin Selagea, and Robert Sommer. 2013. *Self-Help That Works: Resources to Improve Emotional Health and Strengthen Relationships*, 4th ed. New York: Oxford University Press.

Rapping, Elayne. 1996. *The Culture of Recovery: Making Sense of the Self-Help Movement in Women's Lives*. Boston: Beacon Press.

Reading Agency. 2013. "Reading Well Books on Prescription Launches." http://readingagency.org.uk/news/media/reading-well-books-on-prescription-launches.html.

Salerno, Steve. 2005 *SHAM: How the Self-Help Movement Made America Helpless.* New York: Random House.

Sanneh, Kelefa. 2010. "What's Behind Rhonda Byrne's Spiritual Empire?" *The New Yorker*, September 13. http://www.newyorker.com/arts/critics/atlarge/2010/09/13/100913crat_atlarge_sanneh?currentPage=all.

Simonds, Wendy. 1992. *Women and Self-help Culture: Reading between the Lines.* Piscataway, NJ: Rutgers University Press.

Starker, Steven. 1988. *Oracle at the Supermarket: The American Preoccupation with Self-help Books.* New Brunswick: Transaction Publishers.

Vernon, Polly. 2003. "Feel the Fear . . . and Read It Anyway." *The Observer* (Sunday, October 26). http://www.guardian.co.uk/books/2003/oct/26/booksonhealth.lifeandhealth.

Whelan, Christine B. 2004. "Self-Help Books and the Quest for Self-Control in the United States 1950–2000." D.Phil. dissertation, Oxford University. http://christinewhelan.com/wp-content/uploads/Self-Help_Long_Abstract.pdf.

Titles

For publishers and booksellers, a title is a lure to attract readers. And readers report that it often works—when browsing, they say, "sometimes a title will catch my eye." According to research at Thomas Nelson (Hyatt n.d.), the first thing that readers look at is the title. If they are sufficiently attracted by the title, they look next at the following: the cover, the back cover, flaps (on hardcover books or trade paperbacks with "French flaps"), the table of contents, the first few paragraphs of the book itself, and finally the price. Each is a test, and the book may fail at any stage (see BEFORE READING). But not every reader puts the book through all seven tests. As Daniel, a 49-year-old plant mechanic, said when asked how he chose books, "I look for a pleasing title first. I don't know how I pick it out, but I look at the titles—I read the titles. I very seldom read a flyleaf." Maurice (professional engineer, age 57) uses titles as a way to identify and rule out whole categories of books: "I wouldn't even pick up a book that was called *The Andromeda Strain* or *Jurassic Park*, because they would immediately say to me, 'That's monsters or Sci-Fi.'" Sometimes readers take a flyer on a book on the basis of an intriguing title alone. One reader said about once a year he bought a book "simply because the title is outrageous" and had not yet been disappointed. A selective list of titles bought this way included: *Uppity Women of Ancient Greece*; *Canned Goods as Caviar*; and *Sabotage in the American Workplace*.

There are connoisseurs of book titles. Each year since 1978 *The Bookseller* in the United Kingdom has sponsored the Diagram prize, which "celebrates the oddest book title" presented at the Frankfurt Book Fair. After an "intensive judging process," the Longlist gets whittled down to six titles, which are voted on by visitors to the *Bookseller* Web site. One of my favorites, which won in 2007, is Julian Montague's *The Stray Shopping Carts of Eastern North America: A Guide to Field Identification*. Unlike the deliberate spoof of the *Stray Shopping Carts*, some titles seem to be inadvertently amusing such as Graham West's *Innovation and the Rise of the Tunnelling Industry*. In other cases, it is the topics, rather than the titles as such, that seem odd: *Collectible Spoons of the Third Reich*; *Knitting with Dog Hair*; *Greek Rural Postmen and Their Cancellation Numbers*.

In case you were wondering, the *Greek Rural Postmen* book, published by the Hellenic Philatelic Society of Great Britain, is all about Greek postage stamps, which have to be cancelled by postmen. This notable title won the Bookseller/Diagram prize in 1994 and in 1996 was distinguished by the "Diagram of Diagrams" prize for "having the oddest title of any book over the past 30 years." Philip Stone, co-ordinator of the Diagram Prize, said that the prize "draws welcome attention to an undervalued art. Publishers and booksellers know only too well that a title can make all the difference to the sales of a book. *A Short History of Tractors in Ukrainian* has sold almost a million copies to date, while books such as *Salmon Fishing in the Yemen*, *The Guernsey Literary and Potato Peel Pie Society* and *The Hundred-Year-Old Man Who Climbed Out of the Window and Disappeared* perhaps all owe some of their success to their unusual monikers" (Allen 2013).

Representing the Book versus Selling It

In the early days of the novel, authors gave their books the name of the main character to enhance the claim that novels are biography: *Tom Jones*, *Pamela*, *Moll Flanders*, *Robinson Crusoe*, *Emma*, *Jane Eyre*, *David Copperfield*, *Anna Karenina*, *Dracula*. Then came some new types: thematic titles such as *Sense and Sensibility*, *Vanity Fair*, *The Scarlet Letter*, and *Heart of Darkness*; titles that highlight setting such as *Wuthering Heights*, *The House of Seven Gables*, and *A Tale of Two Cities*; titles that suggest a mystery such as *Lady Audley's Secret* and *The Strange Case of Dr. Jekyll and Mr. Hyde*; and titles based on quotations such as *The Golden Bowl*. One problem from a marketing point of view is that before the book becomes well known, the main character's name is not a big draw. Hence the advantage of combining the name with the promise of excitement or mystery: *The Adventures of Tom Sawyer* or *Harry Potter and the Philosopher's Stone*.

Romance writer Jennifer Crusie (2007) acknowledges the conflict between two functions of a title: selling the book and representing it. On the one hand, the marketing function is to get noticed and tempt the reader to pull the book off the shelf. On the other hand, during reading itself the title is a crucial part of the structure of the book's meaning. She says, "Titles, like covers, are a marketing tool. The key is to come up with a snappy title that sells the book while representing it."

Publishers and editors usually come down on the marketing side of this balancing act between selling the book and encapsulating its meaning structure. The book by André Bernard (1995) on the story behind famous book titles contains many accounts of editors who complain that sales will be hurt by their authors' proposed titles. They say variously that specific titles are "too foreign"

(Monteriano for E. M. Forster's *Where Angels Fear to Tread*), "too cumbersome" and "too foreign" (John Nichols's *The Milagro Beanfield War*), "hopeless" (Poisonville for Dashiell Hammett's *Red Harvest*), "too obscure" (Mr. Norris Changes Trains for Christopher Isherwood's *Berlin Stories*), "meaningless" (Eugene O'Neill's *Mourning Becomes Electra*), too "peculiar" (J. D. Salinger's *The Catcher in the Rye*), and "flabby" (O Lost for Thomas Wolfe's *Look Homeward Angel*). Publishers quoted by Bernard have theories about what makes a good title. It should smite the reader in the eye; it should be easy to remember and short enough to say; it shouldn't contain internal punctuation or words that are hard to pronounce; it shouldn't contain an initial rebus such as a crucifix that makes it hard for librarians to put the title in alphabetical order; it shouldn't resemble some other popular title (Catch-18 got changed to *Catch-22* to avoid confusion with Leon Uris's just published *Mila-18*). And it should be easy to say and remember. The title of Alice Munro's ninth short story collection, *Hateship, Friendship, Courtship, Loveship, Marriage* was changed for the mass paperback edition to *Away from Her*, the title of a film made from one of the stories.

Readers also have ideas about what makes for a good title. In *Howards End Is on the Landing*, Susan Hill says (2010, 10): "A good title beckons, attracts, seduces, remains. . . . A good title makes a pattern, has a rhythm and can be rolled very satisfactorily round in the mouth, even recited like a verse to cheer up dull moments." She provides a rollcall of 18 seductive titles, each of which has "a certain ring." Here are the first nine:

The Heart Is a Lonely Hunter

The Ballad of the Sad Café

The Tenant of Wildfell Hall

Salmon Fishing in the Yemen

Tinker, Tailor, Soldier, Spy

The Mysterious Affair at Styles

A Woman's Guide to Adultery

All Fun and Games until Somebody Loses an Eye

The Curious Incident of the Dog in the Night-Time.

On the social media site Goodreads, members were asked to suggest, and then vote for, books on the Listopia list, "Best Book Titles: Most eyecatching or distinctive book titles." Here are the top 10:

1. *Do Androids Dream of Electric Sheep?* By Philip K. Dick

2. *Pride and Prejudice and Zombies* by Seth Grahame-Smith

3. *The Gordonston Ladies Dog Walking Club* by Duncan Whitehead

4. *Something Wicked This Way Comes b⌐ ⌐y Bradbury*

5. *The Hitchhiker's Guide to the Galaxy* ⌐Douglas Adams

6. *I Was Told There'd Be Cake* by Sloan ⌐sley

7. *The Hollow Chocolate Bunnies of the Ap⌐ ⌐alypse* by Robert Rankin

8. *Eats, Shoots & Leaves: The Zero Toler⌐ ⌐e Approach to Punctuation* by Lynne Truss

9. *The Curious Incident of the Dog in the N⌐ ⌐t-Time* by Mark Haddon

10. *Are You There Vodka? It's Me, Chelsea* ⌐y Chelsea Handler

At least half of these Goodreads titles are interte⌐ ⌐l. Two (2 and 10) echo already existing book titles. Two (4 and 9) are quot⌐ ⌐s from *Macbeth* and a story by Arthur Conan Doyle, respectively. In fact, ⌐ ⌐ations from other literary works supply titles for many well-known books, ⌐ th certain sources being especially fruitful. The Bible, for example, is the source for Henry James's *The Golden Bowl*, William Faulkner's *Absolom, Absolom!*, Ernest Hemingway's *The Sun Also Rises*, Dorothy Sayers's *Clouds of Witness*, James Agee's *Let Us Now Praise Famous Men*, Katherine Patterson's *Jacob Have I Loved*, John Steinbeck's *East of Eden*, and many others. There's Shakespeare of course: for example, Faulkner's *The Sound and the Fury* and Aldous Huxley's *Brave New World*. There's Milton: Thomas Wolfe's *Look Homeward, Angel*, Howard Spring's *Fame Is the Spur*, and Philip Pullman's *His Dark Materials*. There's Yeats: Cormac McCarthy's *No Country for Old Men*, Chinua Achebe's *Things Fall Apart*, and McMurtry's *Horseman, Pass By*. And of course T. S. Eliot: Evelyn Waugh's *A Handful of Dust* and Iain M. Banks's *Consider Phlebas*. The use of familiar quotations in a title has the advantage that it provides a readymade sense of familiarity.

Fitzgerald's preferred title for his third novel was *Trimalchio in West Egg*, but his editor, Maxwell Perkins of Scribner's, said "various gentlemen here don't like the title,—in fact none like it but me." Fitzgerald (1924) wrote back: "The only other titles that seem to fit it are *Trimalchio* and *On the Road to West Egg*. I had two others *Gold-hatted Gatsby* and *The High-bouncing Lover* but they seemed too light." Another suggested title was *Among the Ash Heaps and Millionaires*. In the end both Perkins and Zelda Fitzgerald liked *The Great Gatsby*, which fortunately won the day. Once a book is published under a particular title and becomes popular, the new title takes on the aura of inevitability and rightness, as in these examples of paired previous titles and final published titles:

James Agee. *Three Tenant Farmers*	*Let Us Now Praise Famous Men*
Jane Austen. *First Impressions*	*Pride and Prejudice*
William Burroughs. *Meet Me in Sargasso*	*The Naked Lunch*
Anthony Burgess. *A Robotic Banana*	*A Clockwork Orange*

T. S. Eliot. *He Do the Police in Different Voices*	*The Waste Land*
Ford Maddox Ford. *The Saddest Story*	*The Good Soldier*
Stella Gibbons. *Curse God Farm*	*Cold Comfort Farm*
Ernest Hemingway. *Fiesta: A Novel*	*The Sun Also Rises*
D. H. Lawrence. *John Thomas and Lady Jane*	*Lady Chatterley's Lover*
Carson McCullers. *The Mute*	*The Heart Is a Lonely Hunter*
Stephenie Meyer. *Forks*	*Twilight*
Margaret Mitchell. *Pansy*	*Gone with the Wind*
George Orwell. *The Last Man in Europe*	*Nineteen Eighty Four*
Robert Louis Stevenson. *The Sea Cook*	*Treasure Island*
Bram Stoker. *The Dead Undead*	*Dracula*
Jacqueline Susann. *They Don't Build Statues to Businessmen*	*Valley of the Dolls*
Tennessee Williams. *Blanche's Chair in the Moon*	*A Streetcar Named Desire*

When publishers consider the marketability of titles, they have in mind a particular national readership, and they have ideas about what those readers are likely to know and how they are likely to respond. Hence titles sometimes get changed when a book originating in one English-speaking country gets published in another. A Robert Parker mystery sold as *Hundred Dollar Baby* in the United States is sold as *Dream Girl* in the United Kingdom. Agatha Christie's titles seemed to have been especially susceptible to transformation. Here's what happened to some of Christie's United Kingdom titles when they were published in the United States: *4:50 from Paddington* became *What Mrs. McGillicudy Saw!*; *Why Didn't They Ask Evans?* became *The Boomerang Clue; One, Two, Buckle My Shoe* became *The Patriotic Murders*; *Dumb Witness* became *Poirot Loses a Client*, and so on. To help readers keep straight books with multiple titles and different covers, the official Lee Child Web site shows both the U.S. and the U.K. covers for his Jack Reacher novels: for example, the U.K. title *The Visitor* is shown as the counterpart of the U.S. title *Running Blind*.

Sometimes a key word or phrase in the title resonates well with one national audience but not at all or badly with another. Canadian writer Alice Munro published her third collection of short stories under the title *Who Do You Think You Are?* This take-you-down-a-notch phrase didn't impress the American publisher, who changed it to *The Beggar Maid* in reference to the King Cophetua story. The book known in most parts of the world as *Harry Potter and the Philosopher's Stone* got changed to *Harry Potter and the Sorcerer's Stone* in the United States on the grounds American readers could be confused by the British title. And, most dramatically, the award-winning novel *The Book of Negroes* by Canadian author Lawrence Hill became *Someone Knows My Name* when published in the United States. In an article on the *Guardian* book blog after his novel won the Commonwealth Writer's Prize, Hill (2008) reported that his New York editor sent him a worried email saying that "the title had to change. 'Negroes' would not fly, or be allowed to fly, in American book-stores." Hill explained: "I used *The Book of Negroes* as the title for my novel, in Canada, because it derives from a historical document of the same name kept by British naval officers at the tail end of the American Revolutionary War. . . . Unless you were in the Book of Negroes, you couldn't escape to Canada." On his American book tour, African American readers said they were glad he had changed the title because "they would never have touched the book with its Canadian title." Although the original title better represents the histori-cal reality, Hill wisely deferred to readers: "I'd rather have the novel read under a different title than not read at all."

Authors of course always want to attract readers, but they are apt to argue, in cases less dramatic than Hill's, that the title is key to the book's meaning. The title should convey "the soul of the book." According to Andre Bernard (1995, 29), when Harper Brothers advised Joyce Cary that his title *The Horse's Mouth* would hurt sales, Cary strongly resisted any change. He objected, "The point is that my titles are essential parts of the book. I don't forget for a moment that they appear at the top of each page." The title becomes what Peter Rabinowitz (1987) calls a "rule of notice" that lets readers know which elements, in a lengthy text, they should read with extra close attention. Any theme, image, or incident that is directly related to the title gets special weight. The title works as a kind of magnet, pulling into the reader's field of attention any element in the book related to it. F. Scott Fitzgerald's titles—*This Side of Paradise* and *The Beautiful and the Damned*—for example, focus readers' attention on an elegiac sense of loss. Jane Austen's original title, First Impressions, and the title she ended up with, *Pride and Prejudice*, both focus attention on thematic matters, albeit somewhat different ones.

Italian semiotician and novelist Umberto Eco (1984, 3) explains why he ended up choosing *The Name of the Rose* as the title of his book about the solv-ing of a series of bizarre murders of monks in a fourteenth-century Benedictine monastery. His working title had been *The Abby of the Murder*. A rose appears only at the very end of the book in an untranslated Latin quotation from a poem by a twelfth-century Benedictine, Bernard of Morlay, on the transitoriness of the things of this world:

> The idea of calling my book *The Name of the Rose* came to me virtually by chance, and I liked it because the rose is a symbolic figure so rich in meanings that by now it hardly has any meaning left . . . The title rightly disoriented the reader, who was unable to choose just one interpretation. . . . A title must muddle the reader's ideas, not regiment them.

References

Allen, Katie. 2013. "Six Picked for Oddest Book Title Shortlist." *The Bookseller*, February 22. http://www.thebookseller.com/news/six-picked-oddest-book-title-shortlist.html.

Bernard, André. 1995. *Now All We Need Is a Title: Famous Book Titles and How They Got That Way.* New York: W.W. Norton & Company.

Cruisie, Jennifer. 2007. "The Romance Writer's Novel's Fabulous Title." *Jenny Cruisie's page.* July 13. http://www.arghink.com/2007/07/13/the-romance-writers-fabulous-title/.

Dexter, Gary. 2007. *Why Not Catch-21?: The Stories behind the Titles.* London: Frances Lincoln Limited.

Eco, Umberto. 1984. *Postscript to* The Name of the Rose. Translated by William Weaver. San Diego, CA: Harcourt Brace Jovanovich.

Fitzgerald, F. Scott. 1924. Letter to Maxwell Perkins, November 7, 1924. Reprinted in blog edited by Shaun Usher. *Letters of Note: Correspondence Deserving of a Wider Audience.* Tuesday, July 3, 2012. "The novel is a wonder." http://www.lettersofnote.com/2012/07/the-novel-is-wonder.html.

Hill, Lawrence. 2008. "Why I'm Not Allowed My Book Title." *Guardian Books Blog.* May 20. http://www.theguardian.com/books/booksblog/2008/may/20/whyimnotallowedmybooktit.

Hill, Susan. 2010. *Howards End Is on the Landing.* London: Profile Books.

Hyatt, Michael. n.d. "Four Strategies for Creating Titles That Jump off the Page." http://michaelhyatt.com/four-strategies-for-creating-titles-that-jump-off-the-page.html.

Rabinowitz, Peter J. 1987. *Before Reading: Narrative Conventions and the Politics of Interpretation.* Columbus: Ohio State University Press. https://ohiostatepress.org/index.htm?/books/complete%20pdfs/rabinowitz%20before/rabinowitz%20before.htm.

The Bookseller. The Diagram Prize. http://www.thebookseller.com/diagram-prize.

Further Reading

Gary Dexter's blog, *How Books Got Their Titles*, started in March 2009 with A. A. Milne's *Winnie-the-Pooh* and George Orwell's *Nineteen Eighty-Four* and finished up with Howard Spring's *Fame Is the Spur*, having provided the story behind 181 titles. http://garydexter.blogspot.ca/.

Unreadable Books

You may have a personal list of books that you consider "unreadable"—for example, *Finnegan's Wake*, *Peyton Place*, *American Psycho*, or anything written in any of the Cyrillic alphabets. However, these books are not universally unreadable. What I'm considering here are books that *no one* can read. Some of these unreadable books are bibliographic ghosts—books that were advertised but never published and got into bibliographies anyway. Some are books that used to exist but all copies have disappeared, such as the lost books in the destroyed Alexandria Library, which had contained, among other treasures, the world's only copy of *The Complete Works of Aeschylus*. Manuscripts are forever being lost, stolen, or thrown into the fire (Kelly 2006). Ernest Hemingway's early writings vanished when his first wife Hadley's unattended luggage was stolen as she waited for a train in the Gare de Lyon in Paris. Thomas Carlyle entrusted his only manuscript copy of volume 1 of "History of the French Revolution" to John Stuart Mill who, some time later, rushed to Carlyle's house in an excited state, with the story that his housemaid had used the manuscript to start a fire. (In this case, Carlyle rewrote volume 1 from memory.)

Dr. Watson tantalizes his readers by referring to cases solved by Sherlock Holmes but not written up. In "The Five Orange Pips," Watson tells us that his files contain records for "the adventure of the Paradol Chamber, of the Amateur Mendicant Society, who held a luxurious club in the lower vault of a furniture warehouse, of the facts connected with the loss of the British barque *Sophy Anderson*, of the singular adventures of the Grice Pattersons in the island of Uffa, and finally the Camberwell poisoning case." "Who wouldn't wish to hear more of 'Wilson, the notorious canary trainer' and 'Huret, the boulevard assassin,'" asks Michael Dirda (2012, 101–2) in his intriguing book on Conan Doyle. Some books were thought about, and possibly planned, but never actually written. Raymond Chandler's *Notebooks* (1976, 11) contain a list of titles that he never got around to writing. Here are some of them: "The Man with the Shredded Ear," "The Corpse Came in Person," "Too Late for Smiling," "Deceased When Last Seen," "No Third Act," and "A Night in the Ice Box."

Sometimes the unreadable book is the product of an elaborate hoax. Umberto Eco (Carriere and Eco 2011, 283–84) tells the story of a prank perpetrated at the Frankfurt Book Fair by publishing bigwigs who were tut-tutting over the silly craze of overbidding untested new authors. One of them came up with the idea of inventing an author and talking him up. Voila: the birth of the soon-to-be-famous Milo Temesvar, author of "Let Me Say Now." By the end of the day, an Italian publisher was overheard to say, "Don't waste your time. I've just bought the global rights to 'Let Me Say Now'!" Milo Temesvar has been important to Eco ever since. In a conversation with Jean-Claude Carriere, Eco tells the story of the genesis of Milo Temesvar and adds:

> I once wrote an article reviewing one of his books, a parody of apocalyptic conspiracy theories called *The Patmos Sellers*. I described Milo Temesvar as an Albanian exiled from his country for being too left-wing, who had written a book inspired by Borges about the use of mirrors in chess. I even mentioned the obviously invented name of the publisher of the apocalypse book. (Carriere and Eco 2011, 283)

The most tantalizing unreadable books may be those that exist only in the pages of other books. Some examples are Prospero's book in *The Tempest*, Gilderoy Lockhart's "Voyages with Vampires" in *Harry Potter and the Chamber of Secrets*, or Sherlock Holmes's "little monograph on the ashes of 140 different varieties of pipe, cigar, and cigarette tobacco." The ultimate in invisibility is the book in *Harry Potter and the Prisoner of Azkaban*: "Invisible Book of Invisibility" by Unknown. Such books are eligible to be collected in *The Invisible Library*, a term used by Brian Quinette for a Web site he maintained from 2001 to 2006, until one day the site vanished. Quinette's Web page formerly listed "imaginary books, pseudobiblia, artifictions, fabled tomes, libris phantastica, and all manner of books unwritten, unread, unpublished, and unfound." When the original invisible library site was discontinued, others opened their own branches, for example, Levi Stahl and Ed Park's Invisible Library (blog) and the Invisible Library, Malibu Lake Branch. Of course, long before Quinette's Web site, people have been intrigued by the idea of books existing only in other books. Max Beerbohm (1914) called this phenomenon "books within books" and said that he yearned to read "Walter Lorraine" by Arthur Pendennis, "Passion Flowers" by Rosa Bunion, or "Who Put Back the Clock?" by Gideon Forsyth. Different readers have favorite invisible books. David Barnett (2008) would like to read "The Blind Assassin" by Laura Chase, which appears in Margaret Atwood's novel *The Blind Assassin* (2000).

Books and Writers within Books

Novels that include fiction writers are fertile sources of books eligible for the invisible library. Rosie M. Banks, a popular romance writer from the pages of P. G. Woodhouse's Bertie Wooster stories, has written many unreadable novels, including "Only a Factory Girl." Literary detectives often seem to write as a sideline to investigating—P. D. James's Adam Dalgleish writes books of poetry and Dorothy Sayers's Harriet Vane writes detective stories. Many people say that they would like to read the work of Kilgore Trout, a writer who appears in Kurt Vonnegut books. Trout fans would have a goldmine to choose from— 117 novels and 2,000 short stories—albeit largely underappreciated and published mainly as filler in pornographic magazines.

Anthony Powell has generated a whole library of unreadable books. His 12-volume roman-fleuve, *A Dance to the Music of Time*, is filled with fictional authors who have written imaginary books. The following are only a few tantalizing samples: Evadne Clapham's "Engine Melody" (formerly "The Pistons of Our Locomotives Sing the Songs of Our Workers"), St John Clarke's "Dust Thou Art," Nicholas Jenkins's "Borage and Hellebore: A Study," J. G. Quiggin's "Unburnt Boats" (never completed), Odo Stevens's "Sad Majors," and X. Trapnel's "Dogs Have No Uncle" and "Camel Ride to the Tomb," this last title being an encapsulation of Trapnel's view of what life is like. In response to Ed Park's *New York Times* piece, "Titles within a Tale" (2009), readers offered their own suggestions of fake books they would like to read. One Powell fan (Barrett 2009) said that a big pleasure in reading *Dance to the Music of Time* is "savoring the titles of the many books, articles and poems [Powell's] characters have written":

> I for one would love to be able to read Evadne Clapham's 35th novel, *Cain's Jawbone*. And Ada Leintwardine has left us, at least in Powell's pages, her novels *I Stopped at the Chemists* (later filmed as "Sally Goes Shopping"), *Bedsores* and *The Bitch Pack Meets on Wednesday*.

As Ed Park (2009) observes about books within books, "Sometimes these interior texts inform the plot or enhance the theme, other times they are just lively bursts of color, sparks thrown off during the authorial process." And sometimes, as Max Beerbohm (1914) put it, there are "imaginary great books that are as real to us as real ones are." Beerbohm singles out Henry James's novella, "The Author of *Beltraffio*," as a story in which "a great book itself is the very hero of the story." In this novella, we see the English novelist Mark Ambient through the eyes of the narrator, a young, star-struck American disciple, and learn that the narrator considers Ambient to be "quite the greatest of living authors" and *Beltraffio* to be his masterpiece. We hear about "the high finish of his printed prose," Ambient's love of beauty, and his wife's view that her husband's art-for-art's-sake novels are "immoral and his influence pernicious." On the subject of his new book, Ambient says that he expects his detractors will "dislike this thing (if it does turn out well) most." With his new book, he says, "I want to be truer than I've ever been. . . . I want to give the impression of life itself. No, you may say what you will, I've always arranged things too much, always smoothed them down and rounded them off and tucked them in—done everything to them that life doesn't do." As Beerbohm observed, we never learn the title of the new book "which Ambient's wife so hated that she let her child die rather than that he should grow up under the influence of its author."

Reading Transactions with Imaginary Books

A reading transaction with an invisible book often reveals something significant about the character who reads. Certainly, this is the case with *Beltraffio* and the unnamed work in progress. Mark Ambient works ceaselessly to produce a beautiful work of art with a surface that is "firm and bright." He says, "Perhaps I care too much for beauty. . . . I delight in it, I adore it, I think of it continually, I try to produce it, to reproduce it. My wife holds that we shouldn't cultivate or enjoy it without extraordinary precautions and reserves." The fate of their young son is sealed by the striking difference in what his parents see when they read the same work—for the father it is something beautiful, for the mother something "most objectionable" and morally contaminating. Mrs. Ambient couldn't destroy the book, and so she allowed its future reader to die.

Characters reveal a lot about their values and outlook when they recommend a book to others or talk about their favorite book. In the first chapter of *The Great Gatsby*, the narrator Nick Carraway introduces us to some of the book's central characters when he visits the house of Tom and Daisy Buchanan. At dinner, Tom Buchanan unexpectedly announces, "Civilization's going to pieces. . . . Have you read 'The Rise of the Colored Empires' by this man Goddard? . . . The idea is if we don't look out the white race will be—will be utterly submerged. It's all scientific stuff; it's been proved. . . . It's up to us, who are the dominant race, to watch out or these other races will have control of things."

In *The Catcher in the Rye*, the mention of a favorite story introduces a key theme of childhood innocence and vulnerability. A favorite with Holden Caulfield is "The Secret Goldfish," written by his brother. According to Holden, before his brother D. B. sold out to Hollywood, he was just a "regular writer": "He wrote this terrific book of short stories, *The Secret Goldfish*, in case you never heard of him. The best one in it was 'The Secret Goldfish.' It was about this little kid that wouldn't let anybody look at his goldfish because he'd bought it with his own money. It killed me."

Lost, Unfinished, or Destroyed Books

Some books are doubly unreadable. That's because, even within the fictions in which they appear, they can't be read because they are destroyed, they are never completed, or like Miss Prism's three-volume novel in Oscar Wilde's *The Importance of Being Earnest*, they are abandoned, lost, or mislaid. In George Eliot's *Middlemarch*, Dorothea's mistaken marriage choice, Mr. Casaubon, spends his time putting documents into pigeonholes, fruitlessly constructing a "Key to All Mythologies" that will never be finished and is already out of date (Casaubon hasn't read "the Germans"). More upsetting are the masterpieces that are deliberately destroyed. *Books Do Furnish a Room*, the 10th novel in Powell's *Dance to the Music of Time*, provides an excellent example of a doubly unreadable book destroyed through spite: X. Trapnel's unpublished masterpiece, "Profiles in String," the unique manuscript copy of which was thrown into the Regent's Park Canal by his departing mistress, Pamela Widmerpool.

In Umberto Eco's *The Name of the Rose*, the plot turns on the lost, second book of Aristotle's *Poetics*, which dealt with comedy just as the first book dealt with tragedy. This second book was lost for centuries, but in Eco's novel it was brought from Spain, along with some other books, by the librarian Jorge of Burgos, who is the librarian of the abbey where the novel is set. Regarding laughter as the worst of heresies, Jorge locked away the book on comedy for decades in the abbey's labyrinthine library, having poisoned its pages to kill off any potential readers. By the end of the novel, Aristotle's second book has been both eaten and burned. In fact the whole library is burned and the abbey is in ruins. When the narrator returns many years later, he finds scattered remnants:

> At times I found pages where whole sentences were legible; more often, intact bindings, protected by what had once been metal studs. . . . Ghosts of books, apparently intact on the outside but consumed within; yet sometimes a half page had been saved, an incipit was discernible, a title.

Fire also destroyed six books of prophecy that the Sibyl of Cumae burned when King Tarquin the Proud, seventh and last king of Rome, quibbled at her price. According to Roman legend, the Sibyl approached King Tarquin and offered to sell, for an immense price, nine books that were oracles of the gods and recorded all the future. The king laughed her to scorn, thinking she was in her dotage. "Okay," said the Sibyl and burned to ashes three of the volumes. Then she calmly offered the remaining six at the original price. "That's extortion," said the king. "Okay," said the Sibyl and burned to ash three more volumes. "What part of the future was that?" asked the king. "We'll never know," was the answer. Much shaken, King Tarquin paid the original price for the remaining three books of prophesy and carried them back to Rome, where they were housed in the temple of Jupiter on the capital.

Parody Titles

Parody titles poke fun at particular genres or types of writing but don't usually inspire in real readers a desire to read the imaginary book in question.

For example, in David Lodge's *Nice Work*, there are those academic studies written by Robin Penrose titled "Domestic Angels and Unfortunate Females: Woman as Sign and Commodity in Victorian Fiction" and "The Industrious Muse: Narrativity and Contradiction in the Industrial Novel." In Book III, Chapter 5 of *Gulliver's Travels*, Gulliver visits the grand academy of Lagado where scientists and "projectors" were hard at work at various scientific projects such as extracting sunbeams out of cucumbers: "I saw another at work to calcine ice into gunpowder; who likewise showed me a treatise he had written concerning the malleability of fire, which he intended to publish" (noted in Blumenthal 1966). Raymond Chandler (1976, 11) invented a writer, Aaron Klopstein, who died at 33 of suicide in Greenwich Village, having shot himself with an Amazonian blowgun. Before his sad death, he published two novels, "Once More the Cicatrice" and "The Seagull Has No Friends," two volumes of poetry, "The Hydraulic Facelift" and "Cat Hairs in the Custard," and a book of critical essays, "Shakespeare in Babytalk."

In her dystopian novel, *Oryx and Crake* (2003), Margaret Atwood provides a list of SELF-HELP titles, at least some of which are made up. The story of Snowman (once known as Jimmy), who is the sole survivor of a biological disaster, is told through an interweaving of Snowman's post-catastrophe present with memories of Jimmy's pre-catastrophe past. One such memory is a term paper Jimmy wrote for his applied rhetoric course titled "Self-Help of the Twentieth Century: Exploiting Hope and Fear." This work "supplied him with a great stand-up routine for use in the student pubs." Mixed in among real book titles, such as *How to Make Friends and Influence People* and *Entertaining Without a Maid*, are some almost-real book titles such as "Access Your Inner Child" and "Total Womanhood!" Then there are "Cosmetic Surgery for Everyone," "Raising Nutria for Fun and Profit," and "The Twelve Step Plan for Assisted Suicide," which seem to me to be genuinely made-up titles, but you never know—maybe they are real or soon will be real. "Grief Management for Dummies" wasn't a real title in 2003 when *Oryx and Crake* was published, but in 2007 *Grieving for Dummies* appeared. We have the narrator's assurance that at least one title is made up: "Sometimes [Jimmy would] make up books that didn't exist—'Healing Diverticulitis through Chanting and Prayer' was one of his best creations—and nobody would spot the imposture." Park (2009) claims that "invisible books are charged with the uncanny. No one can possibly have read, or even heard of, every book ever written, so how can we distinguish the fake from the real?"

Shelves of Unreadable Books

The next step after locating imaginary books is to arrange them on imaginary shelves. Beerbohm (1914) considers the satisfaction of getting "ocular evidence" for the existence of his favorite books within books: "I want to see them all ranged along goodly shelves. . . . How well they would look there, those treasures of mine! And, most of them having been issued in the seemly old three-volume form, how many shelves they would fill!" Aldous Huxley's

Chrome Yellow (1921) provides an example of what Park (2009) calls "second-degree invisibles: a bookcase of pageless spines . . . camouflaging a secret door." Charles Dickens went one step further in giving a physical presence to the unreadable books. When he moved into Tavistock House in 1851, he wanted to furnish some shelves in his study with faux books whose titles he had invented. He wrote to the bookbinder Thomas Robert Eeles, giving him a "list of imitation book-backs." Here are some of the titles (Usher 2012):

History of a Short Chancery Suit. 21 vols.

Catalogue of Statues of the Duke of Wellington

Five Minutes in China. 3 vols.

Forty Winks at the Pyramids. 2 vols.

Kant's Ancient Humbugs. 10 vols.

King Henry the Eighth's Evidences of Christianity. 5 vols.

Miss Biffin on Deportment.

Lady Godiva on the Horse.

Munchausen's Modern Miracles. 4 vols.

Hansard's Guide to Refreshing Sleep. As many volumes as possible.

In a further step toward making real the invisible book, an artist collective turned the Tenderpixel Gallery in London into a library filled with books mentioned in other books (Dimitrov 2009). Forty titles chosen from books in the Stahl and Park's Invisible Library blog were turned into physical books with covers created by the collective's artists and with opening and closing pages written in advance by novelists. Featured books included Elisabeth Ducharme's "When the Train Passes" mentioned in Vladimir Nabokov's *Bend Sinister* (1947), Benno von Archimboldi's famous second novel "The Endless Rose" mentioned in Chilean author Roberto Bolaño's novel *2666* (2004), and books from Italo Calvino's *If On a Winter's Night a Traveller* (1979). Partly an art installation and partly a metafictional exercise in reading and writing, this exhibition invited participants to sign out a book temporarily from the library and contribute to the collaboration by helping to write the story. Alex Dimitrov (2009) reported that "At the close of the exhibit the once-empty pages of the books had been transformed into vivid narratives, full of various voices and shifts in perspective and style, making the library a postmodern literary experiment."

Writing the Invisible Book

In rare but satisfying cases, a book that starts off as unreadable gets written and published later. The seven Harry Potter books are crammed with references to invisible books, but two such books got a second life. *Quidditch through the*

Ages and *Fantastic Beasts and Where to Find Them* were published as a box set in 2001. In the Harry Potter world, "Fantastic Beasts" is a school textbook written by Newt Salamander that Harry takes to Hogwarts. "Quidditch" by Kennilworthy Whisp is a popular library book to be found in the Hogwarts Library. When Comic Relief, a British charity, asked Rowling to write something for them, Rowling (2001) thought it would be fun to take some fragments she had written as background for her Harry Potter world and extend them into fully written books.

Apart from a note from J. K. Rowling describing Comic Relief and thanking readers for buying the book, *Quidditch through the Ages* has all the earmarks of a book wholly existing in the Harry Potter world. There is a page of laudatory quotations ("Whisp's painstaking research has uncovered a veritable treasure trove of hitherto unknown facts about the sport of warlocks"—Bathilda Bagshot, author, *A History of Magic*); a short biography of the author ("His hobbies include backgammon, vegetarian cookery, and collecting vintage broomsticks"); a foreword written by Albus Dumbledore ("*Quidditch Through the Ages* is one of the most popular titles in the Hogwarts school library"); and a borrower's plate with entries in the hand of Librarian Irma Pince showing the names of borrowers and due dates (H. Granger was the 17th student to borrow the book, following F. Weasley and before H. Potter). The copy of *Fantastic Beasts* made available through the Comic Relief project is Harry Potter's personal copy, enlivened by MARGINALIA by Hermione, Ron, and Harry. Comic Relief (2012) reported that sales of these two books over the past 11 years had raised 18 million ($30 million) for education of children in the poorest parts of the world.

Sometimes we never know what motivates the writer to bring an invisible book to life, but readers are usually grateful when it happens. In response to a question about reading books recommended within other books (see LITERARY LOGROLLING), one reader commented:

> My mom and I have done this [read books recommended in other books] so often, we started calling it "the Old Books Network." One of the major disappointments of my life was reading a book called *The Tightrope Walker* [by Dorothy Gilman] in which a character describes a children's fantasy that had an incredible impact on her life—and then it turns out to have been made up for the plot.

In *The Tightrope Walker* (1979), the central character, Amelia Jones, is a shy, troubled owner of an antique shop, who finds in a barrel organ a faded note that says, "They're going to kill me soon . . . my name is Hannah." Amelia sets off on a journey to uncover the truth, strengthened in times of danger by remembering a favorite childhood book, "The Maze in the Heart of the Castle." The book sounded so wonderful that many *Tightrope Walker* readers declared themselves disappointed to discover that both it and its sequel, "In the Land of the Golden Warriors," were unreadable. Then came a satisfying turn in which Gilman wrote and published *The Maze in the Heart of the Castle* (1983). As one happy reader reported, "*The Tightrope Walker* is one of my fave books of all time, so when

I learned that Gilman had actually written the book that saved Amelia's life, I was on fire to read it."

References

Barnett, David. 2008. "Which Are the Best Books That Never Existed?" *Booksblog*, October 15. *The Guardian*. http://www.guardian.co.uk/books/booksblog/2008/oct/14/imaginary-books-borges-irving.

Barrett, Robert. 2009. "Titles on the Wish List." *New York Times*, August 7. http://www.nytimes.com/2009/08/09/books/review/Letters-t-TITLESONTHEW_LETTERS.html?_r=0.

Beerbohm, Max. 1914."Books within Books." In *And Even Now*. London: William Heinemann. http://web.archive.org/web/20050310063943/http://www2.cddc.vt.edu/gutenberg/etext99/evnow10h.htm.

Blumenthal, Walter Hart. 1966. *Imaginary Books and Phantom Libraries*. Philadelphia: G.S. MacManus. http://web.archive.org/web/20050308175054/http://www.invisiblelibrary.com/Blumenthal.htm.

Carriere, Jean-Claude, and Umberto Eco. 2011. *This is Not the End of the Book: A Conversation Curated by Jean-Philippe de Tonnac*. Translated by Polly McLean. London: Random House.

Chandler, Raymond. 1976. *The Notebooks of Raymond Chandler and English Summer: A Gothic Romance*. Edited by Frank MacShane. New York: The Ecco Press.

Comic Relief. 2012. "Harry Potter Companion Books, Now Available as eBooks!" *Comic Relief News*, August 16. http://www.comicrelief.com/news/harry-potter-companion-books-now-available-ebooks

Dimitrov, Alex. 2009. "The Invisible Library." *Poets & Writers*, September. http://www.pw.org/content/invisible_library_0?cmnt_all=1.

Dirda, Michael. 2012. *On Conan Doyle: Or, the Whole Art of Storytelling*. Princeton, NJ, and Oxford: Princeton University Press.

Invisible Library, Malibu Lake Branch. http://webspace.webring.com/people/ph/hermester/hbinvisiblelibrary.html.

Kelly, Stuart. 2006. *The Book of Lost Books: An Incomplete History of All the Great Books You'll Never Read*. New York: Random House.

Park, Ed. 2009. "Titles within a Tale." *The New York Times*, July 23. http://www.nytimes.com/2009/07/26/books/review/Park-t.html?_r=0

Rowling, J. K. 2001. "Transcript of J.K. Rowling's Live Interview for Comic Relief." *Scholastic*, March 12. http://web.archive.org/web/20070607001251/http://www.scholastic.com/harrypotter/books/author/interview3.htm.

Stahl, Levi, and Ed Park. *The Invisible Library* (blog), August 17, 2008. http://invislib.blogspot.ca/.

Usher, Shaun. 2012. "The Fake Books of Charles Dickens." *Lists of Note*, March 5. http://www.listsofnote.com/2012/03/fake-books-of-charles-dickens.html.

Vampires, Zombies, and the Undead

Many cultures have told tales about the undead—creatures of the night who rise from the grave to prey on humans. There are werewolves, zombies, and living dead creatures that come out of the fog to terrorize readers and movie watchers. Zombies—those cannibalistic, reanimated corpses made popular in movies such as *Night of the Living Dead* (1968) or more recently *World War X* (2013)—typically appear as an undifferentiated horde that relentlessly keeps on coming. The zombie has been used as a vehicle of social criticism for phenomena that turn people into mindless automatons, such as ideological political movements, war, or class struggle. The Centers for Disease Control and Prevention (2011) used the "Zombie Apocalypse" concept as a gimmick for selling the need for disaster preparedness against a natural disaster (establish a safe stronghold and stock it in advance with water, crucial supplies, tools, and flashlights). But the vampire story trumps them all in popularity because of its capacity for variety, change, adaptation, and renewal. Zombies, let's face it, have poor personalities. Vampires, though scary, can be enticingly seductive. In its origins in Slavic folklore, the vampire was a repulsive, reanimated corpse, who preyed on peasants in villages, draining their lifeblood. By the time John William Polidori wrote the first literary vampire story, *The Vampyre* (1819), this gibbering, walking corpse had been transformed into a glamorous, aristocratic seducer who was welcomed into the most exclusive drawing rooms of London. For the first time, we have a vampire who can infiltrate human society, able to pass muster as an acquaintance, a friend, or a fiancé. The shambling, rotting corpse that comes after you at night is a Johnny one-note, but the charismatic, handsome vampire can evoke a wide spectrum of emotional responses. He (and sometimes she) can even evoke readers' fantasies of a hyper-intense and all-consuming love that knows no boundaries.

The vampire seduces its victims, who are complicit, drawn willingly into the encounter like a moth to a flame. Vampires must be invited to cross a threshold. There is a real-life counterpart for the vampire experience in psychological vampirism: a relationship based on one person's feeding off another's energy and eventually absorbing the other's personality. Attraction to a vampire is like an addiction—seductive but also deadly. "Beware," "The Blood Is Life," and "Love Never Dies" are the taglines for Coppola's 1992 movie *Bram Stoker's Dracula*, signaling a mixed appeal: terror, the powerful myth of blood as life force, and also the lure of eternal life and love. Among other things, the vampire story is about shape-changing and transformation. The vampire blurs the boundaries between human and animal, male and female, the familiar and otherness, life and death. Many readers enjoy the frisson they experience when that otherness intrudes into the everyday world. In comparison with mainstream fiction, the range of possibility is bigger—the story can touch upon supernatural terror, the absorption of one character by another, difference, immortality, transformation, and the nature of love.

Some retellings of the vampire story put the emphasis on the vampire hunters who relentlessly track down and kill vampires, often using the classic crucifix-and-garlic defense and the wooden stake. In Stephen King's *'Salem's Lot* (1975), a select group in a small town in Maine band together to hunt down an ancient vampire, Kurt Barlow, who has been preying on townspeople and turning them into vampires. Once the vampire can walk undetected among us, however, it is a short step for writers to imagine sympathetically the vampire as a tragic hero—isolated, filled with angst, marked by difference, and cut off from normal human community. Anne Rice (2007) has said that, when she wrote her first book *Interview with the Vampire* (1976), she "felt that the vampire was the perfect metaphor for the outcast in all of us, the alienated one in all of us, the one who feels lost in a world seemingly without God." However, the vampire differs in one key way from the outcast Being in Mary Shelley's *Frankenstein*, who says, "Everywhere I see bliss from which I alone am irrevocably excluded. I was benevolent and good; misery made me a fiend. Make me happy, and I shall again be virtuous" (see Horror). The vampire's need for human blood requires him to kill to survive—hence he can be seen as a tragic figure compelled to do evil.

Unlike the western, whose popularity has waned, the vampire story has renewed itself as authors have reimagined the vampire from frightening fiend to tragic figure to romantic love interest to Bunnicula, the vampire rabbit, in a children book series by James Howe. Some authors have fused the vampire story with other genres such as the post-apocalyptic "last man" story, the detective story, historical fiction, or romance. For example, in Richard Matheson's *I Am Legend* (1954), a pandemic caused by an infectious virus has turned *everyone* on earth into vampires—all but one sole survivor, who is left to explore the ultimate in human loneliness. In the television cop series, *Forever Knight*, the 800-year-old homicide detective Nicholas Knight seeks redemption and restitution for past sins by using his vampire powers to bring murderers to justice in contemporary Toronto. In contrast, Chelsea Quinn Yarbro, who has written more than 25 books featuring the 3,500-year-old vampire Count Saint-Germain, sets each of her stories in a different historical period such as Nero's Rome, Florence, at the time of the Medicis, Germany during the rise of the Nazis, India during Tamurlane's invasion, France during the reign of terror, St. Petersburg at the time of Peter the Great, and Africa on a pilgrimage to underground churches in southern Egypt.

In the television series *Buffy the Vampire Slayer* that premiered in 1997, Buffy is a high school cheerleader with a difference: she has been singled out by fate to be a Chosen One in the fight against vampires, but she has the problem that she falls in love with two bad-boy vampires, Angel and Spike. Once consensual sex with vampires is presented as a thrilling possibility, the way is open for a vampire love story with a Romeo and Juliet theme. Stephanie Meyer's *Twilight* series is about an unconditional love between Bella Swan and the vampire Edward Cullen that transcends a barrier stronger than the barriers of class, caste, or race. Liisa Ladouceur (2013, 31) says, "It simply cannot be overstated just how much the *Twilight* Saga changed vampires."

Reading *Twilight*

At the height of the popularity of *Twilight* series, a student in my graduate course on reading theory and practice presented a research seminar to the class, based on her analysis of discussion boards devoted to the *Twilight Saga*. The Twilight phenomenon proved an interesting seminar topic because of the phenomenal popularity of *Twilight* (2005), *New Moon* (2006), *Eclipse* (2007), and *Breaking Dawn* (2008) and the ready availability of reading statements posted on discussion boards. Reading discussion sites are a gift to researchers because they provide rich, unmediated accounts of readers' experience with particular books. What do readers like or dislike about the book in question? What is their relationship to the characters? What kind of special satisfaction does this particular book provide? The discussions are reader-generated, reflecting the interests of readers themselves, not those of researchers.

The seminar focused on the *Twilight Saga* reading experience as revealed by readers' posted questions and answers. One reader explained *Twilight*'s appeal as "the right mix" of real life, mixed with fantasy: "It's fantasy enough that it keeps your imagination going, but real enough that you can relate to it on some level. I think another good example of this type of literature is *Harry Potter*. Same concept with this fantasy world hidden within the real world." Readers discussed the characters as real people, asking questions such as "Which would you choose, Jacob or Edward?" (Edward because of his courtly manners, many said—"more men need this sort of chivalry towards women.") One 29-year-old reader, who described herself as "totally hooked," asked, "Why are you addicted? Why are they addictive?!?!." One reader explained, "I think the character Edward is the biggest part of the appeal. What girl wouldn't love to have a guy that's not only unhumanly beautiful but is protective of her and will do anything for her?" Another reader agreed, "Who doesn't want their own vampire who is totally obsessed with you??"

Twilight is a crossover phenomenon, a coming-of-age vampire romance for teens that has recruited a large adult readership, mostly female. Reading *Twilight* and its sequels was evidently a social affair—readers posted accounts of how they had pressed copies on their female friends or how they had read *Twilight* when urged on by a daughter and then became a huge fan. In one thread on vampires, a poster explained that all vampires originated in Alaska, which was their natural home. This was news to us in the seminar, even although we had already acquired a fair amount of specialized knowledge on the care and feeding of vampires from *Dracula* movies, Anne Rice's novels, the television series *Buffy the Vampire Slayer* (1997–2003), and so on. But it goes to show how the portrait of the vampire has been evolving since its first literary appearance in Polidori's *The Vampyre*.

Vampire Prototypes

Personal physician to Lord Byron, John Polidori had been present at the famous supernatural storytelling sessions, along with Byron and the Shelleys, at the Villa Diodati (see HORROR). Polidori's own story of a skull-headed woman was apparently a dud, but he struck pay-dirt when he took over Byron's abandoned story and made it the groundwork for the spectacularly successful work, *The Vampyre*. Translated almost immediately into French, Spanish, and German, the story was adapted into vampire operas and dramas and also inspired a whole line of vampire novels including Sheridan LeFanu's *Carmilla* (1872) about a female vampire and Bram Stoker's *Dracula* (1897), which itself generated a huge following of books, plays, and some 200 film adaptations (Miller 2009, 296). In Byron's story, published later as "Fragment of a Novel," a younger narrator begins by describing his attraction to Augustus Darvell, "a man of considerable fortune and ancient family," who was "a being of no common order, and one who, whatever pains he might take to avoid remark, would still be remarkable." Byron's fragment breaks off at the point at which Darvell dies near Ephesus, making his younger companion swear an oath to "conceal [his] death from every human being." Byron's story, according to Polidori's letter to his publisher (1819, 15), "depended for interest upon the circumstances of two friends leaving England, and one dying in Greece, the other finding him alive upon his return, and making love to his sister."

Polidori took Byron's outline and developed the completed story of an overly trusting young man Aubrey and his fatal attraction to the predatory Lord Ruthven (pronounced Riven). Polidori endows Lord Ruthven with Byronic qualities, making him seductive but deadly, "a man entirely absorbed in himself." The story begins, "It happened that in the midst of the dissipations attendant upon a London winter, there appeared at the various parties of the leaders of the *ton* a nobleman, more remarkable for his singularities, than his rank."

Polidori's novel, like Byron's originating story, features two companions, Ruthven and young Aubrey, who travel together to Europe; bad outcomes for people who get too close to Ruthven; Ruthven's death in Greece and the solemn oath to reveal the death to no-one; and Aubrey's horrified discovery back in London society that Lord Ruthven, whom he now recognizes as a fiend, is courting his own sister. Bound by the oath (Lord Ruthven keeps whispering in his ear, "Remember your oath"), Aubrey falls into a state of tormented illness and dies, helpless to separate his sister from the seductive Lord Ruthven, who shares with Satan the serpent tongue that flatters and deceives:

> Who could resist [Lord Ruthven's] power? His tongue had dangers and toils to recount—could speak of himself as of an individual having no sympathy with any being on the crowded earth, save with her to whom he addressed himself;—could tell how, since he knew her, his existence, had begun to seem worthy of preservation, if it were merely that he might listen to her soothing accents;—in fine, he knew so well how to use the serpent's art . . . that he gained her affections.

Not unexpectedly, falling for a vampire works out badly for the sister. In the story's concluding sentence, we learn that Lord Ruthven disappeared immediately after his wedding night, and "Aubrey's sister had glutted the thirst of a VAMPYRE!"

The vampire, par excellence, is of course Count Dracula of Transylvania. He is the compelling, evil presence presiding over Bram Stoker's *Dracula* (1897), a novel that has never been out of print since its first publication. For 21 years the personal assistant and theatre manager of the magnetic Irish actor Henry Irving, Bram Stoker knew at first hand what it was like to have one's life absorbed into that of a mesmerizing, dominant personality. In *Dracula*, Stoker heightens the depiction of psychological absorption by turning it into the vampire's kiss. The novel begins with Jonathan Harker's journal account of his unnerving journey to Transylvania to help in a real estate transaction. He arrives, in the best GOTHIC fashion, at a "vast ruined castle, from whose tall black windows came no ray of light." Greeted by the count who is "clad in black from head to foot, without a single speck of colour about him anywhere," Harker notes that the count's handshake is bone-crushing and "seemed cold as ice, more like the hand of a dead than a living man." Nor is the appearance of the count reassuring, however courtly and polite his manner:

> His face was a strong, a very strong, aquiline, with high bridge of the thin nose and peculiarly arched nostrils, with lofty domed forehead. . . .
> The mouth, so far as I could see it under the heavy moustache, was fixed and rather cruel-looking, with peculiarly sharp white teeth. The general effect was one of extraordinary pallor.

In creating Count Dracula, Bram Stoker introduced many of the characteristics that we now associate with vampires: pallor; sharp white teeth; failure to cast a shadow or a reflection in a mirror; the ability to communicate with wolves and change into mist; the need to sleep on their native soil; and their weakness in the face of the crucifix-and-garlic deterrent. Following Stoker, the prototypical vampire is tall and dark, is associated with bats and wolves, is dressed in black and walks at night in his black cloak, and can disappear into mist.

The Sexy Vampire: One Reader Describes His Appeal

Readers who dislike horror and are repelled by the idea of being kissed by a 300-year-old vampire say that they can't understand why vampire fiction has become so very popular. That's why it is illuminating to overhear a committed fan of vampire books talk about what she finds so appealing about the sexy vampire. Morag is a very knowledgeable and articulate fan of vampire fiction, interviewed by Kim Kofmel (2002) for her doctoral research interviewing avid readers of science fiction and fantasy. A 35-year-old who works for a publishing company, Morag is a knowledgeable and eclectic reader. Her apartment, where the interview took place, is filled with books with floor-to-ceiling shelves. Morag says that her favorite books are grounded in the everyday world but then they make a leap. They "start off in a place where everybody's been . . . and they just sort of jump, leaps and bounds, into imaginary things and imaginary places which you would love to visit, if you ever had the chance." She says, "Vampires have been a fascination with me for a very long time," ever since as a child she watched Todd Browning's *Dracula* with Bela Lugosi. At the time, she thought, "I want to be there. I want him to try it on me. Or, 'Yes, I like the idea of being a vampire.' They became the character that you wanted."

In this edited and condensed excerpt, Morag talks about her own reading, which is based primarily on an emotional response to the text. Vampire fiction provides, in an especially intense form, the emotional involvement that she hopes for from fantasy. She looks for "that hook" in a book that draws her in to a world where she wants to be for a while. She says sometimes it can be just a few sentences "that evoke a time, a place, a feeling that I have to continue with." Morag is not drawn to any particular storyline but rather to the concept of the vampire itself, which can be variously developed for different emotional effects, including sexual seduction. She looks for "these great intense, emotional feelings that you get—where the vampire caresses you and, then all of a sudden, takes that bite out of your neck." She says, "I've fallen in love with Count Saint Germain, fantasizing about him through my entire life." She contrasts the monster with fangs in Stephen King's *'Salem's Lot* "terrorizing the neighborhood" and "evoking all those childhood fears" with Chelsea Quinn Yarbro's Saint Germain, "who is very sexy, sensual, non-violent, and non-threatening." She says, "You can sit there and fantasize for hours about the pleasure that you would receive from him. There is no fear, no horror, involved. I want to marry Saint Germain. I want to be the one woman he can have after I turn into a vampire."

Kofmel: What do you look for when you are picking up a vampire novel?

Morag: I'm looking for that hook, that drawing power. And then when I read it, I have to find the rhythm. I have to find a voice within the story. It's looking at the first page and then realizing, all of a sudden, you've hit page five, without counting the pages. That is what I look for; that's what gets me.

Kofmel: Can you tell me a bit more about the hook?

Morag: It can be just this one or two sentences that evoke a time, a place, a feeling that I have to continue with. Or even a descriptive sentence that evokes a visual that I can see, can feel—it can draw me in. It's like visualizing walking down a very, very cold street at night and, all of a sudden, you see a warm, lit shop window that's just drawing you in. And you don't necessarily know what's in there. At first it's just that initial light and then you get closer and it might be the warmth and then you get closer still and it might actually be the things in the shop that bring you in.

Kofmel: If you could get an author to write a perfect book for you, what would it include?

Morag: Definitely a vampire. It would have to be sensual—and I don't mean that in a sexual way, but just sensuous and very sense-driven, where you've a lot of descriptions. It has to be based in some type of reality—there has to be this base in reality, before you jump off. Probably there would be some sort of "dreamworld"—whether a character comes from the other world or whether a character is drawn into another world. It should take place, or at least end up, somewhere in New Orleans, just because it's got that little bit of mystery to it, that humid quality.

Kofmel: What would you find satisfying about this perfect book?

Morag: Other than the fact that it's a perfect book and it makes me feel good and I have wonderful dreams about amazingly good-looking men who come and sweep me off my feet and bite my neck and take me to live down in an old antique-filled house in New Orleans with a ghost who's searching for something, and I'm it? We're talking about that me-driven book.

References

Centers for Disease Control and Prevention. 2011. "Preparedness 101: Zombie Apocalypse." Public Health Matters Blog, May 16. http://blogs.cdc.gov/publichealthmatters/2011/05/preparedness-101-zombie-apocalyp.

Kofmel, Kim Grace. 2002. "Adult Readers of Science Fiction and Fantasy: A Qualitative Study of Reading Preference and Genre Perception." Doctoral dissertation. London, Ontario: The University of Western Ontario.

Ladouceur, Liisa. 2013. *How to Kill a Vampire: Fangs in Folklore, Film and Fiction.* Toronto: ECW Press.

Miller, Elizabeth, ed. 2009. *Bram Stoker's Dracula: A Documentary Journey into Vampire Country and the Dracula Phenomenon.* New York: Pegasus Books.

Polidori, John. 1819. "Letter to Henry Colburn, London, April 2." In *The Diary of Dr. John William Polidori, 1816, Relating to Byron, Shelley, etc.* Edited by William Michael Rossetti. London: Elkin Mathews. http://www.archive.org/stream/diaryofdrjohnwil00polirich/diaryofdrjohnwil00polirich_djvu.txt.

Rice, Anne. 2007. "Essay on Earlier Works." AnneRice.com: The Official Site, August 15. http://www.annerice.com/Bookshelf-EarlierWorks.html.

Westerns

Oh, to be riding a horse through a Wyoming blizzard, half-unconscious from a bullet hole in your shoulder, 50 miles from Hat Creek Station, with a murderer on your trail and nothing in your belly but coffee boiled in an old tin can. That's life, stripped down to its essentials with nothing between you and death but your endurance, courage, and resourcefulness. There are no artificial codes of behavior, no social hierarchies based on hereditary wealth, and no fancy dress codes. You have few material possessions to tie you down—no home, furniture, tea sets, or silver forks. All you need is your horse, your saddle, your bedroll, and your six-guns. And that's the appeal to readers of the western, according to Jane Tompkins in her compelling book *West of Everything* (1992). When life is stripped down to the essentials of keeping alive in a hostile environment, claims Tompkins (12), the activities of everyday domestic living become insignificant. Faced with death, real men have no energy to waste on words, emotions, social distinctions, relationships, appearance, or even physical comfort. A cowboy lives alone under the open sky on nothing but boiled coffee and hand-rolled cigarettes. Not words but actions count: the decisive confrontation of the hold-up, the shoot-out, and the chase. And what pleasure does the reader get out of all this pain, violence, and death? According to Tompkins (13–14), "It's when your own life doesn't require of you the effort, concentration, and intensity of aim that [Western] heroes need to stay alive that you want to be with them in a Wyoming blizzard . . . fifty miles from Hat Creek Station . . . [L]ife on the frontier is a way of imagining the self in a boundary situation—in a place that will put you to some kind of ultimate test."

Even if you don't read westerns, you probably know a lot about them. Popular understanding of the genre comes from crisscrossed and overlapping images and themes drawn from Wild West shows, country and western songs, television reruns, and western gear such as hats and boots. Such knowledge is drawn intertextually from comic books such as Roy Rogers and Zorro; songs such as "The Streets of Laredo"; television reruns such as *The Lone Ranger, Gunsmoke,* and *Bonanza;* and movies such as *Shane* (1953), *The Searchers* (1956), *Rio Bravo* (1959), *The Magnificent Seven* (1960), *A Fistful of Dollars* (1964), *Unforgiven* (1992), *Tombstone* (1993), *Seraphim Falls* (2007), and *True Grit* (1969/2010). Therefore you probably have little difficulty in conjuring up a whole western repertoire of landscape, characters, plot devices, and tonalities. You can anticipate the characters who may venture into this story—the dance-hall girl, the school teacher, the widow being driven off her ranch, the saloon owner, the gambler, the stagecoach driver, the broken-down lawyer or doctor on the run from failure in the East, the sheriff, the tracker who has learned native skills, the bounty-hunter, the cruel cattle baron and his gang, the Indians, the Mexicans, the rustlers or train robbers, and, of course, the lone stranger who rides into town. You know the costumes—the buckskin shirt faded by wind and rain, the bandanna, the battered Stetson, the worn Levis, leather chaps, scuffed boots, and the Colt six-gun and the Winchester rifle. You can hear the country music tone of loss and longing—"Beat the drum slowly and play the fife lowly/And play the dead march as you carry me along." And above all, you can imagine the setting—the frontier town, the ranch, the homestead, and beyond that the arid desert broken by buttes, pinnacles, and arroyos, the circling buzzards, the white bones.

In comparison with the DETECTIVE story, with its single-minded preoccupation with investigating a crime, the traditional western offers a greater variety of plots. John G. Cawelti (1999, 19) quotes Frank Gruber (1955), veteran writer of pulp westerns and detective stories, as saying that there are seven basic western PLOTS, namely:

1. The Union Pacific Story, which centers on bringing transportation and communication to the West through the building of a railroad, a telegraph line, or stagecoach line.

2. The Ranch Story, which centers on conflicts between free-range ranchers and marauding rustlers or between sheepmen/homesteaders and the tyrannical cattle barons who want to prevent the fencing of open grazing land.

3. The Empire Story, which is a RAGS TO RICHES story of building a powerful ranch or oil empire, which may be threatened by advancing civilization.

4. The Revenge Story in which the hero chases the villain or the villain chases the hero, each with killing in mind.

5. The Cavalry and Indian Story, which draws on episodes in the Indian wars and recounts the conquest by force of arms of indigenous peoples.

6. The Outlaw Story, which recounts sympathetically the adventures of the outlaw gang (until their inevitable death).

7. The Marshal Story, which focuses on the exploits of a lawman in taming outlaws.

These seven plots provide the overall shape of the story. But into each of these stories can be dropped one or more motifs drawn from a large pool of available story elements: a fire deliberately set that kills an entire family; a gunfighter who has hung up his six-guns but buckles them on again to protect the town; a man whose desire for vengeance turns him into the savage enemy that he hates; a gunfighter who gets into a showdown with someone who used to be his best friend or mentor; a journey across hostile territory; a captivity in which a white woman and/or child is stolen by Indians and has to be rescued or kidnapped back; flight and pursuit; a concealed identity of the hero or the villain; betrayal by a trusted friend or family member; a sudden change in fortune that propels a character into a new life; and so on. In fact, the only limitation on the importation of common plot devices into the western is whether or not the particular device can be adapted to the western setting. And what holds all these materials together is a set of concerns or recurring themes. Lee Clark Mitchell (1996, 3) lists the problems that recur in westerns in "endless combination": "the problem of progress, envisioned as a passing of frontiers; the problem of honor, defined in a context of social expedience; the problem of law or justice, enacted in a conflict of vengeance and social control; the problem of violence, in acknowledging its value yet honoring the occasions when it can be controlled; and subsuming all, the problem of what it means to be a man, an aging victim of progress, embodiment of honor, champion of justice in an unjust world."

Life in a Boundary Situation: The Frontier

The western, more than any other, is the genre of place. In his Foreword for *To the Last Man* (1921), best-selling western writer Zane Grey said, "My inspiration to write has always come from nature. Character and action are subordinated to setting." But in the best westerns, character and action grow out of setting, which is the American frontier—both as a historic place and as a symbolic landscape. Landscape foreshadows plot, as in this description in Louis L'Amour's *Hondo* (1953): "the tips of the cottonwoods turned gold, like the sun-tipped lances of a moving army." The opening sentence of Grey's *Riders of the Purple Sage* appears to be a description of the landscape, but it anticipates the providential arrival of Lassiter, the hero-in-black: "A sharp clip-clop of iron-shod hoofs deadened and died away, and clouds of yellow dust drifted from under the cottonwoods out over the sage." According to Tomkins (1992, 3), "Physical sensations are the bedrock of the experience Westerns afford." These sensations are all related to place: eyes squinting against the dessert sun, the clip-clop of horses' hooves, the creak of the leather saddle, the coolness of water on a parched tongue and throat, the smell of roasted venison, the chill of crawling out of a bedroll into a spring morning, driving rain that hammers into the bodies of men and horses in savage gusts, the bone-weariness being chased for days across a hostile landscape, the smash of a fist to the nose, and the iron taste of blood.

Popular culture theorist John G. Cawelti (1999, 9) has argued that *everything* in the western is generated by the frontier—that boundary between social order and lawlessness, between old and new, between civilization and nature. He says, "It is this setting which generates certain kinds of crises which involve certain kinds of characters and call for the intervention of a particular kind of hero." The western setting is a symbolic landscape with three elements. There's civilization, associated with the eastern seaboard and all that it stands for: church, schools, courts of law, art and culture, rules of gentility, codes of dress, civil contracts, mediation by documents such as land titles and legislation, reason, prudential behavior, language, diplomatic solutions to conflict, femininity, and softness. Then in opposition, there's untamed nature, associated with indigenous peoples and all that that stands for in this genre: the wilderness, natural beauty, wide-open spaces, regeneration, freedom from institutional regulation, survival skills of tracking and hunting, irrationality, silence, the settling of conflict by violence, masculinity, and hardness.

The fragile new settlement represented by the fort, the town, and the homestead is the third space that occupies the in-between zone—the borderland between civilization and the wilderness. It shares qualities of both. The town is dominated by the saloon with its whiskey drinkers and gamblers—mostly young, single men, who outnumbered the women 40 to 1. The agents of the East are present in the town—the surveyors and land agents who parcel out the land, the schoolteachers from Boston who teach manners and grammar, and the Quakers who counsel the ways of peace. But the institutional structures of civil society are weak and ineffective—for example, the only lawyer in town may be an alcoholic who came west to escape failure in the East; the sheriff is often in the pay of the feudal cattle baron whose cowhands terrorize the town.

So, in the absence of an effective state, everything depends on the resolute individual. It takes a hero with steely courage and a quick trigger finger to win the showdown against the unruly forces of disorder. In this setting, the violence of the western hero is a moral necessity as well as a historical fact. The cover blurb on the Bantam paperback of Frank Gruber's *The Marshal* (1958) says, "He wanted to be peace marshal—but the town made him a killer." At the end of Jack Schaefer's *Shane* (1949), the young narrator, Bobby Starrett, recalls the final "single flashing instant" when Shane whirled to shoot Fletcher: "I would see the man and the weapon wedded in the one indivisible deadliness."

The western celebrates that brief, turbulent in-between time period *before* women and a civilized lifestyle and temperance unions prevailed. The western depicts a world scoured clean of all the elements associated with female values:

domestic interiors; the protected space of the house; the centrality of children and community; the importance of language, communication, and relationships; and the power of love and forgiveness. The only emotions sanctioned for the western hero are pride, loyalty to comrades, anger over insults, hatred for enemies, and the desire for vengeance. His virtues belong to a tribal, primitive world: refusal to compromise or negotiate; loyalty to family members and blood kin; and a willingness to die or kill for his concept of honor. For fans, the world of the western is more heroic than the present. It satisfies the reader's hunger for meaning—for a place where individual action can still make a difference. One reader said, "I used to love westerns because they hinged on the ability of the hero to resolve his problems on his own in an empty land, without the social structures that exist in civilization."

The Western Hero: Hard, Tough, and Unforgiving

The book that is credited as the founding text of the popular western genre is Owen Wister's *The Virginian* (1902), which explores this dynamic of East and West, female and male, civilization and the empty land. Jane Tompkins claims, in *West of Everything* (131–42), that the key to *The Virginian*, as well as to the genre to which *The Virginian* gave rise, lies in Owen Wister's relationship with his mother, Sarah Butler Wister. Sarah was a woman of strong intellect, keen artistic interests, thwarted talents, and a censorial disposition, who was at odds with her more practically minded husband. Sarah wanted culture and gentility for her son, while her husband recommended a practical career in a Boston bank. In response to this conflict, Wister had a nervous breakdown, and his doctor sent him west to a Wyoming ranch for fresh air. There Wister slept in a tent, spent his days in the saddle, bathed in an icy creek, hunted and fished, and worked with cattle. Within weeks he had recovered his health. Out of this transformative experience, he wrote a book, *The Virginian*, which set the pattern for the popular genre of the western. In a key scene, Molly, the schoolteacher from New England, says she won't marry the Virginian if he risks his life against the outlaw, Trampas. The Virginian does it anyway, kills Trampas in a main street shoot-out, and then what happens? Molly takes him back and loves him all the more. With the conflict in his own life still unresolved, Wister invented the West as a place where a man can take risks, face ultimate danger, and discover his masculine identity in defiance of female authority. The West got written as a place of self-transformation, regeneration, and renewal, where the spirit can heal itself in the wide-open spaces of nature.

Wister's Virginian is a prototype of the rugged hero in tune with the untamed natural world—wild animals, rocks, the land itself. In the first paragraph, the Virginian is described as moving "with the undulations of a tiger, smooth and easy, as if his muscles flowed beneath his skin." In *Riders of the Purple Sage* (1912), Zane Grey describes Lassiter's face as having "the leanness, the red burn of the sun, the set changelessness that came from years of silence and solitude." In *Hondo* (1952), published 50 years later, Louis L'Amour describes Hondo Lane as "a man as bleak as the land over which he rode." "To be a man in a Western," says Tompkins (1992, 73), "is to seem to grow out of the environment, which means to be hard, to be tough, to be unforgiving."

Despite his hardness and toughness, the western hero, even in his first introduction, was a breed on the way out. The more successful he is at killing Indians and suppressing outlaws, the more he paves the way for the flood of settlers who will fence in the open spaces, parcel out the land, and destroy the wilderness. James Fenimore Cooper's Leatherstocking novels (1823–1841) made that point first: it was the tragedy of the character variously called Hawkeye, the Pathfinder, and the Deerslayer to be an agent of a civilization to which he could never belong. Like Cooper's Hawkeye, the typical western hero "knows" Indians, having in many cases lived among them. He has learned their skills in tracking, fighting, wilderness survival, and enduring and inflicting pain—all useful abilities for defending the new community. But his violence makes him a perpetual outsider. That's why the western hero so often does not get the girl in the end. If he doesn't die sacrificially in a gunfight, he rides off into the sunset, as Shane does in Jack Schaefer's novel or as Ethan Edwards does in John Ford's movie *The Searchers*. There's an unmistakably elegiac tone to the western.

Where Have All the Readers Gone?

With all this going for it—a mythologized setting linked to the identity of a nation (Slotkin 1992), significant themes, great costumes, a loner hero, and horses—the western is nevertheless a genre in decline. It is losing readers to more successful genres such as the DETECTIVE story, science fiction, and ROMANCE. A 2010 Harris poll on what Americans are reading asked respondents to check off all categories of books that they had read in the past year. Among those who said they had read at least one fiction book in the past year, the breakdown of genres read was as follows: mystery, thriller, and crime—79 percent; science fiction—26 percent; romance 21 percent; chick lit—8 percent; westerns—5 percent. When readership was broken down demographically, western readers were far more likely to be male rather than female, older rather than younger. Only 4 percent of women had read a western in the past year in comparison with 7 percent of men. Only 3 percent of the 18-to-33 age group had read a western in comparison with 9 percent of readers age 65 and up.

In fact, the western has lost ground on all counts: fewer readers, fewer authors, fewer books being written and published, and fewer films and TV series produced than before. The space dedicated to the western has shrunk from 54 pages in the sixth edition of *Genreflecting* (2006) to 22 pages in the seventh edition (Orr and Herald 2013). There is a only a modest body of notable critical work on the popular western novel as opposed to, say, critical work on literary fiction set in the west or on the western film (for some examples of the good stuff on the popular western, see Cawelti 1999; Etulain and Marsden 1974; Jones 1978; Mitchell 1996; Smith 1950; Tompkins 1992). Librarians describe the difficulty of finding suitable books for readers—usually older men—who ask for westerns but have read everything written by Zane Grey, Louis L'Amour, Max Brand, Elmore Leonard, and Elmore Kelton, now alas all dead. Fewer and fewer writers are producing new westerns, as publishers rely increasingly on reprinting their backlists of older books. In its heyday in the late 1950s, westerns accounted for 10.75 percent of fiction books published in 1958; eight of the top ten television programs in 1959, when 35 western shows were running; and at least 54 feature films in 1959 (Cawelti 1999, 1). So what happened? How could a genre that was so quintessentially American and that had a popular appeal that dated back to Cooper's Leatherstocking tales and the 1860s dime novels—how could this genre just fizzle out?

Well, some advocates for the western, such as John Mort, argue that the western spirit is still alive. In *Read the High Country* (2006), which describes and categorizes some 2,000 western titles, Mort points out that, while there is a hard core of continuing fans for the traditional western, there are also new readers recruited by such literary writers of western settings and themes as Larry McMurtry, Cormac McCarthy, Louise Erdrich, Annie Proulx, and Barbara Kingsolver. In addition, some elements of the western have been adopted selectively to live on in other genres. The cowboy, the western landscape, and the ranch often appear in romances set in the West, such as the Calder ranch saga by Janet Dailey. The loner PI with a gun is the hero of hard-boiled crime fiction. Then there are mash-ups. In Scott Snyder's *American Vampire* series of graphic novels, a new VAMPIRE bloodline is started in the American West in the late 1800s by outlaw Skinner Sweet, who returns from the dead to wield new powers of strength and speed. In Doug TenNapel's steampunk graphic novel *Iron West*, homicidal robots invade the Old West and start killing everyone in sight until a small group of survivors fight back under the reluctant leadership of small-time outlaw Preston Struck.

An analysis of what readers themselves say about reading westerns provides some clues about the readers' experience. When avid readers were asked if there were genres that they particularly liked (see QUESTIONS ABOUT READING), fans of the western tended to be male. Maurice (professional engineer, age 57) explains concisely the main element of the genre's appeal: "Westerns fit right into the type of book I like. There's usually a well-defined hero and a linear story with a beginning, middle and end. Then there's the good guys and bad guys, and the good guy comes out on top." Philip (history student, age 20) adds another element—the traditional western is usually short and written in a style that presents few stumbling blocks to quick reading: "Westerns are for when you feel like reading and you just want to relax with something that's easy reading and a good story." Angus (student, age 27) describes *The Virginian* as "one of these universal stories" that yields up new meanings and pleasures when read at different ages.

Female readers, on the other hand, were apt to mention westerns in response to the question, "Are there any genres you do *not* enjoy and wouldn't choose?" Pearl (housewife, age 55) said, "I find them all to be much the same: the good guys and the bad guys." Lorraine (elementary school teacher, age 27) said, "I'm not really interested in anything 'western'—the horses and the trail, the cowboy notion, and all the rest of that stuff." Mia, an 80-year-old grandmother who was born and raised in Eastern Europe, was very clear about why she wouldn't read westerns: "Cowboys, all these men. Dirty, stinky, big mustaches, dirty clothes, boots. I don't like cowboys, they kill animals, I can't stand that."

That's the problem for many female readers: cowboys kill animals, they kill Indians, and they kill each other. The men have all the big action roles, while the women get kidnapped or driven off their homesteads. Mitchell (1996, 3) argues that a "persistent obsession with masculinity marks the Western." But Madeline (student, age 22) says, "I'm not too interested in a bunch of men killing each other. I like books where there are good women characters." When female readers complain that westerns are predictable and formulaic, they often mean that they don't like the formula in question, with its limited roles for women. Petra (student, age 24) says, "I like to adopt the role of whoever is in the book. I can become either the heroine or the hero." But she can't do that with westerns: "I have yet to find one that I relate to. In Westerns I find that females aren't portrayed in a good light. They're usually the hookers in the town. I don't want to read that." Tompkins (1992, 16) says that in her study the women who have some familiarity with westerns are "split into two camps: those who identified with the hero and those who didn't or couldn't." One female reader quoted by Tompkins said she could identify with the male heroes, but only with the non-white, non-WASP ones such as Tonto or Zorro. Another said that she identified with the horse.

Female readers have not been won over by the "adult Western" that emerged in the 1980s—for example, George G. Gilman's *Edge* series (advertised by his U.S. publisher as "The Most Violent Westerns in Print") and the Longarm series written under the house name Tabor Evans. Six-time winner of the Western Writers Association's Spur Award, Richard S. Wheeler (2012, 91–92) claims that earlier western fiction used to be broader in its appeal but that publishers and editors in the 1980s and 1990s "were sharply limiting what they would be willing to purchase from us":

> The effect of all this was a precipitous narrowing of western fiction. No longer was it written for a general audience. It became men's fiction, and it was loaded with "action," a word that really meant a lot of shooting, ambushes, fist fights, and various other forms of mayhem such as whippings, torture, sniping, lynching, high noon shootouts, and gang warfare.

The Western through Female Eyes; or, the Captivity Story

Successful genres such as detective fiction have a tent large enough to accommodate a variety of subgenres, some appealing more strongly to men and others appealing more strongly to women. Suppose we were to reimagine a western with a broader appeal? What sort of western subgenre might appeal to women? What would it look like? One line that seems ripe for development is the revisioning of standard western stories through the eyes of the women involved. As a test case, we could consider the Indian captivity narrative, which has a long history. Thousands of stories have been written about settlers—usually women and children—who were taken prisoner in a surprise Indian attack on a fort or a house. Many have been historical accounts (see Derounian-Stodola 1998); others take real events as starting points for fiction; and still others are entirely invented. Because some captivity stories have been told from the point of view of the women involved while others have focused exclusively on the searchers, this subgenre seems to offer an interesting test case for the idea of gendered appeal.

Mary Rowlandson's first-person account of her captivity has been called the first American bestseller. In *The Sovereignty and Goodness of God* (1682), Rowlandson tells the story of how she was abducted in 1675 by Narragansett Indians, was held hostage for almost three months, but was preserved throughout her ordeal by God's grace. As she described it, "On the tenth of February came the Indians with great numbers upon Lancaster. . . . Some in our house were fighting for their lives, others wallowing in their blood, the house on fire over our heads, and the bloody heathen ready to knock us on the head if we stirred out. . . . Thus were we butchered . . . standing amazed, with the blood running down to our heels."

Rowlandson includes elements that later became standard fare in captivity narratives: the suddenness of the event that drags a life onto a totally different path; the initial shock of witnessing a violent attack in which loved ones are beaten, killed, disemboweled, or scalped; the physical pain of travelling great distances, while wounded and carrying a dying child, on foot and on horseback through the snowy wilderness; the sorrow of witnessing her six-year-old child Sarah die of wounds; the initial revulsion at eating unfamiliar food—deer intestines, partially cooked horse liver, a piece of bear foot—which later became "sweet and savoury to my taste"; the unaccustomed labor she was required to perform for her master and his three wives, even on Sunday; various unpredictable acts of harsh treatment (hot ashes thrown in her eyes) interspersed with kindness (offerings of corn and groundnuts and a place by the fire); and, throughout, the inexplicable behavior of the captors, who seemed "unstable and like madmen." For Mary Rowlandson, who was ransomed for £20 after almost 12 weeks, the story ended in deliverance and redemption. Mary had crossed the line that separates regulated community from savage nature, and she had returned, with her religious faith tested and strengthened.

The historical kidnappings of Mary Rowlandson and others lay behind the many fictional accounts that followed. The kidnapping of the Munro sisters—dark, self-reliant Cora and fair, simple-minded Alice—by the treacherous Huron Magua sets off the chain of events in James Fenimore Cooper's *The Last of the Mohicans* (1826) (Haberly 1976). Similarly the capture of the heroine Ina by Mohawks and her pursuit by Seth Jones is the subject of Edward S. Ellis's wildly popular *Seth Jones: Or, the Captives of the Frontier* (1861), the Beadle and Adams publication that kick-started the dime novel western (Jones 1978, 8). In the only independent action that she takes in the entire narrative, Ina in Chapter 3 unwisely decides to jump out of the canoe against all advice, whereupon she falls immediately into the hands of the Mohawks. After an agonized cry ("Oh, father! mother! The Indians have got me!"), Ina isn't heard from again for many chapters, during which time interest centers on the adventures of the searchers.

A century later, in Alan LeMay's *The Searchers* (1954), the captured Debbie Edwards is seen only in traces—pieces of her clothing, hoofprints of her captors' horses—as the narrative focuses on the five-year pursuit by Debbie's Uncle Edwards and her adopted brother Martin. LeMay's retelling of the captivity story falls into the category that Frank Gruber calls the revenge story. Returning home to find that his brother's family has been slaughtered by a Comanche war party, Edwards sets off on a relentless pursuit, motivated by his fierce hatred of Indians and his zeal to find Debbie in order to kill her (a white woman who has lived with and slept with Indians is dishonored beyond repair). This plot also happens to be listed in Georges Polti's *The Thirty-Six Dramatic Situations* (1921) as plot 35: "Recovery of a Lost One. Elements: The Seeker; the One Found" (see PLOTS).

For those on the settlers' side of the dividing line, the historical captivity story had the potential to be deeply troubling. In contrast to the Mary Rowlandson rescue narrative, many documented captives—for example, Eunice Williams, Mary Jemison, Frances Slocum, and Cynthia Ann Parker—transferred their allegiance to the Indian world, learning the language, eating the food, and wearing the clothing of their captors. As a mark of their changed identity, they took on a new Indian name. To the would-be rescuers, the transformation was as frightening, distasteful, and inexplicable as it would have been had the stolen-away women turned into vampires. In the real-life story on which *The Searchers* was based, Cynthia Ann Parker became a Comanche woman called Naudah, or Keeps Warm with Us. In 1836, a Comanche war party attacked Parker's fort in eastern Texas, killing and torturing many and taking five captives, including nine-year-old Cynthia Ann Parker. When, after a long search, Cynthia Ann was finally found in 1846 at the age of 19, she refused to speak to her would-be rescuers and ran away and hid (Frankel 2013, 62). She lived with the Comanches for 24 years in total, until she was very unwillingly recaptured in 1860 by the U.S. Cavalry after a murderous raid on her Comanche village. At the time of her recapture, she was the wife of a Comanche and the mother of three, including Quannah, who became one of the last great Comanche warriors and political leaders (Gwynne 2010).

Cynthia Ann Parker herself left no oral or written record of her experience, but her story has been told and retold, reimagined and fictionalized, both at the time and subsequently. *The Searchers* told the story from the perspective of the rescuers. In contrast, *Ride the Wind: The Story of Cynthia Ann Parker and the Last Days of the Comanche* (1982) by Lucia St. Clair Robson puts the focus on the captive's experience as she gradually adapts to, and eventually embraces, the culture of the Comanche and its people. As in most westerns, there is a lot of pain, suffering, and death; flight and pursuit; terrific horses; and the wide-open spaces of the "wind-scoured plain." In good western fashion, the main character is stripped bare of almost everything—her home, her family, her clothes, her language, her name. But then, unlike the male western hero, she recreates for herself a new family, establishes strong friendships, and eventually achieves a new domesticity of husband, children, and family life. So is it really a western?

The Western Writers of America Association thinks so. *Ride the Wind* won the Western Writers Spur award, made the *New York Times* best-seller list, and has been frequently reprinted. To judge from the enthusiastic comments of readers on the Amazon site (85% of some 250 reviewers gave it five stars), Robson's story has an army of fans, the majority of whom seem to be women. Readers said that they had reread *Ride the Wind* many times—four times, ten times, twenty times, every year; that they had bought multiple copies to lend and give away to friends; that because they had read to tatters their original copy, they were happy to have an e-copy on Kindle; that they put *Ride the Wind* high on their list of all-time favorites; and so on. Many readers enjoyed what one called the "strong heroine character." Megan said that "you are drawn into the story" through "the growth and development of the main character as she adjusts to her new life and to the adventures that new life brings her."

Ride the Wind passes a key test for the western genre: it evokes the physical sensations—the sounds, sights, and smells that give the reader a sensuous experience of being "right there." Lorri says that the author "made you feel what it was like to be a Comanche." Frank says, "We smell the smoke, the coffee, and the animals. We taste the food, feel the bitter winters and scorching summers." Anudah said, "You can almost sense the smell of fire, hear the deep voice of the drums, and feel the joy and pain." One reader, who said that *Ride the Wind* was a book "to be kept and passed down like a family heirloom," recalled, "My mother read this book years ago, and spent 7 years looking for it in dusty used book stores and flea markets. Finally she found it and gave it to me. I can almost imagine myself as Cynthia . . . riding through the prairies on my own horse."

References

Cawelti, John G. 1999. *The Six-Gun Mystique Sequel.* Bowling Green State University Popular Press.

Derounian-Stodola, Kathryn Zabelle. 1998. *Women's Indian Captivity Narratives.* New York and Toronto. Penguin.

Etulain, Richard W. and Michael T. Marsden. 1974. *The Popular Western: Essays Toward a Defininition.* Bowling Green, Ohio: Bowling Green University Popular Press.

Frankel, Glenn. 2013. *The Searchers: The Making of an American Legend.* New York and London: Bloomsbury.

Gruber, Frank. 1955. "The Basic Western Novel Plots." *Writers' Year Book*, 49–53, 160. Cincinnati: Writers Digest.

Gwynn, Sam C. 2010. *Empire of the Summer Moon: Quanah Parker and the Rise and Fall of the Comanches, the Most Powerful Indian Tribe in American History.* New York: Scribner.

Haberly, David T. 1976. "Women and Indians: The Last of the Mohicans and the Captivity Tradition." *American Quarterly* 28, 4 (October): 431–44.

Harris Interactive. 2010. "Stephen King Is America's Favorite Author; Mystery, Crime and Thriller Novels Are the Genre Most Read." *The Harris Poll*, October 7. http://multivu.prnewswire.com/mnr/harrisinteractive/44732/.

Jones, Daryl. 1978. *The Dime Novel Western.* Bowling Green, OH: Popular Press, Bowling Green State University.

Mitchell, Lee Clark. 1996. *Westerns: Making the Man in Fiction and Film.* Chicago: University of Chicago Press.

Mort, John. 2006. *Read the High Country: A Guide to Western Books and Films.* Westport, CT and London: Libraries Unlimited.

Orr, Cynthia and Diana Tixier Herald. 2013. "Westerns." *Genreflecting: A Guide to Popular Reading Interests,* 7th ed., 207–29. Santa Barbara, CA: Libraries Unlimited.

Polti, Georges. 1921; 1991. Translated by Lucille Ray. *The Thirty-Six Dramatic Situations.* Boston: The Writer, Inc. Available in the Internet Archive: http://archive.org/details/thirtysixdramati00polt.

Slotkin, Richard. 1992. *Gunfighter Nation: The Myth of the Frontier in Twentieth-century America.* University of Oklahoma Press.

Smith, Henry Nash. 1950. *Virgin Land: The American West as Symbol and Myth.* New York: Vintage Books/Harvard University Press.

Tompkins, Jane. 1992. *West of Everything: The Inner Life of Westerns.* New York and Oxford: Oxford University Press.

Western Writers of America. http://westernwriters.org/.

Wheeler, Richard S. 2012. *An Accidental Novelist: A Literary Memoir.* Sunstone Press.

X-traordinary Readers

This section is about superreaders—people who not only are amazing readers in themselves but also help other people become joyous readers. The four considered here—Cindy Orr, Nancy Pearl, Joyce Saricks, and Neal Wyatt—are pioneers in a new brand of readers' advisory (RA) that has taken hold in North American public libraries starting in the early 1980s. *Readers' advisory* is the term used by librarians to refer to all the various activities involved in brokering a good match between a reader/listener/viewer and the materials that person might enjoy—print books certainly, but also audiobooks, films, music, and videogames. In the 1920s in North American public libraries, RA was a huge program, but the term meant something different then. It meant helping readers "read with a purpose" in a sequenced, systematic self-education program focused on socially significant topics (Ross et al. 2006, 211). RA in that earlier period was thought of as a form of adult education. When RA returned to public libraries in the 1980s, it was transformed into a different animal—helping readers find books for leisure reading. A big part of this transformation involved jettisoning the earlier notion that the librarian's job was to push the reader up the reading ladder from "weaker works" such as popular fiction to higher grade stuff. Cindy Orr, Nancy Pearl, Joyce Saricks, and Neal Wyatt were all, in one way or another, part of this transformation.

These superreaders live right across the continent, from Virginia to Seattle, Washington, but I was fortunate to be able to interview the four of them at various American Library Association (ALA) conferences during intervals snatched from between other events that these library leaders were attending and sometimes convening. The locations for the interviews were variously a hotel room, a restaurant, and a seating area outside an auditorium. As I was transcribing the recorded interviews, I could sometimes also hear background music or nearby conversations or the clinking of silverware—in one case the sounds of the audience filing into the Carnegie Medal presentation in Chicago, in 2013, to celebrate the previous year's best fiction and nonfiction. As a starting point, I had some questions thought up in advance, but each interview took its own shape, following the particular interests of the interviewees. Here are some of the questions that I asked:

- How old were you when you first began to think of yourself as a reader?

- What for you would be the perfect book?

- You have made a career out of helping other people connect with books they will enjoy. How did this happen? What were the steps that brought you to where you are today?

- What do you know now about reading that novice readers don't yet know?

- What are the most important things you learned about readers' advisory that you didn't know when you started out in RA work?

All four of these readers *extraordinaire* believe passionately in the power of pleasure reading to transform lives. Right from earliest childhood, they all thought of themselves as readers, and they read voraciously. All four turned their own love of reading and talking about books into a career in public librarianship. Drawn to RA work, they have all been innovators in finding ways to promote the pleasures of reading. They all agree that a *good book* is one that the reader enjoys. They have shared their innovations in RA through books, articles, Web sites, columns in library journals, and presentations at library conferences. All have received significant national and international awards for their contributions to RA. They all have taught courses in RA in graduate library programs in different regions of the country. They believe that public libraries are not just about providing access to information but also about helping people find enjoyable books to read. Above all, they believe that the key to promoting reading is pleasure.

Each of these four extraordinary readers has made a unique contribution to RA. Here is a brief introduction:

Cindy Orr is a library consultant with a long history of RA work in public libraries. She has been a pioneer in the use of Web resources, working with Janet Lawson beginning in 1996 to create Bookbrowser as a site for avid readers, featuring lists of series books in order (a site later acquired by Barnes & Noble). Currently she edits the blog for Library Unlimited's *Reader's Advisor Online*. She is the coeditor, along with Diana Tixier Herald, of the 7th edition of *Genreflecting: A Guide to Popular Reading Interests* (2013). A long-time fan of Betty Rosenberg, who wrote the first edition of *Genreflecting* (1982), Cindy supports Rosenberg's First Law of

Reading, "Never apologize for your reading tastes," and adds her own corollary: "Never belittle anyone else's reading tastes."

Nancy Pearl is the only interviewee to have her own Librarian Action Figure, complete with "shushing action." Her 1998 program If All Seattle Read the Same Book has been widely imitated in One City, One Book programs as well as in statewide programs and countrywide programs such as Canada Reads. The former executive director of the Washington Center for the Book at Seattle Public Library, she regularly comments on books on National Public Radio's Morning Edition. For her role as an advocate for reading, she was chosen by *Library Journal* as the 2011 Librarian of the Year. She has helped others find books they would enjoy through her many books—the *Now Read This* series, *Book Lust, More Book Lust, Book Crush, Book Lust to Go*—all of which provide reading recommendations "for every mood, moment and interest." In 2012, she partnered with Amazon in the Book Lust Rediscoveries program that annually will reprint six overlooked gems published between 1960 and 2000. These are books that Nancy Pearl had loved and recommended in her *Book Lust* series but which sadly had gone out of print. Her first pick was Merle Miller's *A Gay and Melancholy Sound*. Her second pick was *After Life* by Rhian Ellis, which starts off, "First, I had to get his body into the boat."

Joyce G. Saricks is the busiest retired person possible, continuing since her retirement in 2004 from Downers Grove to be engaged in reading, listening to, and talking about books, giving workshops and conference presentations, and writing voluminously. She is the author of two influential books on how to help readers find that next good book: *Readers' Advisory Service in the Public Library*, 3rd ed. (2005) and *The Readers' Advisory Guide to Genre Fiction*, 2nd ed. (2009). She is a founding member of the Adult Reading Round Table (ARRT), a Chicago-based group of librarians who have been engaged in genre study since 1984. First hired in 1983 by the Downers Grove Public Library in Illinois, Joyce Saricks turned the library into a living laboratory for experimenting with ways to help readers. She has been especially influential for her work on *appeal*, a term that refers to elements in a book to which readers respond. She has spread the word nationally and internationally in hundreds of RA workshops and she frequently offers the online ALA-sponsored course Readers' Advisory 101. Her regular At Leisure column in *Booklist* provides a series of micro-training articles on RA. An enthusiast for audiobooks, she is the author of *Read On—Audiobooks: Reading Lists for Every Taste* and is the audio editor for *Booklist*, the ALA's chief tool for collection development. In 2000, the Romance Writers of America named her Librarian of the Year.

Neal Wyatt worked as a collection development and RA librarian in Virginia before attending graduate school. She now holds a PhD in Media, Art, and Text from Virginia Commonwealth University and specializes in collection development, RA, new media, and digital humanities. She is also a one-woman band. She produces multiple columns for *Library Journal*, writing "RA Crossroads," editing "Reader's Shelf," and compiling the online feature "Wyatt's World," all of which draw attention to the pleasures of reading and sometimes of watching and listening. She is a strong advocate of what she calls "whole collections" RA, which draws on everything—fiction, nonfiction, audiobooks, movies, music, Web sites, databases—in short, the works. Demonstrating this inclusive approach, her column "RA Crossroads" starts with a single title such as *A Game of Thrones* and suggests "Read-Alikes," "Read-Arounds," "Listen-alikes," and "Watch-Arounds." In *The Readers' Advisory Guide to Nonfiction* (2007b, 241), Wyatt explains the value of "reading maps" as a hypertextual tool to chart "the internal world of the book itself and all the threads of reading interest that stem from it" (see NONFICTION). She designed ALA's RA 101 course and has written a series of articles on the RA renaissance for *Library Journal*. In 2013, she won the Isadore Gilbert Mudge award for her "significant contributions to the field of reference librarianship."

Becoming a Reader

Unlike frustrated readers who avoid reading, these superreaders thought of themselves as readers right from early childhood. The majority of early readers come from a reading family, but others, like Cindy Orr, find reading on their own. Her parents weren't pleasure readers themselves, Cindy said, but "somehow I had that desire." One of her earliest memories is "standing in the kitchen with a bubblegum and opening the cartoon and thinking, 'One of these days I won't have to ask my mother to read this to me.' " Neal Wyatt had been encouraged all along by her mother but turned into a real reader when she found that first wonderful book that provided a pleasure that can be found in no other way—in this case Ellen Raskin's *The Westing Game*. She said: "What turned me into a reader was when I found a book that made me want to read another book just like it—that made me want to continue having those kinds of experiences. It was the process of finding books that made me deeply happy, of exploring the library and finding more books that did the same, and of knowing there were even more to find next time that helped me become a reader."

Nancy Pearl started thinking of herself as a reader when she was "very young—seven or eight at the oldest." *Ellen Tebbits* by Beverly Cleary and *Whirligig House* by Anna Wright were important books. Nancy recalled, "[The children in these books] just had different lives than I had and, for the most part, they were lives that were happier. That was a relief to know that there were other families that handled things differently than my family did." She became a committed reader as soon as she was able to distinguish that the world of books "was a different world from the one I was living in and that the world in books was the one I wanted to live in." The sense of escaping to different and happier worlds was the payoff: "So for me it's always been the transformative power of books. It's all escape for me, one way or another."

Similarly, Joyce Saricks described the draw of reading in childhood as escape, in her case from boredom: "It was certainly escape. It was something to do. In a town of 1250, in a rural area, there's not much happening. It was an escape. I remember one summer day reading when I was supposed to follow the tractor in the pick-up. Unfortunately it was stick shift, which made it harder to read when driving at ten miles per hour." Reading was variously associated with independence, with a pleasurable and repeatable experience, with escape to another world closer to the heart's desire, and with a way to avoid boredom.

Finding that first book that makes you want to re-experience "another book just like it" is often the turning point in the making of avid readers. Because readers want to recreate that pleasurable experience, it helps if they can identify the elements in the satisfying book that draws them in. The four superreaders have all reflected deeply on their own reading preferences, and so I asked them what they themselves look for (or what they avoid). Here's what they said when I asked the perfect book question—although Neal Wyatt qualified her answer by saying "any wonderful book is perfect at the time":

Orr: Sympathetic strong characters is the first thing that's important. I like a good story too. It's wonderful when you find both. I don't like to be pulled out of the story. So if it's poorly edited or something's really wrong and I get pulled out of the story, I hate that. I like to be pulled in and just lose myself in the characters and the story. I don't like distance. The book I'm carrying with me now is an Ian MacEwan, but there's a distance between him and the characters. I can admire that it's beautifully written and the descriptions are wonderful, but I feel really removed from the characters.

Pearl: It would have to be a smart book. So many books have given me such pleasure and they are so different from one another. The only thing that they have in common is that the characters are really interesting and the language is distinguished. What I like crosses genres and it crosses the fiction/nonfiction divide. I think as a child I read more for story. I certainly wasn't conscious of the language at all. What I've learned is my limits of what I'm willing to tolerate in a book. I don't like books where you are in the head of a killer. I don't like books where the narrator dies or is killed off. I don't like psychological edginess too much—that makes me too edgy. I know my limits and my tolerations.

Saricks: It would have a good story in it—and an element of romance. I like that sense of time and place in books. I don't like books with really obscure language—I don't know that I'll ever get to *Ulysses*. I like books where there's a secret in the past, so that you get the two time lines. And I love treasure books. Give me Fabergé eggs any day! I know I say I read for story, but I don't remember plot details. It's just the *experience* of story that I like. And how I feel about what's happening is really important to me. . . . I don't like books where I don't like any of the characters. It makes me unhappy. I have to have that connection.

Wyatt: It would be one that was witty, clever, and smart. One that made me think. One that thrilled me to be in its company, one that surprised and enthralled. It would be long and meaty so that I could sink inside of it for some time. The author would pay attention to style, have a point of view, and exhibit a deft hand at description and dialogue. A "perfect" book is one that I would want to delay finishing so I could stay within its hold. It would be one that I might start again, or dip back into, as soon as I did finish; one that would make me start suggesting it to others before I was even halfway through.

    In describing their perfect book, all four readers balanced a discussion of the features of the book itself (sympathetic characters, a good story, deft description, etc.) with a discussion of the *experience* of the book—the way the book would affect them or make them feel. They wanted to be "pulled into" the story; to "sink inside [a meaty book] for some time"; to have a close "connection" with the characters; to be stimulated to think; to be "surprised and enthralled"; and to be able to prolong or repeat the pleasurable experience.

How Did These Superreaders Get Started with Readers' Advisory?

Joyce Saricks described being thrown into RA at the deep end and learning to swim with a little help from her friends. At the Downers Grove Public Library in Illinois, Saricks was head of technical services when in 1983 the new director, Kathy Balcom, invited her to start a RA department in 1983. Joyce recalled that she said, " 'What is it?' Because I knew *nothing*. At the University of Chicago library school, we had some very good professors, but we didn't talk about readers' advisory. Or fiction books." Realizing that that she would have to learn a lot and invent a lot, she recruited Nancy Brown from a library school to help set up the department. They started with Betty Rosenberg's first edition of *Genreflecting* (1982) and used that to create their popular fiction list. Joyce has described her career as a readers' advisor and coauthor with Nancy Brown of *Readers' Advisory in the Public Library* as "pure serendipity":

        We did a workshop for a group of south suburban reference librarians. Someone there talked to an editor at ALA Editions and she said, "Don't you want to write a book?" And so we did. And it was just the right time. You know, it's all this stuff happening together . . . And then we started the Adult Reading Round Table in 1984. We created the market, I guess, for that. But we couldn't have done it, if people hadn't wanted to do it. If it hadn't been the time.

Neal Wyatt also said, "I learned about readers' advisory on my own." But she had a head start—a long history of talking about books, right from childhood: "I would say to people: 'Have you read *The Westing Game?*—you won't believe what happens in that book!' " In Virginia, when Wyatt began working in a public library, few were actively doing RA in the libraries she knew well. But then in 1996 she got on the ALA committee to pick the list of Notable Books. Through participation on the Notable Books Council, she met others of like mind with an interest in RA—Nancy Pearl and Brian Kenney and Cathleen Towey. And then she found Saricks and Brown's *Readers' Advisory in the Public Library* (1989) "at the right time in my career to think that readers' advisory is what I wanted to do." Neal recalled, "The prospect of doing something new and creative was deeply appealing." She found others of like mind when she served on ALA's Notable Books committee: "Nancy Pearl, Cathleen Towey, and so many others on Notable Books were all deeply engaged readers—smart readers who wanted to push RA forward. I think Notable Books made me a readers' advisor."

Cindy Orr understood the value of good public libraries from growing up in their absence. She said, "I grew up in the middle of Kansas and there was no library in my little, tiny town except a room of discarded books that people had donated with volunteers keeping it open one day a week." In her first library job, which was in the Lakewood Public Library, a suburb of Cleveland, she learned the nuts and bolts of RA by modeling "those older women when users asked for some good books to read." These more experienced librarians "weren't saying, '*I* like this.' They really listened and talked to people." Orr said, "We made displays, we made booklists, we talked about books that felt like other books. There was no language for that," but the Lakewood Public Library was doing it.

By 1995, the Internet was the new big thing. In a new job as manager in charge of building a new building and hiring staff, Cindy felt that new technology was leaving her behind: "So I bought a computer at home and decided to get online. I joined Dorothy-L [an online discussion list for mystery lovers] and got into some of the early discussions about mysteries." Cindy started with what she loved—pleasure reading and especially mysteries—and turned that love into a project that used technology to expand the reach of RA. She met Janet Lawson online, and together they codeveloped BookBrowser, a "site dedicated to readers," which was used extensively by public libraries for RA. Beginning with BookBrowser and more recently with the *Reader's Advisor Online*'s blog, which she edits, Cindy has used Internet resources to amplify the reach of readers' advisory activity. As a regular Monday morning feature of the *Reader's*

Advisor Online blog, Cindy Orr and Sarah Statz Cords produce the RA Run Down, which pulls together the past week's book news from some 100 blogs, newsletters, magazines, newspapers, and television. Cindy says, "Nowadays I scan blogs. I think I subscribe to about 100 blogs and I just scan them very quickly. I scan a lot of magazines—*Locus* and *Mystery News* and *Romantic Times*. I go to bookstores and walk around. Trying to put myself in the patron's shoes is what it's all about."

Nancy Pearl knew from the age of 10 onward that she wanted to be a librarian, the result of having encountered a "wonderful librarian, Miss Whitehead." Pearl recalled that Miss Whitehead "recognized something in me that needed to be supported and fed. She would say to me, 'Nancy, I have a brand new dog book that just came in to the library. You can be the first person to read it. Oh wait, but first I'd like you to read *The Five Children and It*.'" Having received the gift of reading from Miss Whitehead, Nancy thought that being a librarian would be a good way of making the world a better place: "I couldn't think of what would be better than for me to give the gift of reading—which is what she gave to me—to somebody else, to other children. And I did." When I asked about some of the other steps that got her to her current role as a super-reader, she said, "Everything I do now, I've always done, but now it's just on a larger scale." Throughout a sequence of jobs—children's librarian; book-mobile librarian; bookseller in a small, independent bookstore; then returning to the library world—she was always hand-selling and talking about books and reviewing books. Nancy recommends two books a week on National Public Radio radio and selects books for the "Pearl's Picks" library service, which provides subscribing libraries with 12 recommended titles a month that they can link to their catalogs. But the secret, she says, is "I only have to read the books that *I* want to read. I'm never under any obligation to finish a book. I stop at whatever point the book starts to bore me." About readers' advisory, she says:

> I'm pathologically pessimistic about everything except reading. I've always felt that, even as a young librarian, that I could find a book for every reader. It was just a question of figuring out what they wanted and not what I wanted them to read. You can intuit from the way people talk the kind of book they would like. I was able to make those magical connections, intuitive leaps, between who this person is and what they might want to read.

Reading as a Collaborative Enterprise

The meaningful part of what happens when someone reads is invisible to an observer. Hence we may think that everyone's reading experience resembles our own, and it takes a reality check to discover that's not the case. We all create our own versions of the books we read. Nancy Pearl makes this point explicitly: "Reading is a very interactive activity in the sense that a reader is collaborating with the author on writing the book. Every reader therefore reads a different book from every other reader." What meanings we bring to life when we read the book and what we remember about the experience later can vary dramatically from one person to the next. Joyce Saricks provided her own example of readers creating different versions of the same book: "I was talking to a friend about one of my favorite books I've read recently, which is *The Mistress of the Art of Death*. And he said he *hated* that book—it was all the romance in it. And I'm going 'romance'? I don't remember *any* romance in it. So his version was totally different."

In describing her early RA work, Joyce Saricks told me that collaborating with Nancy Brown in the Downers Grove Public Library brought home to her the differing ways in which readers experience books. The seed for the concept of appeal elements was that Joyce and Nancy themselves were "so different as readers." Joyce remembered, "Nancy read for character and I read for plot. So we could almost never suggest books to each other." First described in Saricks and Brown's *Readers' Advisory Service in the Public Library* (1989) and elaborated subsequently, the concept of appeal elements has become bedrock for thinking about RA work. In the transactional model of reading that underlies the concept of appeal, the reading experience depends partly on identifiable elements in the text itself and partly on what the particular reader brings to the experience in terms of preferences, ways of reading, and mood. Saricks (2005, 42) captures the two collaborative agents of book and reader by defining appeal as the "elements of books to which a reader relates."

Saricks has identified four main appeal factors—pacing, characterization, story line, and frame/tone—to which is added language or style (2005, 40–66). Unlike a list of subject headings, an articulation of appeal elements captures the *feel* of the book and provides readers with helpful clues for deciding whether or not the book is likely to be worth their picking up. A particular reader at any given time may be looking for, say, a slowly unfolding book with strong character development or a fast-paced book with plot twists. A reader may want a hard-hitting, edgy book that explores the heart of darkness or alternatively may be looking for an upbeat book that provides reassurance. That's where the "conversation about books" becomes important. Readers' advisors learn to listen closely. Does the reader use terms such as *fast-paced* or *hard-to-put-down*, or does the reader talk about quirky characters or exotic settings? What does the reader say he does *not* enjoy (e.g., no psychological horror, no three-generational sagas)? *Readers' Advisory Service in the Public Library* gave momentum to a new perspective on RA that put the emphasis on the quality of the reading *experience* for the reader, not on the literary quality of the book.

Instead of talking about appeal elements, Nancy Pearl talks about the "four doorways" (see also Pearl 2012a, 2012b). Although Joyce Saricks's model of reading is transactional, it is possible to talk about appeal elements as if they are a set of characteristics inhering in the book alone—that "appeal is in the book" (Dali, 2014). The doorway metaphor more clearly foregrounds the collaborative nature of reading and the active role of the reader who prefers one or another of the doorways. Nancy Pearl says the doorways idea is more intuitive: "It's the same thing as the appeals, generally, but it's a terrific metaphor. Ever since I've started using that in the classroom, it's been smoother sailing." When I asked how she described the doorways to her students, she said:

> That every book has the same four doorways—character, language, setting, and story. But every book does not have the same size doorways. There are some books where 99 per cent of the people who love that book have entered through the very same doorway. Then the next biggest doorway—in terms of the numbers of readers or in terms of the numbers of books that you have in the library collection—is character. Then setting is smaller, and language is the smallest. Then I ask students to make the connections between fiction and nonfiction. So if the doorway is story, where would you send readers [to find nonfiction where the doorway is primarily story]?

Neal Wyatt has taken the concept of appeal and dreamed it forward. Wyatt (2007a) has declared that the concept of appeal is undergoing "an RA Big Think." She herself wanted to find a way to recognize something that she found true of her own experience of reading—what she calls "the internal life of the book," which is different from appeal. In addition to read-alikes, readers' advisors need another way to help readers—what Wyatt calls "read-arounds." After reading an Amish romance featuring a heroine who made quilts, Neal wanted to read more about the quilts: "If a readers' advisor said to me, 'Here are some other Amish romances,' that would be the completely *wrong* answer. I wanted to see the quilts. I thought, 'Well, where's this?' This is as important to me as the appeal elements are."

Thinking about the "where's this?" question lead Neal into her breakthrough work on whole collections and reading maps. In her RA position in Virginia, her job was to buy nonfiction. She started talking to people about how to bridge the Dewey divide, including Joyce Saricks, who said, in the back of a taxi at an ALA conference, "Why don't you write a book about it?" So the seed for *Readers' Advisory Guide to Nonfiction* (2007) wasn't just nonfiction but the need to break down compartments between fiction and nonfiction and between different formats in order to help library users: "The whole point was that RA needed to step beyond fiction and do nonfiction and movies and music and audiobooks—the whole world of the library and all its possibilities." The last chapter of the book "lays out the world of whole collections—and says it's not just read-alikes; it's read-arounds too. You need to create this universe that supports their reading interest that's beyond appeal." One conceptual tool was the reading map, which grew out of Neal's interest in visualizing the internal life of the book.

So what are reading maps exactly? Here's how Neal Wyatt (2006) defines them: "Reading maps are Web-based visual journeys through books that chart the myriad associations and themes of a title via other books, pictures, music, links to Web sites, and additional material." In 2004 at the Public Library Association conference in a program in with Nancy Pearl and Cathleen Towey, Neal introduced her concept of reading maps, illustrating it with her map of *Jonathan Strange and Mr. Norrell*. Since then the concept of reading maps has caught the imagination of readers' advisors, and students in RA programs are being taught how to make them (Spratford and Hawn 2004). Neal says, "Once I became a reader, I grew up *knowing* that there was a living life inside of a book. I really wanted to figure out a way to reveal it."

What Novice Readers *Don't* Know

As is evident by now, my four interviewees have had a long apprenticeship in reading. So what do superreaders know that novices and frustrated readers don't know? Perhaps if we could figure out the answer to that question, we could help scaffold the experience for less experienced readers. Joyce joked, "The biggest answer for novice readers is that they have to read more!" But no one accumulates the 10,000 hours of practice that it takes to become an expert unless they are enjoying it. So here are some suggestions on how to maximize enjoyment.

• *If you are not enjoying the book, put it down*

Beginning readers sometimes think that if they are missing a detail or are confused about who all the characters are and their ranks in the Russian civil service, they need to start all over from the beginning and read more slowly. Practiced readers know that, on the contrary, it's better to forge ahead—or, in some cases, it's better just to put the book down. Joyce said, "Surely one of the things novices may not know is that they have permission *not* to read it." It may not be their right time to read a particular book. Nancy's advice for novice readers is to follow her "rule of 50," which was inscribed on a Starbucks cup: if you are 50 years old or younger, read 50 pages before giving up on it; if you are older than 50, the magic number is 100 minus your age: "I know that, if I'm not in the mood for this book today, that does not mean that I am not going to get into the mood for that book six months down the line. Or 6 years or 60 years. Or the next day."

• *Don't be too constrained, because there are lots of possible experiences to try*

All the superreaders said that a big challenge for beginning readers is that they can't know the range of possible experiences out there. Overwhelmed by the sheer number of choices available, novices often stick to the familiar, but the downside is that readers may be missing a lot of what they would enjoy.

Cindy Orr said that in her first job, she learned the hunger that readers have for something new by the way the phones would start ringing whenever a book was recommended on the radio by Dorothy Fuldheim, "the Oprah of Cleveland of her time." At the end of one program, when she had 10 seconds left to fill, she said, "Well, I'm reading this other wonderful book right now and I can't remember the name but it's about w[h]ales." People wanted that book: "They didn't know if it was Wales the country or whales the sea animal, and they didn't care."

"One of our goals," Nancy Pearl says, "should be to broaden the way people experience the world of books. People often don't know that they would like a book, because no one has thought to suggest it to them before." As a way to provide "reach," Nancy tells students in her RA course about Nordstrom's and "the three-shoe solution." At Nordstrom's Department Store, shoe salespeople are trained to bring out three pairs of shoes: the pair you asked for, "another shoe that's very similar, but more expensive maybe," and "a third shoe that often has very little connection to those first two shoes, but it has *some* connection."

> That's how we should do readers' advisory—we should think of three books. So if someone comes in and says, "I just love Lee Child" or a mystery, then you recommend another book that is a mystery, a second book that isn't shelved with the mysteries but has the same doorway, and then you do a reach book. That reach, I think, should take you to a different part of the library. So I ask students for each of those doorways, what would it correspond to in their mind in the nonfiction section.

Tips for Readers' Advisors

Finally I asked the superreaders what important things they had learned about readers' advisory that they didn't know when they first started out. They all said, "It's not about you." That's Cindy Orr's seventh *golden rule* for readers' advisors (2013). Nancy Pearl said, "The first thing is that readers' advisors have to know it's not about them. We should make those little plastic bracelets and have them say, 'It's not about you.' Everybody could look down at it and be reminded: it's not the book that I just read and loved or hated." The tips from these four experts all involved, in one way or another, the following elements: read a lot and read broadly; build your knowledge of books and genres; listen to your readers; it's a conversation; remember that it's all about pleasure; and give back.

Orr: Number one is read. Read, read, read. There's just no short-cut. Don't fake it, because they'll call you out, they'll catch you. Don't say, "Yes, I've read that" when you haven't. It's not about you; it's about what this person would like. "Never apologize for your reading taste"—I always give them that quote [from Betty Rosenberg's first edition of *Genreflecting* in 1982]. Keep a reading log. There is no one right answer. Give back. Have fun—it should be fun; that's the whole point.

Pearl: When I suggest a book, I don't talk about the plot. I just talk about the experiential aspects of it—what a reader will find in this book. Even in formal booktalks, what the book is about should be taken care of in a sentence. The rest should be the *experience* that the reader will get from this book. People tend to tell too much. They tend to tell the story of the book. When I talk about booktalking in my class, the big thing I stress is "Don't overtell."

Saricks: You have to be a good listener. You've got to be able to get readers to talk to you. You've got to listen so that you can hear what they are saying about what they like. There's no way around the fact that you have to read—read reviews, read books, talk to readers. Pump the readers for things that they're reading. You have to build that knowledge. There are fifty thousand correct answers to the request, "Give me a good book." Readers Advisors need to know that—and that it's about setting up relationships, that it's fun, and that readers love it.

Wyatt: The three most important things are: Read as widely as you can. Don't worry about depth as much as you worry about breadth. Without wide reading, you're working in the dark. Second, you have to understand that your reaction to what they say to you can stay with them forever. It is incumbent upon you to *only* have a reaction of being thrilled and delighted that they liked what they liked. Don't make anyone feel badly—that's not your job. If you fail at that, you've failed at everything. And finally, remember that this isn't a quiz; it's a conversation. Those conversations have affirmed what they like, have given them a chance to talk about their preferences, and have taught them that the library is a place where such conversations are fostered. If you can, give them a range of materials and let them go play. But if you can't, know that you have done the right thing just by having the conversation.

References

Dali, Keren. 2014. "From Book Appeal to Reading Appeal: Redefining the Concept of Appeal in Readers' Advisory." *Library Quarterly* 84, no. 1: 22–48.

Orr, Cynthia, ed. *Reader's Advisor Online* (blog). Libraries Unlimited. http://www.readersadvisoronline.com/blog/.

Orr, Cynthia. 2013. "Cindy Orr's Golden Rules of Readers' Advisory Service." http://www.cindyorr.com/Golden_Rules_of_RA.html.

Orr, Cynthia, and Diana Tixier Herald. 2013. *Genreflecting: A Guide to Popular Reading Interests*, 7th ed. Santa Barbara, CA: Libraries Unlimited.

Pearl, Nancy. 1999. *Now Read This: A Guide to Mainstream Fiction, 1978–1998.* Englewood, CO: Libraries Unlimited.

Pearl, Nancy. 2002. *Now Read This II: A Guide to Mainstream Fiction, 1990–2001.* Greenwood Village, CO: Libraries Unlimited.

Pearl, Nancy. 2003. *Book Lust: Recommended Reading for Every Mood, Moment, and Reason.* Seattle, WA: Sasquatch Books.

Pearl, Nancy. 2005. *More Book Lust: Recommended Reading for Every Mood, Moment, and Reason.* Seattle, WA: Sasquatch Books.

Pearl, Nancy. 2010. *Book Lust to Go: Recommended Reading for Travelers, Vagabonds, and Dreamers.* Seattle, WA: Sasquatch Books.

Pearl, Nancy. 2012a. "Check It Out with Nancy Pearl: Finding That Next Good Book." *Publishers Weekly*, March 16. http://publishersweekly.com/pw/by-topic/columns -and-blogs/nancy-pearl/article/51109-check-it-out-with-nancy-pearl-finding-that -next-good-book.html.

Pearl, Nancy. 2012b. "Reading with Purpose: Why We Like the Books We Like." Nancy Pearl at TEDxSeattleU, http://www.youtube.com/watch?v=WjDMbix PSeQ.

Pearl, Nancy, and Sarah Statz Cords. 2010. *Now Read This III: A Guide to Mainstream Fiction, 2002–2009.* Santa Barbara, CA: Libraries Unlimited.

Rosenberg, Betty. 1982. *Genreflecting: A Guide to Reading Interests in Genre Fiction.* Littleton, CO: Libraries Unlimited.

Ross, Catherine Sheldrick, Lynne (E. F.) McKechie, and Paulette Rothbauer. 2006. *Reading Matters: What the Research Reveals about Reading, Libraries, and Community.* Westport, CT: Libraries Unlimited.

Saricks, Joyce G. 2005. *Readers' Advisory Service in the Public Library,* 3rd ed. Chicago: American Library Association.

Saricks, Joyce G. 2009. *The Readers' Advisory Guide to Genre Fiction,* 2nd ed. Chicago: American Library Association.

Saricks, Joyce G. 2010. "Training 101—First You Read." At Leisure column. *Booklist* 106, no. 11 (February 1): 27.

Saricks, Joyce G. 2011. *Read On—Audiobooks: Reading Lists for Every Taste.* Santa Barbara, CA: Libraries Unlimited.

Spratford, Becky, and Christi Hawn. 2004. "Reading Maps Made Easy. *NoveList.* http://www.ebscohost.com/novelist/novelist-special/reading-maps-made-easy.

Wyatt, Neal. 2006. "Reading Maps Remake RA." *Library Journal* 131, no. 18 (November 1): 38–42.

Wyatt, Neal. 2007a. "An RA Big Think." *Library Journal* 132, no. 12 (July 1): 40–43. http://lj.libraryjournal.com/2007/07/ljarchives/lj-series-redefining-ra-an-ra-big-think/.

Wyatt, Neal. 2007b. *The Readers' Advisory Guide to Nonfiction.* Chicago: American Library Association.

Wyatt, Neal. "RA Crossroads." *Library Journal.* http://reviews.libraryjournal.com/category/readers-advisory/ra-crossroads/.

Wyatt, Neal. "Wyatt's World." *Library Journal.* http://reviews.libraryjournal.com/category/readers-advisory/wyatts-world/.

Year of Reading

On January 1 some people make a New Year's resolution to start a new fitness program or lose 20 pounds. Others launch themselves into ambitious year-long projects. One such challenge that turned into a best-selling book is *The Happiness Project: Why I Spent a Year Trying to Sing in the Morning, Clean My Closets, Fight Right, Read Aristotle, and Generally Have More Fun* (2009). In this best seller, Gretchen Craft Rubin spends a month each on different targeted ways for boosting happiness: January/vitality; February/marriage; March/work; April/parenthood; September/books. But why limit yourself to just the month of September for books? Why mess around with cleaning your closets when you could be reading for the whole year? That's exactly what a number of avid readers have decided.

But if you plan to embark on a year-long reading challenge, first you need to figure out what kind of reader you are. Do you enjoy the serendipity of exploring byways and picking a book just because it catches your eye? Do you notice in retrospect that there are patterns in your reading where a link from one book leads to the next in unexpected ways—say, a shared setting or a common time period or similar subject matter? Or do you prefer the reassuring structure of a disciplined plan that systematically lays out in advance the whole year's reading: for example, the complete works of Charles Dickens (see IMPORTANT BOOKS VERSUS INDISCRIMINATE READING) or a list of all the great Russian novels you have always thought you should read, starting with *Anna Karenina, The Idiot*, and *The Master and Margarita*? Systematic readers have the advantage that they can use the structure of the book challenge to justify not doing something else (I can't sort the sock drawer; I'm behind on reading *Bleak House* for my year-of-Dickens project). Or perhaps you like to discuss the books you read? In which case, you might want to recruit others to read along with you. This is what Amy Elizabeth Smith (2012) did when she took a sabbatical year to travel to six South American countries, where she lead book discussions of Jane Austen novels in

Spanish. Smith had the extra challenge of first having to learn Spanish. But maybe you prefer something that seems less strenuous and less like, well, work.

Naomi Beth Wakan exemplifies the first kind of reader, who reads serendipitously, following heterogeneous interests and influences. A lifelong avid reader and writer of poetry, she recorded her year's reading in 12 chapters, one a month starting in January. Wakan (2010, 10) says, "*Book Ends* is ostensibly my reading record for a year, which I invite the reader to dip into and to note down books that they too might want to journey into." Her reading takes her off the beaten path into a promiscuous selection that includes the following: duty reads (Thomas Mann's *Doctor Faustus*, which she abandoned); history (Ronald Wright's blistering *What Is America?*); spy stories (John Le Carré's *The Little Drummer Boy*, which she loves for the way characters undergo changes of identity); books about Japan (Lafcadio Hearn's *Daruma*); books about mathematics (Peter J. Bentley's *The Book of Numbers*); books on death (Julian Barnes's *Nothing to Be Frightened Of*); and books on gardening (Rosemary Verey's *The Garden in Winter*). Given her belief that "the reader is the final contributor to the creation of a book" (Wakan 2010, 10), it is appropriate that she tells her readers what kind of reader she is. Hence her monthly reading record interweaves her responses to the books together with references to what is going on at the same time in her life on Gabriola Island, off the coast of British Columbia. In March she says, "I have to report that I am now halfway through *The Tale of Genji*" (65). In May, she read Christopher Beha's *The Whole Five Feet* (see FIVE-FOOT SHELF OF BOOKS).

In the case of Nina Sankovitch (2011), the year-long reading project was a way of reading her way out of a personal crisis. In *Tolstoy and the Purple Chair* (20), Sankovitch describes how she began her year's reading on October 28, 2008: "as an escape back to life. I wanted to engulf myself in books and come up whole again." The year of "magical reading" began with her sitting on a wooden bench at the edge of a cliff on Long Island facing the Atlantic Ocean and reading Bram Stoker's *Dracula*. As she describes it (2), "I travelled over mountains and past crazed villagers, dodging vampires and accompanied by the good guys, Jonathan Harker, Van Helsing, and Mina. We were fighting to save the world from vampire takeover" (see VAMPIRES, ZOMBIES, AND THE UNDEAD). The next day, she announced her project: she would read a book a day for 365 days. This reading was a way of reclaiming herself after three years of frantic activity that hadn't worked. Following the death at age 46 of her eldest sister Anne-Marie of bile duct cancer, Sankovitch had been running faster and faster as a way of keeping grief and guilt at bay. For the next year, she would sit in her purple chair and read—for comfort, for hope, and for answers about how to live. And what more natural form of self-therapy for this particular individual? She says, "I've used books my whole life for wisdom, for succor, and for escape" (21). She describes the year-of-reading project both as a gift to herself and as a discipline. She would have rules. She would write a review of each book, which she would post on her already-existing Web site called *Read All Day*. Here's her summary of her year of magical reading: "My year of reading one book a day was my year in a sanatorium. . . . During my yearlong respite filled with books, I recuperated. Even more, I learned how to move beyond recuperation to living" (217–218).

Other Approaches

The years of reading that we know most about have been documented, often first in a blog or diary, followed sometimes by a full-length book. Here are some other documented approaches to the year's reading challenge.

- *A Book a Week*

  For most people, Sankovitch's book-a-day would be too strenuous. Better to start with something more manageable, such as a book-a-month or a book-a-week, as many bloggers are now doing. For example, on January 1, Ethan (2012) announced his goal on his *A Book a Week* blogspot. Feeling that other activities were crowding out reading, Ethan decided that he needed the discipline of a goal and a weekly deadline for posting a review to his blog. He says, "I invite others to join me in this challenge." In this approach, book choices can be anything—books for children as well as for adults, nonfiction as well as fiction, older books as well as new ones. The reader is free to be eclectic and serendipitous.

- *Turn Yourself into an Experimental Subject by Combining Reading and Doing*

  In *Helping Me Help Myself*, Beth Lisick (2008, xvi) describes how on January 1, 2006, she "decided to pick twelve things I wanted to improve in my life, find an established guru in each field, and devote one month to each of them." Deciding to begin with a life coach, she settles on Jack Canfield, originator of the *Chicken Soup* franchise and gets the first month of her SELF-HELP project off to a shaky start. In February, she reads Stephen Covey's *The Seven Habits of Highly Effective People*, decides she needs to see Covey in person, and signs up for the Twelfth Annual International Franklin Covey Symposium at McCormick Place in Chicago. On the whole, it's another bust. However, she does discover a few things about herself and, overcome with "a low surge of self-empowerment," she thinks suddenly, "If I want to be a professional writer, I can. I can do it!" (52).

- *Read Systematically in a Single Genre*

  Learning about popular fiction, one genre at a time, was a founding goal of the Adult Reading Round Table (ARRT), a group that Chicago-area public librarians started up in 1984. ARRT members spend a year on a single genre, reading classic prototypes and good examples of the genre, considering the characteristics of the genre, and identifying elements that appeal to readers. Posted on the ARRT Web site are notes from past years of genre study, where the focus has been on such genres as nonfiction, mystery, fantasy, science fiction, adventure, romance, and young adult fiction. In 2013, the form chosen for study was graphic novels; in 2014 it was crime fiction. A founding member of ARRT, Joyce G. Saricks has published *The Readers' Advisory Guide to Genre Fiction*, 2nd ed. (2009) to provide a good starting point for genre study for the rest of us (see X-TRAORDINARY READERS).

- *Read Alphabetically*

To avoid the problem of getting stuck indefinitely on one letter, you could first read a book written by an author whose last name begins with A, then move on to B, and so on through the alphabet. Admittedly X will be a problem. If you want to choose from the 42,000 free eBooks in the Gutenberg project, you could pick an A-book from among Henry Adams, Louisa May Alcott, Horatio Alger, Hans Christian Andersen, Victor Appleton, Jane Austen, and so on. Then pick a B-book from among Honoré de Balzac, J. M. Barrie, Frank Baum, Annie Besant, James Boswell, Max Brand, Anne (or Emily or Charlotte) Brontë. And so on. For other suggestions, see Z TO A, A TO Z READING.

- *Read According to Some Other Arbitrary Category*

In *One for the Books*, Joe Queenan (2012) describes his various reading challenges: a year reading only short books; a year reading books that he always thought he would hate; and a year reading books picked with his eyes closed. Then there is novelist Susan Hill, who spent a year reading nothing but books already on her shelves. She wrote an engaging memoir about the year's reading entitled *Howards End Is on the Landing* (2010). As she explained, "I wanted to repossess my books, to explore what I had accumulated over a lifetime of reading, and to map this house of many volumes" (2).

- *Reread*

Reread books that you have read before at different times of your life. That's what Patricia Meyer Spacks did when she launched herself on a year-long project of rereading dozens of novels: childhood favorites, old standbys, canonical works that she had never really liked, guilty pleasures, books she had read often because she taught them in her courses. In *Rereading* (2011, 2) Spacks says that the distance between the remembered reading and the present reading is "a way to evoke memories . . . of one's life and of past selves."

- *Combine Approaches*

  In "My Year of Rereading Dickens," Katherine Ashenburg (2012) combines rereading with the systematic reading of a single author. She describes how, in the 200th anniversary year of Charles Dickens's birthday, she set herself the task of rereading *all* of the Dickens novels, something she did 40 years ago for her PhD thesis but not since. Ashenburg started with *Great Expectations*, remembered as "a masterpiece of psychological insight, moral exploration and obsessive love," and went on to *David Copperfield*, *Edwin Drood*, and *Bleak House*, "one of the first mystery stories and still an incomparable one." Her assessment part way through the year of reading: "for all his faults, there is still no one to touch him—for breadth, for depth . . . for moral seriousness, hilarious comedy, social criticism and for filling a room with characters you suddenly know better than some of your closest friends."

References

Adult Reading Round Table (ARRT). http://www.arrtreads.org/home.html.

Ashenburg, Katherine. 2012. "My Year of Rereading Dickens." *The Globe and Mail* January 27. http://www.theglobeandmail.com/arts/books-and-media/my-year-of-rereading-dickens-a-writer-revisits-the-master/article1359971/.

Ethan. 2012. *Book a Week* (blogspot). http://e135-abookaweek.blogspot.com/2012/01/goal-how-i-plan-to-read-new-book-each.html.

Hill, Susan. 2010. *Howards End Is on the Landing*. London: Profile Books.

Lisick, Beth. 2008. *Helping Me Help Myself: One Skeptic, Ten Self-help Gurus and a Year on the Brink of the Comfort Zone*. New York: HarperCollins.

Queenan, Joe. 2012. *One for the Books*. New York: Viking.

Rubin, Gretchen Craft. 2009. *The Happiness Project: Why I Spent a Year Trying to Sing in the Morning, Clean My Closets, Fight Right, Read Aristotle, and Generally Have More Fun*. New York: Harper.

Sankovitch, Nina. 2011. *Tolstoy and the Purple Chair. My Year of Magical Reading*. New York: HarperCollins.

Sankovitch, Nina. *Read All Day* (blog). http://www.readallday.org/blog/.

Smith, Amy Elizabeth. 2012. *All Roads Lead to Austen: A Yearlong Journey with Jane*. Napierville, IL: Sourcebooks.

Spacks, Patricia Meyer. 2011. *On Rereading*. Cambridge, MA: Harvard University Press.

Wakan, Naomi Beth. 2010. *Book Ends: A Year between the Covers*. Hamilton, ON: Poplar Press.

Z to A, A to Z Reading

I admit it—there is something decidedly artificial and arbitrary in the alphabetic arrangement. Why should "Alexia" be juxtaposed with "Bad reading" or "Unreadable Books" with "Vampires"? But the pay-off can be unexpected connections, oppositions, and surprising synergies as unlikely juxtapositions spark new ideas.

So here are several other ways in which avid readers have used the alphabetic arrangement to highlight their love of reading. Sarah Statz Cords, librarian, readers' advisor, and reader *extraordinaire* of NONFICTION, has posted her answers to an A to Z Bookish Survey on her Web site *Citizen Reader*. Cords credits the survey itself to Jamie's blog *The Perpetual Page-Turner*, where in turn the idea is traced to "back-in-the-day" surveys that used to be created on various topics on Xanga and MySpace. This meme focuses on the reading experience itself, using such categories as these:

Author you have read the most books from

Best sequel ever

Currently reading

Drink of choice while reading

E-reader or physical book?

Fictional character you probably would actually have dated in high school

Glad you gave this book a chance

Hidden gem book

Important moment in your reading life

. . .

Three of your all-time favorite books

Unapologetic fangirl for

Very excited for this release more than all the others

Worst bookish habit

X marks the spot: Start at the top left of your shelf and pick the 27th book

Your latest book purchase

ZZZ-snatcher book (last book that kept you up *way* late)

Jamie says that she is "definitely a physical book girl" but loves her Kindle for the gym and for vacations (see E-READING). Cords confesses that her worst bookish habit is to jump right to the last chapter of thrillers when she is becoming bored. And of course she is an unapologetic fangirl for all nonfiction. I find that reading other people's answers to this survey reminds me all over again how differently people read and how varied people's reading experiences can be. This meme, copied enthusiastically from one blog to another, has generated many reading profiles with answers that can be compared across readers. What do people say is their greatest "reading regret"? What is the "one book" people say they have read multiple times? You can check it out. A Google search on "A to Z Bookish Survey" conducted in December 2013 turned up 143 readers who have posted answers on their own blogs to the Bookish Survey, along with comments such as it "seemed like far too much fun to pass up," "[surveys] about stories and books are the absolute best," "Jumping on the bandwagon too!" and "What better way to spend time than by thinking about all things book-related?" Moreover this alphabetic survey may inspire you to make up your own categories in a variant survey. How about:

Audiobooks: yes or no?

Best first sentence in a novel

Changed your life

Didn't finish

Escaping into a fictional world—which books do it for you?

First book you remember reading

Guilty reading

Another alphabetic approach puts the spotlight on favorite books. On his blog *Stuck in a Book*, Simon introduced the "A to Z favorites" meme, which was taken up with alacrity by others. The starting point was Simon's challenge: "if I had to pick a favorite author for each letter of the alphabet, and the accompanying novel, how would that go?" Here are Simon's first eight entries:

A = Austen, Jane	*Pride and Prejudice*
B = Baker, Frank	*Miss Hargreaves*
C = Crompton, Richmal	*Frost at Morning*
D = Delafield, E. M.	*The Provincial Lady*
E = Eliot, George	*The Mill on the Floss*
F = Fadiman, Anne	*Ex Libris*
G = Gibbons, Stella	*Cold Comfort Farm*
H = Hanff, Helene	*84, Charing Cross Road*

Once you have read his list, Simon predicts, "you won't be able to resist making your own." Other readers have enthusiastically taken up the challenge, with suggestions for tricky letters, for example, Anna Quindlen for Q; Barry Unsworth or John Updike for U; and Emile Zola, Yevgeni Zamyatin, or Stefan Zweig for the very challenging letter Z. Bookgirl (2008) drew up her own alphabetic list starting with Margaret Atwood's *The Handmaid's Tale* and ending with Markus Zuzak's *The Book Thief*. She commented, "It was fun to come up with this list because I got to think back on the books I've read. . . . Who else has done this or wants to play?"

Don't hold back. Take up the challenge by developing your own list A to Z, Z to A of favorite authors and books. I tried my hand at a specialized listing in the section Books about Books and Reading. Over to you.

References

Bookgirl. 2008. *Bookgirl's Nightstand*. April 24. http://www.bookgirl.net/a-to-z/.

Cords, Sarah Statz. 2013. "A to Z Bookish Survey." *Citizen Reader*. September 30. http://www.citizenreader.com/citizen/reading-process/.

Jamie. 2013. "Some Friday Fun: A to Z Survey." *The Perpetual Page-Turner*. August 9. http://www.perpetualpageturner.com/2013/08/some-friday-fun.html.

Thomas, Simon David. 2008. "A-Z Favorites." *Stuck in a Book*. April 18. http://stuck -in-a-book.blogspot.ca/2008/04/z-favourites.html.

Index

About the Author

CATHERINE SHELDRICK ROSS, PhD, is professor emeritus of library and information science at Western University, Ontario, Canada. Her published works include Libraries Unlimited's *Reading Matters: What the Research Reveals about Reading, Libraries, and Community*; *Conducting the Reference Interview*, second edition; and *Communicating Professionally*, third edition. Ross holds a doctorate in English and a master's degree in library and information science from Western University.